FRANCE
A HISTORY
IN ART

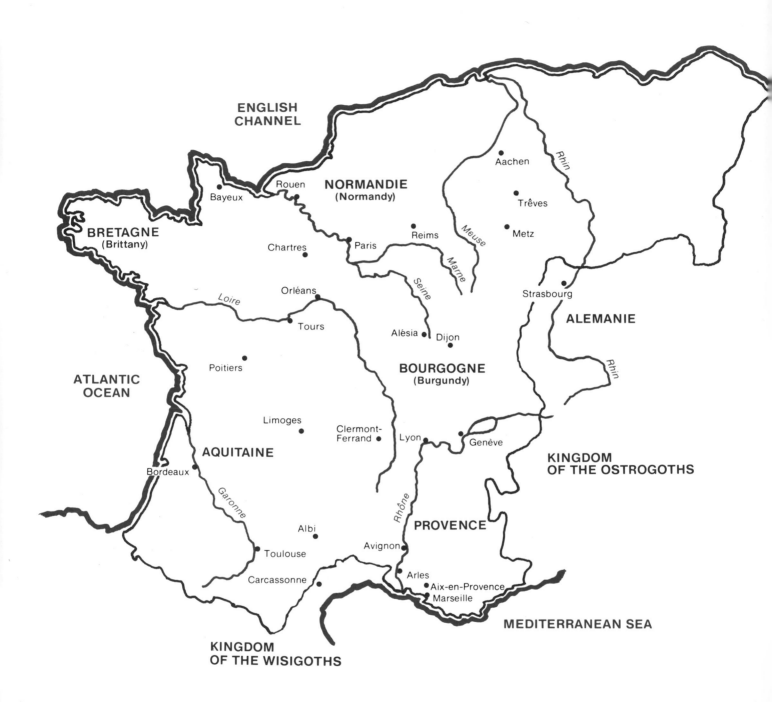

ENGLISH
CHANNEL

Rouen NORMANDIE
(Normandy)

Bayeux

Aachen

Rhin

Trêves

Metz

BRETAGNE
(Brittany)

Reims

Chartres

Meuse

Paris

Marne

ALEMANIE

Orléans

Seine

Strasbourg

Loire

Tours

Rhin

Alésia • Dijon

Poitiers

ATLANTIC
OCEAN

BOURGOGNE
(Burgundy)

Limoges

Clermont-
Ferrand •

Lyon

Genève

AQUITAINE

KINGDOM
OF THE OSTROGOTHS

Bordeaux

Garonne

Rhône

Albi

PROVENCE

Toulouse

Avignon

Carcassonne

Arles
Aix-en-Provence
Marseille

MEDITERRANEAN SEA

KINGDOM
OF THE WISIGOTHS

ANCIENT
FRANCE

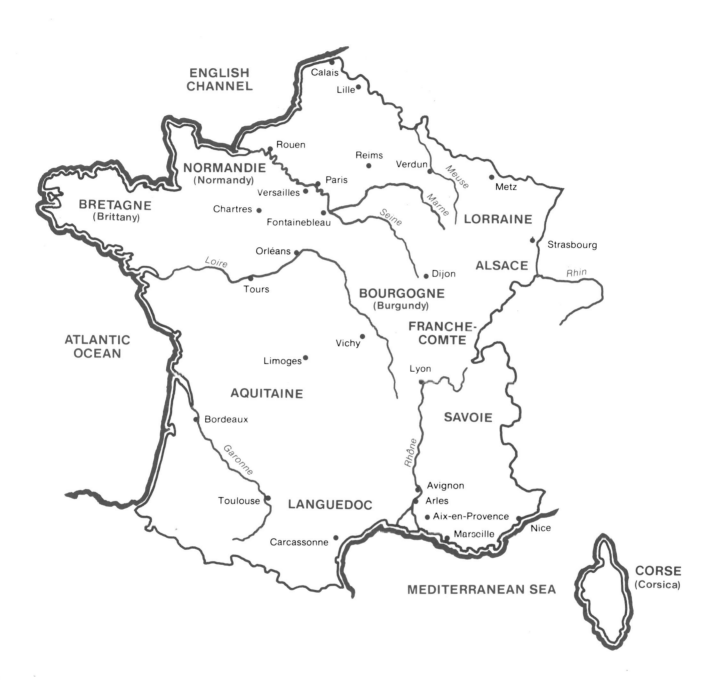

ENGLISH CHANNEL

Calais

Lille

Rouen

NORMANDIE
(Normandy)

Reims

Verdun

Meuse

Metz

Paris

Versailles

Marne

LORRAINE

BRETAGNE
(Brittany)

Chartres

Fontainebleau

Seine

ATLANTIC
OCEAN

Loire

Orléans

Strasbourg

Tours

Dijon

ALSACE

Rhin

BOURGOGNE
(Burgundy)

Vichy

FRANCHE-
COMTE

Limoges

Lyon

AQUITAINE

SAVOIE

Bordeaux

Garonne

Rhône

Toulouse

LANGUEDOC

Avignon

Arles

Aix-en-Provence

Carcassonne

Marseille

Nice

MEDITERRANEAN SEA

CORSE
(Corsica)

MODERN FRANCE

FRANCE

A HISTORY IN ART By Bradley Smith

A Gemini-Smith, Inc. book published by Doubleday & Company, Inc., Garden City, New York

A Gemini Smith, Inc. Book

Written and photographed by Bradley Smith

Producer:
Elisabeth Girard Smith

Text Editor:
Leonard Slater

Research Consultant:
Marci Sortor

Translator:
Elisabeth Girard Smith

Graphics:
Mary Farris

Production:
Lorraine Ortiz

Permissions:
S.P.A.D.E.M., Paris/V.A.G.A., New York;
A.D.A.G.P., New York

Published by:
Doubleday & Company, Inc.
245 Park Avenue
New York, N.Y. 10017

Printed in Italy by G. Canale S.p.a., Torino.

Library of Congress
Smith, Bradley.
   France, a history in art.
   "A Gemini Smith, Inc. book."
   Bibliography: page 290
   Includes index.
   1. Art, French. I. Title.
N6841.S58 1984   709.'44   84-5932
ISBN   0-385-18211-2

France A HISTORY IN ART

CONTENTS

ACKNOWLEDGMENTS

In the Works of Art section beginning on page 279 the paintings and sculpture used in this book are described and the museums and private collectors that contributed are identified. Yet the author wishes to make grateful acknowledgment of the special cooperation and assistance given to him as he traveled about France in search of the art that made the book possible.

In France: Mr. and Mrs. Jean-Luc de Carbuccia; Jacques Vistel, *Direction des Musées de France*; Jacques Hazard, *Ministère des Affaires Etrangères*; Pierre Rosenberg, *Musée du Louvre*; Geneviève Ravaux, *Direction des Musées de France*; Nina Simmons; Alain Girard; Jacqueline Tartarin; Dick Balli, *Balcor; Central Color*; François Avril, *Bibliothèque Nationale*; Michel Faré; Christian de Bartillat, *Editions Presses de la Cité*; Dr. J. M. Lo Duca; Yves Mabin, *Ministère des Affaires Etrangères*; Melle Lefébure, *Musée Condé, Chantilly*; Eugène Braun-Munk; Ronald Barrymore; Mary Sargent d'Anglejean; Mr Lemoine, *Chateau de Versailles*; Melle Lossignol, *Musée des Arts et Traditions Populaires*; Loomis Dean; Catherine Bélanger, *Musée du Louvre*; Jean Hélion; Jean Forneris, *Musée des Beaux Arts Jules Chéret, Nice*; Mrs. Rocher-Jauneau, *Musée des Beaux Arts, Lyon*; Mr Amable Audin, *Musée de la Civilisation Gallo-Romaine, Lyon*; Eric Hild, *Musée de L'Annonciade, St Tropez*; Anne de Marjorie; Christine de Coninck; Janine Girard; André Prudhomme.

In the U. S. A.: Samuel Vaughan, Ferris Mack; Darlene La Madrid; Ronny Schwartz; Marina Bendik; Louise Rose; Jim Luster; Mayo Campos; Françoise Gilot; Martin Peterson, *San Diego Museum of Art*; Philip Bruno; Tom Brouwer.

PREFACE

Artists leave behind a visual chronicle of the spirit and reality of their time and their personal insight into it. The historic moment is arrested and permanently recorded, along with the personal reactions of the painter. Thus, the artist becomes the ultimate witness to events large and small. In art, the prevailing taste and the prejudices of history are all recorded.

Art does more than illustrate reality. It captures moods, recollections, dreams and sensations. One feels, as well as sees, a historical painting. In *France: A History In Art*, I have, therefore, chosen to avoid abstractions. Every image has its historical point to make, usually directly, sometimes obliquely. This book was planned to allow the artist to give his version of events as they happened. The selection of 268 images has been based entirely upon my own personal judgment. My criteria for selections were: Is it valid to me artistically? Does it reveal something of the history of France? And does it help to carry the visual plot of the book forward. To this end, I have included ancient bas-reliefs and jewelry in the Gallo-Roman period; a few of the inexpensive and popular folk-art lithographs from Epinal, and three twentieth-century posters: the one announcing the first motion picture and those for performances by Joséphine Baker and Maurice Chevalier. With these exceptions, I have used paintings. No one will agree with all of my selections. And there are, to be sure, great artists and important paintings that are not included. My only excuse is that they could not be included without creating an entire series of books.

One does not have to imagine a given period in history when the artist sensitively reveals it. Yet, it is important that the viewer be able to "read" the painting. The viewer must be aware that the event as perceived by the artist has shadings of meaning based upon the latter's personality. These color the events and characters depicted—as does

the choice of subjects. Cézanne wrote, "I want to paint the world's virginity," while van Gogh wrote, "With red and green I have tried to depict those terrible things, men's passions." The artist gives his reaction to the events and to the people who made history, just as I—through my selection of events and art—have given my own impression of the evolution of France.

We can learn a great deal from the artist as historian. Yet words are also necessary. I have supplied a historical narrative that, within the limitations of space, relates to both the art and the history. By viewing the characters and reading about them, one's own thinking about history changes. The visual impression will remain longer than that of the text, for art never stops. Toulouse-Lautrec said: "I have tried to paint the true, not the ideal." From the idea and the image comes *France: A History In Art*.

Almost all of these works of art were photographed in the regional museums that exist in all the departments of France. This is neither a Paris collection (although the great Paris museums are represented) nor was it drawn from the museums of the world. There are important examples of French art in other countries but, in my opinion, the preponderance of the best, the broadest and the most representative remain in France where they were created.

No single book, nor even a thousand books, could encompass the art and history of France. I have considered this work as a mosaic made of selected gems brought together in chronological sequence. It is a sketch book of history, with the paintings chosen to evoke the life and spirit of the French people. It does not profess to be a political, economic, social or even an art history. But it has major elements of all of these to give an impression of France and of the French over nearly 2,000 years of fascinating history.

Bradley Smith

9

INTRODUCTION

By Pierre Rosenberg
Chief Curator of the Painting Department,
The Louvre.

On the walls of Paris one could see at the beginning of this century and until World War II, a publicity poster which had its hour of celebrity. The work of Eugène Vavasseur, it advertised the merits of a brand of paint. It showed a building painter who, with a broad stroke of his brush, had just written in large letters the name of the brand — *la peinture Valentine* — on the back of another painter who, in turn, had put the name of the brand on the back of a painter who had painted... and another and another and so on...

This advertising poster has always symbolized

for me the never-ending history of French art.

Its sweep has been broad: from the painted caves of Lascaux, the Celtic art, the Merovingian tombs, the Romanesque churches, the stained-glass of the Gothic cathedrals, the illuminated Books of Hours of the Middle Ages, the castles of the Loire, the palace of Versailles, the pastels of Perronneau, Chardin and Maurice Quentin de La Tour; the design and architecture of towns like Aix-en-Provence, Bordeaux or Nantes; the elegant Paris of Baron Haussmann and the Eiffel Tower up until today, with the Air France terminal at the Charles de Gaulle airport as one example. Even if they are not as numerous as those of the past, there are other contemporary examples. Our new art does not always have the international reputation it deserves.

The fact remains that French art has shown an amazing vitality with an extraordinary continuity. This long span of quality without breakdowns or interruptions is unique among European civilizations. English art, for example, appeared late. Holland had its golden century, but has only that to remember except for van Gogh and later Mondrian. Germany and Spain, however glorious their pasts may have been, have often been eclipsed in modern times. No one thinks of diminishing Italy's seminal role, but even she has not known France's time span nor variety. To match the revolutions of Impressionism, of Fauvism and Cubism, Italy offers only the *Macchiaioli* and the Futurists. She has nothing comparable to the stained-glass of Chartres, the *Très Riches Heures du Duc de Berry* (The Very Rich Hours of the Duke of Berry), the tapestries of the *Dame à la Licorne* (The Lady with a Unicorn), the furniture of Cressent or BVRB or even the porcelains of Sèvres.

Permanency does not mean monotony, however. In the pages that follow, I will take my examples from the field of painting and will point out the major *lignes de force* (directions) of French art. We often assume they are well known but that is not the case.

The geographical position of France is an important factor in the long history of its art. Situated at the crossroads of Europe, it shares borders with Germany, Belgium, Spain and Italy. England and Holland are virtually next door. It is no wonder then that French artists have so often looked over their shoulders and found their inspiration in the creations of their foreign colleagues. It is not my purpose to recount the foreign influences on French artists, but some examples will show their importance and multiplicity.

Watteau is rightly considered one of the symbols of French art in the eighteenth century. His work sums up, all by itself, the grace and elegance of its time. Its influence has been significant, not only inside France but outside its borders, and not only on European decorative arts. It also has inspired writers and poets, couturiers and movie-makers. Yet Watteau owes the essentials of his technique to Rubens and some of his inspirations and the subjects of his works have their sources in the *genre scene* of a Teniers or the Dutch painters of the seventeenth century.

Manet is acknowledged as the father of Impressionism, and justly so. He "liberated" the painting of his time, from the two iron-collars of academic rules and narrative subject matter. But the debt of Manet to Spanish painting—Velasquez above all—and also to Frans Hals of Holland is immense and examples like these could be multiplied.

Without Richard Bonington and John Constable, there would have been no Eugène Delacroix. Without the seventeenth-century painters of Bologna, there would have been no French Classicism. The immense influence of Raphael on French art, from Eustache Le Sueur to Jean Auguste Dominique Ingres, and the more diffuse influence of Caravaggio on Georges de La Tour and Louis David are worth mentioning. One must realize how much Jehan Fouquet owes to Fra Angelico, Claude Lorrain to Adam Elsheimer, Théodore Géricault and Auguste Rodin to Michelangelo. Also the debts that Hubert Robert owes to Giovanni Panini and Théodule Ribot owes to José Ribera.

If the French artists have been so open to the influences of their neighbors, it is because they visited them so often. The only trip Watteau made outside of France was to London. Fragonard knew Holland, Vignon knew Spain, Vouet knew Constantinople, Courbet knew Germany; Houdon, Edgar Degas, Marcel Duchamp and Fernand Léger went under different circumstances and for different reasons to the United States, while Falconet left in Russia — in Saint Petersburg, now Leningrad — his extraordinary monument to the glory of Peter the Great which faces the fortress of Peter and Paul. An endless list of similar examples could be made.

It was Italy, especially, that welcomed French artists. One school, the Villa Medici, invited the best young French artists. Whether directed by Jean François de Troy, Ingres or Balthus, it allowed Boucher and David and composers like Berlioz or Debussy to complete their educations. Each generation saw and was influenced by Italy differently. Sometimes it was by the large Baroque decorations of Annibale Carracci (Farnese Palace, the current French embassy in Rome) or by Pietro da Cortona; sometimes the muse was Antiquity, the influence of which was immense on the work of Poussin, David or Ingres; sometimes the mores, customs and costumes of the working people of Rome provided the artists with their inspiration and the subjects for their works, as early as the

seventeenth century. Because they loved Italy, and especially Rome (Venice was more German and Florence British), two of the greatest French artists never came back to France. The first, Claude Lorrain, depicted an ideal world that had disappeared; the second, Nicolas Poussin, revealed Antiquity and the exemplary lives of its heroes. It is not the least of the paradoxes of the history of French art to think that these two artists, one from Lorraine and the other from Normandy, who did not know their own country very well, became the symbols of French classicism.

If France was open to the outside world, if she knew how to export her art and her artists, she knew even more how to attract foreigners to it. Simone Martini worked in Avignon, then the papal capital. At one time, many miniaturists of the Middle Ages were Flemish, when the Duchy of Burgundy included the Belgium and Holland of today. If the author of the *Pietà* of Avignon, Enguerrand Quarton, is French, there were just as many artists from Italy and the North who, during the fifteenth century, worked in France. It was the same in the sixteenth century: François I attracted not only Andrea del Sarto but also Leonardo da Vinci who died near Amboise in 1519. The first school of Fontainebleau (Rosso, Primaticcio, Niccolò dell'Abate) was Italian; the second (Dubois whose name was actually Bosschaert) was Flemish.

Philippe de Champaigne, the painter of the Jansenist ideal, was born in Brussels in 1602. Rubens painted for Marie de Medici his masterpiece, *The Luxembourg Gallery*, today in the Louvre. Romanelli came to teach the French the art of the Italian style of *grand décor* (his work in Paris can still be seen in the most beautiful ceilings at the Louvre and at the *Bibliothèque Nationale*). Giovanni Pellegrini and the pastelist Rosalba Carriera tried their luck in the beginning of the eighteenth century. Alexandre Roslin, the "Swede," was considered by his contemporaries one of the best portrait painters of his century. In the nineteenth and the twentieth centuries, France welcomed artists from all over the world: from Joseph Turner to James Whistler, from Edvard Munch to Mary Cassatt.

Sisley was half English, while Pissarro was born in St. Thomas, then an island in the Dutch West Indies, now an American possession. The Dutchman Johan Jongkind worked in France; his compatriot Vincent van Gogh would not have been a great genius had he not come to Paris and Arles. Pablo Picasso and Juan Gris, Marc Chagall and Chaim Soutine, Max Ernst and Hans Hartung, Amedeo Modigliani and Jules Pascin are all as French as Poussin is Roman. Wassily Kandinski died in Neuilly in 1944 after becoming a French citizen. Piet Mondrian, the least French of all the artists of the twentieth century, lived in the heart of Montparnasse until the German occupation made him leave the city he had chosen.

From this somewhat tedious series of examples, one will understand that French art has always shown great overtures toward the outside world. It has been able to absorb foreign influences. It has known how to attract some of the greatest creators of all times, sometimes for a few years, sometimes for a lifetime. French art has served as an example and a source of inspiration.

But the French have not always been aware of the richness of their art. A familiar example is that of the Impressionists who were discovered by German and American collectors. It was the late Alfred Barr, the prophetic director of the Museum of Modern Art in New York, who was the first to see that Matisse was the "other" great painter of the twentieth century. The Le Nain brothers were discovered not more than a century ago; Georges de La Tour was discovered more recently, thanks to Hermann Voss. I have no doubt that there are other artists of the same caliber who have not yet found their places in the hall of fame alongside the great creators of the past.

Nothing is more varied than French art: Romanesque and Gothic art flourished here and its Gothic art is the most resplendent. Imagine a country that could produce simultaneously Valentin and Le Sueur, Chardin and Boucher, Monet and Cézanne, the *Douanier* Rousseau and Seurat? At the beginning of the nineteenth century, Delacroix and Ingres were pitted against each other, Delacroix symbolizing Romanticism, Ingres the classical artist *par excellence*. Between the two of them, they seem to sum up the diversity of painting, the multiciplicity of its ambitions, the two extremes, the limits of an art. Yet, these contrasts are more apparent on the surface than they are deep. In the midst of this variety, there is a constant element, a single note, a very difficult thing to analyze, that one must call French. What is it? How can we define it without getting lost in empty and meaningless generalities?

To begin: French artists knew how to be daring. The names of David, Cézanne, Seurat, Braque or Matisse come to mind and sum up some of the more radical mutations of painting in the last century. But these artists, who made such fundamental changes, never lost their sense of proportion. It is that restraint that unites them and brings them closer to the more traditional artists who respected the examples of the past.

Moreover, French artists often appear to be "intellectuals." Its members think of the rules that guide them and that they want to obey. There are numerous artists from France, like Poussin, Maurice Denis, André Lhote, Cézanne and Signac who wrote about their ideas and ideals. However, while French artists may like theory, they are never pedantic. Their art remains the work of moderate people: Fauvism and Cubism are French while Expressionism is German like Bauhaus art. In France, Rococo art never knew the excesses and exuberance, the charm of the very excess of Austrian or Bavarian creations. Neo-classicism in France never had the dryness nor the dogmatic coldness of English or German works. No French painter has ever dared use the unmixed colors of the pre-Raphaelite English artists. Men like Rembrandt and Goya, Füssli and Blake, Mondrian and Kandinski could never have been French. One can regret it and see a limit to the creative genius of French artists. That is the reverse side of the coin of their innate sense of measure.

I have mentioned previously the antagonism between Ingres and Delacroix in the nineteenth century. Ingres was considered by most of the critics of his time to be looking backward, the typical reactionary turning toward the past. Delacroix won the admiration of the Romantics, of Baudelaire and all the modernists. Today the position of both of these artists has been radically reversed. It is Ingres who was considered the modern, audacious innovator by Picasso and Matisse. His audacity as a colorist, the strange character of some of his plastic inventions, his taste for pure line—which on occasion has been wrongly called abstract—seduces our contemporaries while the impetuous style and sometimes muddy workmanship of Delacroix is boring.

This example is revealing. The French painters do not disclose all of their secrets to their contemporaries, to just anybody or at the first glance. Today, La Tour is fashionable while Lebrun who was glorified for two centuries has lost his appeal. Rightly so, he is beginning to be rediscovered. For a long time, we pitted Cézanne, the intellectual, against Monet, the "eye." Postwar American painters have taught us to look at Monet differently and to see in his work something more than an optical experience pushed to its extreme limits.

I would like to give one last example which I particularly like. Nobody in the United States would question the genius of Matisse. His influence, like Cézanne's, remains enormous. He has made a deep impression on the best painting of our century. But the history of art, the history of American art especially (true of American painters, with the exception of Rothko), is much more reserved about his friend Bonnard. According to them, the latter was a bourgeois painter whose work has become belated and passé and whose love of life and joy in painting has something unhealthy about it. In a word, it is deemed superficial. I would bet that the twenty-first century will decide differently and will give Bonnard a place in the sun at least equal to the one that so far has been given to Matisse.

14

Whether turning toward the past or whether they pride themselves on being *avant-garde*, French painters give more room to construction than to improvisation. They favor intellect over imagination. But the surprise is that they do not neglect light and color.

It is easy to see artists who specialize in the line (drawing) as opposed to those who favor color, Florence against Venice. But in what category can one place the French? And is this opposition still meaningful when one mentions the names of Chardin, Ingres, Cézanne or Matisse? French artists were great draftsmen as well as great colorists. They did not favor one over the other. They tried to reconcile the irreconcilable, to unite what seemed opposite. If they succeeded in this desperate effort more often than their neighbors, it is because they gave the major role to light.

Often, when one talks about light in painting, one thinks of the Impressionists, those poets of the light of Paris, both delicate and rich in nuances. But one must not forget that long before the masters of Impressionism — Monet and Pissarro, Sisley and Renoir — French artists had understood the role that light could play in their works. In Georges de La Tour, the artificial light of a candle expresses and sums up the religious feeling; with Claude Lorrain, the Italian light sublimates the Roman countryside. French artists use light to very precise ends which may appear opposite. In fact, whether it is the light of the moon in the *Songe d'Ossian*, or of Girodet or of Ingres, whether it is the sunlight of Hubert Robert or Ziem, it is rarely gratuitous or "decorative." The light permits the artist to say, with only his brushes, what he means.

One more word on what separates French artists from their rivals across the Rhine, across the English Channel, over the Alps and on the other side of the Atlantic. The French painters know how to be solemn, serious, sad or melancholy (Fouquet, Valentin, Chardin, Seurat and Matisse again). However they are not desperate, flayed alive or solitary. The world of Friedrich, one of the great artists of the nineteenth century, one of the few with Turner and van Gogh who was not French, is German just as the world of Ferdinand Hodler is Swiss. The French are modest and do not display their feelings in the daylight as Rembrandt sometimes did. They flee expressionism. French artists know how to be gay, but their laugh is that of Fragonard or Renoir; it does not grate like those of Hogarth or Ensor.

Their art is calm and peaceful, meditative and expressed with *savoir vivre*. It is above all the love of life. They hide their greatest audacities under the appearance of ease — the effort never appears. Their painting is only rarely literature or music, poetry or philosphy: it is and wants to be painting.

I would like to conclude with a famous story and with a personal observation. In 1665, Louis XIV summoned Gianlorenzo Bernini, the Roman architect then at the height of his glory, to Paris. The king wanted Bernini to build the colonnade of the Louvre. But the project was abandoned as Louvre projects sometimes are. (As I write, the future of the pyramid proposed by the American architect I. M. Pei that President Mitterand has decided to build in the courtyard of the Louvre is not certain). Instead Bernini used his time in Paris to sculpt a marvelous bust of the Sun King (which is in Versailles today) and to visit the most famous Parisian art collections of the time. He went to the

collector Cerisier who owned some famous paintings of Poussin. Bernini studied them at great length. Standing in front of the *Cendres de Phocion* (Ashes of Phocion) — now in England — he exclaimed, pointing to his forehead: *"Il signore Poussin é un pittore che lavora di là,"* (Mr. Poussin is a painter who works with his head). And indeed, for Poussin as well as other French painters, painting was never gratuitous. French art is a meditation on the laws which govern the craft, and even more it is a reflection on the human condition. The artists of our country have managed to treat their themes with lightness, without letting either their ambitions be felt excessively or the nobleness of their views.

This brings me to my second point. The reader who looks at this masterful book created by Bradley Smith will be struck by the predilection that French artists have for some colors. As early

as the fifteenth century, blue, red and white occupied first place. Well before our tricolor flag existed, before France was molded into a national entity, before anyone spoke of the *hexagone* or the national territory, long before the notion of a French art or a French school — a notion much more recent than the notion of the Northern school or the Italian school — had appeared, the artists of our country had chosen and juxtaposed the colors which today symbolize it.

The white, the blue and the red; the Italian artist giving homage to his French rival by pointing his fingers at his forehead — to me, these examples seem to best sum up French art, its glorious past and — let us hope — its just as glorious future.

Pierre Rosenberg
Chief Curator of the Painting Department,
The Louvre.

1500 B.C. - 486 A.D.
CELTS AND GALLO-ROMANS

Nomadic Celtic people settle in Gaul. Romans occupy Provincia (Provence). In 50 B.C. Caesar adds all Gaul to the Roman empire. Roads are built and Gauls assimilate Roman culture while Gallic elite is slowly absorbed into Rome's ruling class. Latin replaces the Celtic language as Gauls adopt Roman gods. Germanic settlers and invaders disturb the peace and Christian cells grow into parish churches. By the fifth century the Gallo-Roman elite begin to abandon the cities. Christian bishops become civil and spiritual authorities.

HISTORICAL CHRONOLOGY		ART CHRONOLOGY	
1500—	Proto Celts (called Keltoi by Greeks)	c. 1500 B.C.	Bronze knives and pins, engraved bracelets.
200 B.C.	begin movement into Western Europe and spread into Paris basin and Normandy.	750 B.C.	Gallic ritual sacrifice and funerary cults.
800—	Horse bit introduced by Cimmerian invaders.	150 B.C.—	Expansion of Roman influence, reflected in the
		50 B.C.	replacement of Greek-style jars by Roman ones.
500 B.C.	Development of iron swords.	100 B.C.	Wine trade spreads throughout Gaul.
125—	Roman conquest of Provincia, modern-day	40 B.C.—	Building of towns, of theater in Arles, forum
118 B.C.	Provence. Narbonne founded as the capital.	19 A.D.	in Lyon, aqueduct at Pont du Gard and Temple
58—50 B.C.	Julius Caesar conquers Gaul.		of Jupiter at Vernèques.
46—12 B.C.	Lyon founded as the capital of Gaul. Arles and Autun founded.	12 B.C.	Altar of the Twelve Gods at Lyon, an attempt to unite Gallic and Romanic religious beliefs.
48 A.D.	Tribal leaders granted senatorial status.	17 A.D.	Fusion of Gallic and Roman religions in mythical
97 A.D.	Revolt against Roman colonization in northeastern Gaul.		scenes on pillar erected by boatmen of Paris.
212 A.D.	Roman citizenship extended to free men.	43 A.D.	Emperor Claudius drives Druidic priests out of Gaul.
c. 233 A.D.	Franks, group of Germanic tribes, invade Gaul.	93 A.D.	Emperor Domitian issues decree that half the land
c. 276 A.D.	Roman armies turn back Germans.		devoted to viticulture be converted to grain.
285 A.D.	Trêves becomes new capital of Gaul.	160 A.D.	Mystery cult established at Lyon.
305 A.D.	Emperor Diocletian divides the Empire into the Eastern and Western Empires, with two emperors.	c. 170 A.D.	Images of a Gallic mechanical reaping machine.
c. 358 A.D.	Emperor Julian restores control over Gaul.	177 A.D.	Brutal persecution of Christians in Lyon.
c. 395 A.D.	Prefecture of Gaul transferred to Arles.	c. 200 A.D.	Refined glass-making techniques introduced. Following Roman defeats, earlier religious beliefs are revived.
c. 400 A.D.	Visigoth expansion stopped by Franks.	c. 249 A.D.	Martyrdom of Saint Denis, bishop of Paris.
448 A.D.	Merovech, ancestor of the Merovingian dynasty, becomes chieftain of the Franks.	c. 300 A.D.	Druids officially recognized by the Empire.
451 A.D.	Attila the Hun invades Gaul and is turned back by Romans and Franks.	c. 370 A.D.	Saint Martin, soldier-turned-bishop of Tours, founds monastery.
455 A.D.	End of Roman Gaul.	371 A.D.	Moselle and Bordeaux wines praised by
463 A.D.	Franks conquer and destroy Trêves and Cologne.		Ausonius, poet from Bordeaux. Mentions of Burgundy wines.
464 A.D.	Roman influence in the Visigothic law code.	c. 400 A.D.	The Life of St. Martin of Tours, by Sulpicius
481 A.D.	Clovis becomes chieftain of the Merovingian Franks.		Severus, early example of popular literature.

Celtic horsemen wearing metal helmets and carrying javelins ride across this magnificent silver basin known as the Gunderstrup Cauldron. A unique vessel, it was decorated by northeastern Celts in the first century B.C.

The Celts Become Gauls

Down from the snow patterned foothills of the Alps came an attractive, vigorous and warlike people. The time: some 200 years before Christ; the place: the northeastern frontiers of what is now France. These men, women and children were no uncivilized hoard. The distinguishing characteristics of the warriors and their women had been recorded by such eminent Greek writers as Herodotus, Strabo, Polybius and Pliny. The Greeks called them Celts or Keltoi. The Romans later called them Galli. History knows them as the Gauls.

Celt-Gauls had become widely distributed throughout Europe as early as the fifth-century B.C. Masters of bronze work and later ironwork, they had fashioned swords and daggers effective enough to fight their way through many battles. Warriors first, they were also farmers and breeders of cattle, pigs and horses. Indeed horse training was a special skill. As the Gauls moved westward, they adapted efficient horses' bits and bridles from earlier models developed by the Chinese, Egyptians and Bavarians. The adoption and improvement of these guidance and restraint implements made them master of the horse. Victory in combat was often made possible by their well-controlled animals, for both two- and four-wheeled chariots were used. One expert driver handled the reins

Below the mounted warriors, foot soldiers carry the distinctive oblong Celtic shield. Note the three trumpeters at right. At the far left, the large figure sacrificing a man is probably the Celtic god Teutates.

while the other hurled the javelins. At close quarters battle axes or long iron swords were used. But the hardy and handsome (according to the Greeks) foot soldiers fought nude behind their oblong shields. A contemporary Greek writer tells of foot soldiers marching naked while in the forefront rode their standard bearers proudly wearing gold amulets and gold neckbands. The Gauls were said to be, by early Greek writers, handsome, blond and mostly clean shaven, except for those with drooping mustaches and short beards. Their hair was worn long and washed with lime to make it white. The Greeks described the effect as looking like a horse's mane. Strabo, the Greek geographer wrote "independent Kelti (Gauls), were flamboyant and headstrong on the battlefield."

These Gauls, with an admixture of Ligurian, Iberian Germanic peoples, and later Romans, were the ancestors of the French. It was these stalwart warriors who in 394 B.C. under their chieftain Brennus, defeated Rome and sacked that splendid city. It was these adventuresome Gauls who settled in France and in northern Italy around the year 390 B.C. Again it was these energetic and resourceful people who sent expeditions across the English Channel as early as 450 B.C. to leave there traces of their language and memorials to their Druidic deities. Their literature is the oldest in Europe after Greek and Latin. Theirs was a civilization in motion. In wave after wave over three centuries, a flood of men, women and children poured across the fertile plains that would one day become France.

19

Symbolic head of a Druidic priestess with one arm raised holding a sacred bird is seen in this portion of the famous Gundestrup Cauldron. The fallen man at lower left, his legs around the goddess's breast, is a sacrificial victim.

The loose knit nation of the Celts was held together by the fabric of their rich language and a deep commitment to an oral history. For the Celtic settlers in France and Britain did not develop a written language. Their poetry and songs, legendary tales of heroes and heroines, the accounts of the forging of iron weapons, of making useful and decorative pottery, were all diligently committed to memory. Lessons were chanted aloud to fix forever the culture of the past and the present.

Druids, as the priests and priestesses were called, acted as teachers. Chosen from the wisest men and women of the clan (and because of their apparent knowledge of the supernatural and of magic), they were equal in status to the military leaders. Legends and accounts by the Greeks and Romans identify them as the most revered and feared members of Gallic society. From them students learned of the gods and the lore of the forests and of the punishments that could be meted out.

Druids prophesied the future, and defined the dangers of both natural and supernatural elements. Dim and shadowy folktales tell of spirits of the Earth, of Fire and of Water. A satanic figure, a man with a stag's head having huge twisted antlers appears on some relics. From acute observation, they charted the mysteries of the forest, the animal life that inhabited it and the magic of the seasons. This Druidic class should not be confused with the priests of organized religion in other regions of Europe. They were not supported by a well-defined pantheon of gods but rather by mysterious nature deities.

The wishes of these myriad gods were constantly analyzed by the Druids and proper sacrifices prepared. The priests held an awesome power of life or death for they served not only as the teachers, but as the final judges of men and women. There is irrefutable evidence that the Druids practiced human sacrifice before the second-century B.C. Over the years, this practice faded and animals were used to propitiate the gods. Finally men crafted votive offerings (of bronze, stone, iron, silver and gold) in the form of domestic and wild animals, that were substituted.

Ancient Celtic-Ligurian heads carved in stone date back to some 500 years before Christ. By this time, thousands of Celts occupied central and southern France. This pillar was found at a sanctuary near Aix-en-Provence.

There are no records of kings or queens among the Gauls. Priests, priestesses and military leaders assumed the duties and privileges of these positions. The priestesses and the priests of the Druidic order may well have had more power than many of the kings in other countries during the fifth century before Christ.

Gallic objects, both warlike and artistic, found in grave sites, reveal that the Celts in England and Ireland interacted with the Celts on the Continent. To a high degree they shared a common culture during some four centuries before Christ. Even in the regions that were to become France they identified themselves as Celts. It was only after the Roman invasions that these people became known as Gauls.

At a school of priestesses in Britain, women learned the art of divining and of casting spells, mixing potions and performing sacrifices. Such institutions may have existed in France as well. Women as well as men met at least once a year at a great annual fête held in the center of the country at Carnutes (Chartres). This was the greatest national assembly of the year. Druidic ceremonies, both sacred and profane, were celebrated in the secluded forests that served as sanctuaries.

Much of what we know of Celtic women comes directly from the Greeks. Diodorus Siculus writes of Gallic women as being as tall and strong as their men and, "they rival them in strength as well," he added. Another Greek, Marcellinus, noted that "a whole band of foreigners would be unable to cope with a single Gaul if he called his wife to his aid. She is usually very strong and with blue eyes; especially when swelling her neck, grimacing with her teeth and brandishing her pale arms of huge proportions, she begins to strike blows and kicks, as if they had been sent from the string of a catapult." That women of the higher caste were revered and elevated to important status is evidenced by the great number of female grave sites excavated in central France, especially in the Champagne region. Within many of these rich graves the popular bracelets and especially the neck rings or torques of bronze or gold were found. But no torques were ever found in the graves where weapons were buried.

The distribution of rich deposits of iron ore may well have been the deciding factor in the establishment by the Celts of their settlements in France. Copper and tin were both scarce metals. Bronze was softer and more difficult to produce than iron. Therefore, with the discovery of the uses of iron ore for swords, daggers, knives, axes, rims to reinforce wooden chariot wheels, horses' bits and javelin points, the restless indo-european peoples, who called themselves Celts, began to spread to the warmer climates of France and Italy, especially to those regions rich in iron ore.

This movement began as early as 1000 B.C. Some 250 years later, iron found in those regions where they settled was being used by a mixture of Celts, Ligurians and Iberians. But the Celts dominated these people and established themselves permanently in Alsace, Lorraine, Champagne, Burgundy, Franche-Comté and other iron-mining centers.

From the iron deposits in these areas came the weapons that made the conquests by the Celts possible. It was in the Hallstatt period, 800-450 B.C. (named for a small village in Austria), that the first iron age began. Long swords, daggers and higher quality iron weapons were only part of the equipment used by the Celts in battles. They also had the custom of decapitating the heads of their enemies and suspending these heads from their horses' trappings or on the sides of their chariots. It has been conjectured that this gruesome custom may have had a supernatural base, perhaps a belief that in this way they could control the spirits of the dead.

Knives, daggers and swords were fashioned by the Celts first of bronze and later of iron. Clean-shaven men who sometimes grew mustaches, the Celts crafted semicircular knives to use as razors. This one is ca. 200 B.C.

This Celtic idol was carved from limestone before the time of the Roman conquest of Gaul. It has a prominent nose and round head and seems to be holding an object, perhaps a smaller figure possibly human, in its arms.

23

Celtic Jewelry

A love of wine and war contributed greatly to the arts of the Celts. A fighting, drinking and feasting people, war was a way of life with them. Even when not involved in conflict with the nearby Germans and Italians, Celtic knights with their freemen followers often hired themselves out as mercenaries fighting in other countries far afield. Greek records tell of Celts fighting as far away as Egypt. So, from both nearby and distant places, art objects found their way into the Celtic homeland in central France. Torques or neck rings of both delicate and massive wrought bronze, gold and silver have been excavated in the burial places of the Celts. Necklaces were worn by both men and women. Women also invariably wore two bracelets, one on each arm. Anklets, brooches, gold or bronze earrings, finger rings, bronze belts and chains of bronze, gold or silver bedecked the upper-class females.

While much of the jewelry was influenced by objects brought back by the Celts from their many incursions into other countries, for the most part they were the fabrications of the Celts themselves. While certain designs were adapted, the Celts created a wide variety of original patterns, designs and forms.

Because the Celts were nature worshippers, interesting designs seem to have been inspired by the shapes of leaves, the patterns of bark on trees, the petals of flowers. One pattern, the Celtic palmette, which gives the impression of growth outward from a central stem, is well known. Figurines of men and women on horseback were created. Bronze belts were sometimes decorated in the *repoussé* style, with the craftsman working from the underside of the metal to create a raised impression. Representations of naked goddesses were common as were imaginative figures related to a sun and a moon god and goddess. Various art motifs were incised on metal helmets and shields. Many of the later shields were extensively decorated with complex abstract patterns which included curlicues, multiple heart shapes and interlocking circles.

Because of their love of wine, huge quantities of the essence of the grape were imported from the nearby Greek settlements in and around the ancient port city of Massilia, later Marseille. From these traders came not only wine but containers for it: cups, flagons and pitchers in distinctive shapes originated by Sythians, Etruscans, Greeks and Iberians. So the Celts' own works of art owed much to the highly developed arts of other European cultures.

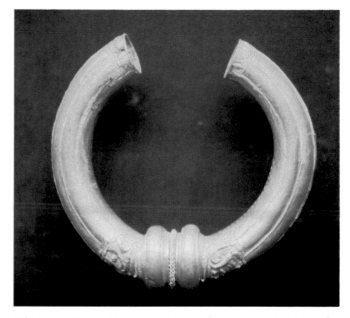

This massive gold torque (necklace) was made before the Romans conquered Gaul. It was worn by a tribal leader.

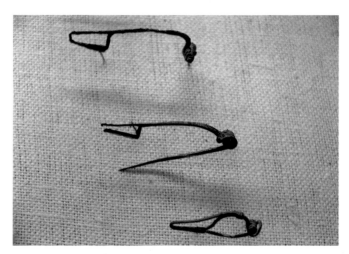

Long cloaks were worn by the Celts and were held up around the shoulders by these ingenious safety pins.

◀ *This extraordinary bronze sculpture created by a Gallo-Roman artist shows exuberance, joy, freedom and motion.*

Dated around 1000 B.C., this elaborate metallic belt with multiple linking parts was created by Celtic craftsmen.

The wild boar, *sus scrofa*, was a favorite subject of Celtic artists. Numerous sculptures, cast in various metals, and found at inhumation sites, have survived the passage of more than 2,000 years. That the forest-oriented, freedom-loving Celts revered the wild boar is not surprising. Their observation of that fierce animal must have shown them that it possessed many of the qualities they admired most in themselves. For like the Celts, the wild boar was a creature of the forests and the groves. In quiet secluded thickets it lived in independent and self-sufficient family groups. A hardy, adaptable animal, it was omnivorous (as were its hunters), feeding on smaller mammals, roots, nuts, fruit and birds. No other European mammal except man was so well equipped to survive. With a grey or black powerful, well-proportioned, narrow body the agile boar could often escape the Celtic horsemen and their hunting dogs by penetrating deep into the thickest underbrush of the woods. When cornered the boar, with its curved, lethal tusks, could, by lifting its head, rip the guts out of a hunting dog or a man. Its ripping bite is believed to be the most damaging of any mammal. Not even the tiger or leopard can inflict so much damage.

The wild boar was hunted for food and for sport. Yet the constant dangers of the hunt served to hone the fighting skills of young Celtic warriors. The full-grown wild boar that roamed the Ardennes forest could reach a height of more than three and one-half feet and weigh up to 350 pounds and was a worthy adversary.

Yet it may well have been the magical qualities that made the wild boar a subject for the artists of this superstitious clan — for the boars with their females and young are nocturnal animals. It is interesting to reflect that the Celts measured time by nights rather than by days. And these truculent wild creatures not only ate the foods that the Celts consumed, but also ate reptiles and were entirely immune from the snake's poisonous bite. It is no wonder that the superstitious Celtic people revered and reproduced the boar in stone and in bronze.

▲ *The energy and power of the wild boar, sacred to the Celts, is represented in this ancient bronze sculpture.*

Bearded and with his long hair tied up, a man in motion ▶ *has been rendered in bronze by a Gallo-Roman sculptor.*

A mature Julius Caesar is shown wearing a laurel wreath, symbol of victory. This silver Roman coin was struck *between 54 and 44 B.C. after his victory over Vercingétorix in Alésia which resulted in Rome's occupation of Gaul.*

The Victor

Julius Caesar was born 100 years before Christ into a rich and influential family. His mother's sister was married to the Roman consul Gaius Marius. At the age of 14, Julius began his rise to political prominence. At 17, he married Cornelia, the daughter of Lucius Cinna, leader of the government's popular party. She was the first of three wives, the others being Pompea, related to Pompey the Great whose support he sought, and Calpurnia whom he married when he was 41. Ten years later he had a love affair with the young Cleopatra.

Even with special connections, only two ways were open for a politician to acquire an army under his exclusive control: to be a praetor or a consul. It took Caesar twenty-four years to achieve his goal.

When he succeeded in having Cisalpine Gaul, the Roman province in northern Italy, awarded to him he used it as a base to mount an attack to bring all Gaul under the rule of Rome. This personal triumph was bought at a high price in the lives of his dedicated legionnaires and of thousands of Celtic soldiers. He was a fearless leader but also a cruel and revengeful one. After the battle of Bourges, Caesar wrote "they (his soldiers) spared neither the old nor the women nor the children." After the battle of Uxellehunum, he noted that "all those who had carried weapons had their hands cut off — but their lives were spared so that everyone could see how evil doers were punished."

The Celtic leader, Vercingétorix, brought Caesar nearest to defeat in his final battle in Gaul. Yet while extolling his opponent's ability and courage, Caesar exhibited him for three years in Rome and then had him publicly executed.

Uncommonly learned and highly intelligent, Caesar wrote lucidly; his works include a play, a book of poetry, two books dealing with linguistics and the well-known commentaries on the conquest of Gaul and on the Civil War in Rome: *De Bello Gallico* and *De Bello Civili*.

In his endless drive for omnipotence, Caesar made jealous and vengeful enemies. Some believed he wanted to be king, others that, as a dictator, he was destroying the Republic. On March 15, 44 B.C. , at the age of fifty-six, he was assassinated by twenty-nine of his colleagues, each driving a dagger into his body at least once.

Leader of the Celts, Vercingétorix is shown on the obverse side of a gold coin used in foreign trade. The inscription and style indicate the influence of Roman art on the Celts in Provincia before the conquest of Gaul.

The Vanquished

Vercingétorix (pronounced Vur'sin-jet-o-riks) was born into a leading Celtic military family, probably between 75 B.C. and 65 B.C. His father, Celtillus, had been chief or commander of the large Arverni clan until his ambition to become king brought about his death. For to the Celts, any attempt to take over the state government was punishable by execution.

The urge to unite his people against the advancing Romans became a crusade for young Vercingétorix. He had observed the slow encroachment of the Romans in Provence which had begun before his father's time but reached its peak in 58 B.C. when Caesar attacked in force. It was then that Vercingétorix was chosen leader of the largest and most powerful tribes: the Parisii (for whom Paris was named), the Pictones, the Lemorices, the Turoni, the Aulerci and other clans.

It is from the descriptions in Caesar's commentaries that we know most about Vercingétorix. He described his young enemy as a man of prodigious energy, a strict disciplinarian, a resourceful strategist and a worthy opponent. It is unfortunate that our only source of information comes from Caesar for it becomes evident that he praises him only to make his own victory seem greater.

Vercingétorix went into the final battle with a force of men larger than Caesar's army. His troops, both infantry and cavalry, were reckless, even fatalistic. But Caesar held the winning cards: superior organization, weapons and strategy.

For the conflict, Vercingétorix chose a hill at Alésia, possibly for two reasons. It was military tradition to occupy high ground, but perhaps more important, it was a sanctuary of the Druidic goddess Epona, a high priestess.

His choice of Alésia was disastrous. Caesar was an expert at siege warfare. The battle raged for two days but the defenders were cut off from reinforcements and supplies when Caesar's men diverted the nearby river and flooded the Celtics' base camp.

Vercingétorix offered his life to his own soldiers in an effort to appease the Romans. They refused. He surrendered by laying his arms at Caesar's feet. At that moment, the Celts became the Gauls.

Protected by their long shields and armed with short swords ready for combat, helmeted Roman legionnaires enter a Gallic city. This stone bas-relief of the Gallo-Roman period was excavated in the south of France, in Saint Rémi de Provence.

30

Rome In Gaul

The Romans called the Gauls barbarians. This was, of course, how the Chinese referred to the Mongols, the Japanese to the Ainus, the Spanish to the Aztecs, even the American Indians to the English, and on and on throughout history. Each country after a certain period of development likes to think of itself as the only civilized people — all others being "barbarians." It is a convenient term of disparagement meaning different things to different people at different times.

Exactly what the Romans meant is repeatedly expressed in their early writings, including those of Caesar. Both the Romans and Greeks accused the Gauls of being superstitious because they worshipped a different pantheon of gods. Since religion is such a strong binding force, the Romans set out to discredit the Gallic deities. One of the first measures imposed after the final battles in Gaul was the official replacement of the Druidic gods and goddesses with Roman deities. Teutates became Mercury (Caesar wrote that Teutates was the most important god of the Gauls). Jupiter, the Roman god of lightning and rain and controller of the heavens replaced Esus and other of the Celtic nature gods; Minerva replaced the priestess of the various arts. The sun god of the "barbarians" became Apollo, who, the Romans believed, cured or drove away disease.

For the Gauls to survive under the strict rule of the Romans it was necessary that they be able to communicate with them. Very few Gauls spoke Latin and their conquerors were completely unfamiliar with the complex Celtic language. The Gauls had no choice but to learn Latin and to learn it quickly.

First came the simple Latin words for food, animals, tools and weapons — but soon through necessity and exposure, Gallic men and women, and especially children, learned the rudiments of spoken Latin. Free men and slaves who worked on the roads learned from Roman road overseers and farm managers. As they became more familiar with Latin some of these captives rose to posts of low-level leadership. The best and brightest were groomed for service to the state.

The Romans, for many years, had developed great expertise in the training of "barbarians" as soldiers. The fighting men of Gaul were not to be an exception. Thousands who preferred battle to slavery quickly became part of the large standing army that protected Rome's ever-expanding borders. In this connection it is worth noting that, at the end of the battle of Alésia which marked the final fall of Gaul, Caesar himself awarded one captured Gaul to each Roman soldier as his slave. Doubtless many of these slaves, when and if they achieved the status of free men, joined a Roman legion. Within a few years, one all-Gallic legion emerged and became famous as the "Legion of the Lark."

When all Gaul had become a Roman colony, its people were exposed to the advanced technology offered by that progressive country. Among the most useful features was the construction of a huge network of roads and bridges (some of which still exist) throughout the captured territory. Such farm-to-market roads allowed Gallic produce to be moved to the villages and towns with increased profits to the farmers. These broad thoroughfares also allowed the military to police the entire country, largely eliminating the almost continuous fighting among the clans. And, as the number of thoroughfares increased, so did the water supply. Huge aqueducts (some still standing) brought water from rivers and lakes to the fast-growing villages and towns. Production of agricultural products and livestock was greatly stimulated.

The first of the Roman colonies, and one that received special treatment, was the well-located village of Lyon. This had previously been an important center of Celtic *Oppidum*, a hill fortress that included Druidic sanctuaries. Other colonies in Trêves and Lutetia (Paris) quickly followed. Because of Rome's liberal citizenship laws, many Gauls became Roman citizens in a relatively short time. Some of the more ambitious men occupied important positions in Roman politics. When the Romans moved in, the Gauls were ready to appear on what was, for them, a new stage of civilization.

In the early days of the occupation, companies of Roman and Gallic soldiers were stationed throughout the country and along its borders to ensure that the peace was kept. This police system worked quite well except for a minor rebellion led by the Druids seventy years after Caesar had defeated Vercingétorix. There were few local and no national rebellions. Much later, some 100 years after Caesar, a few Gallic nobles who had risen rapidly in rank, provoked what could have been a possible revolution, but it was quickly suppressed.

Intermixture and intermarriage between Gauls and Romans was rare, for the Romans, except in small numbers, did not emigrate to Gaul. Roman soldiers, builders and tradesmen must have intermarried or at least fathered many Roman-Gallic children. But this was a small number compared to the huge Gallic population. Most government officials who were forced by their profession to live in Gaul invariably retained their houses in Rome and returned to them whenever possible. So a large scale mixing of Gallic genes with those of their Roman conquerors did not occur.

Within the huge amphitheater chariot races were held on holidays. Chariot wheels grew so hot that one man had to throw water onto the smoking wheels while the agitator whipped the horses on as they rounded the oval track.

Laps were marked off by turning over the central bronze dolphins and taking down one egg. Note the officials in the center, ready to present the winner's palm and the laurel wreath and the chariot accidents at the corners.

33

Long hair flying in the wind, this bronze female figurine reflects both Gallic and Roman sculptural influences.

This bronze figure of a man in motion may represent a juggler or a garlanded winner of Gallo-Roman games.

34

Art And Artists

Very little purely Gallic art was produced in the long 500 years of Roman rule over Gaul. Art was produced by the Gauls, but it was truly a product of two cultures, one primitive, the other classical. Those works that show Gallic influence are almost always overshadowed by their imitation of the Roman style. The Gauls benefited from the Roman influence as is seen in later Gallo-Roman concepts in jewelry, statues and statuettes.

As the 200 years of peace in Roman Gaul continued, the once semi-nomadic Celts fell back on their love of the land, the waters and the forests, to form a peasantry of farmers and stock breeders. Rome needed grain, fruits, cattle and dairy products; the new breed of Gallic farmers supplied it. These founders of an agricultural tradition may never have fully given up their ancient beliefs, rooted as they were in two basic nature gods: the one a mother goddess of the earth, the other a masculine god of fertility and the natural elements.

Both Gaul and Rome prospered for some 300 years, at least 200 of these years at peace. Some Gallo-Romans became rich trading families, others rose to high office in politics, some soldiers even rose to the rank of general. As Romans in Italy deserted the farms for the cities, most of the Gauls stayed with the land, though some moved into Rome. Men and women who had started their lives as slaves worked their way up in the hierarchy of slaves to become indispensable as managers of their masters' huge estates. Others acted as record keepers and as confidants of their owners. A considerable number of these high-status slaves eventually became free men as did thousands of Gallic soldiers who guarded the frontiers.

As the countryside prospered, Rome's colonies in Bordeaux, Poitiers, Marseille (which the Gallo-Romans had largely taken over from the Greeks), Lyon, Toulouse and Autun grew into cities. In these "new" cities, the seeds of a new Gaul took root. Nurtured by the art and literature of Rome, (these were the years of Cicero, Lucretius, Catullus), Gauls read the history of the Roman Republic by Livy. They heard and some read the poetry of Virgil, during the forty years of the reign of Augustus Caesar. The former "barbarians" could see and marvel at Roman architecture such as the Forum Romanum with its exquisite temple of Venus. They heard of eighty silver statues erected in Rome in Augustus' honor. And in Gaul itself, at Nimes, was built the stately Maison Carrée. Other fine examples of Roman architecture rose at Arles (amphitheater, walls and gates still stand) and Vienne. They knew the splendid arches of Orange, St. Rémy and Aix-en-Provence. Gaul benefited immensely from the Roman excellence in architecture and building.

Resembling a singer or an orator, this statue was found near Orléans as were those at left. All may be deities.

35

In a remarkable piece of dynamic sculpture Jupiter makes ready to loose his most dreadful weapon, the thunderbolt.

To the Greeks and Romans, Jupiter was not only the father of the gods but also a universal figure of fertility.

Bacchus, often represented as a precocious child, was born of the union of Jupiter and Semele, a beautiful but human woman. In addition to being god of the grape, he was god of playwriting, acting and all entertainment.

In this revealing action-filled mosaic, the middle-aged Bacchus is extremely drunk. He holds on to Ariane who strokes his chin to calm him down while young Empelus keeps the staggering god of wine from falling down.

The Gallo-Roman state reached the apogee of its economic and cultural evolution within the first 200 years of Roman rule. The citizens of Gaul had become as Roman as the Romans themselves by 150 A.D.

The heritage of Rome became more apparent as wall paintings, frescoes and mosaics (many created by slave artisans) reflecting the lives of gods adorned the residences of the rich. Bath houses, as elaborately decorated as those in Rome itself, became part of Gallic life. Women of Lyon and Paris wore wigs and dyed their hair. Lip rouge, cheek rouge and eye shadow were commonly used.

The Roman religion was fully adopted. Gauls learned to adopt and revere the *numina*, the impersonal nature spirits (not so far from the household gods of the Celts). These spirits helped or hindered individuals depending

Cupid (or Eros) representing innocent sexuality is fighting with Pan, the seducer of women. Pan, half human and half horse, is considered the stronger and is forced to fight with his left hand behind his back.

upon the treatment they received. As the Romans had borrowed earlier from the Etruscans, so the Gauls in turn borrowed religious rituals from the Romans. They learned divination and prophecy; they read the future in the entrails of sacrificed animals. The oracles were revered and their advice followed.

Eros, son of Aphrodite became Cupid, son of Venus; Hermes, messenger of the Greek gods became Mercury; Dionysus became Bacchus, god of the grape and was represented more often in mosaics than the other gods. Zeus became Jupiter and Hera, Juno. These were long lived anthropomorphic gods, some born in ancient Greece, adapted by the Romans and changed again by the Gauls.

Yet it was not all one-way traffic. The Romans used the wild boar, a Gallic symbol, in the magnificent Trajan monument on which the sacred emblem is prominently displayed.

Like the Romans, the Gauls created many decorative objects and wore them. The gold bracelet above is inlaid with a miniature carving of a plump Apollo. The god holds a bow and arrow. His symbolic lyre is at his feet.

The art of the Celts speaks to us even after many years of Roman occupation of Gaul. Their jewelry has survived time and place. One can find traces of Celtic, Roman and Greek influences in the riches that were displayed around the necks, arms and fingers of Gallo-Roman maidens and matrons.

Most Gallo-Roman jewelry still shows the influences of the Celtic gods, even when the decorations seem simple. An echo goes back to ancient times when the carrying of a talisman afforded protection to the wearer, and also displayed status and wealth. It must be remembered that our knowledge of many of the ancient arts of the jeweler goes back to early burials — where the most precious possessions of the owners accompanied them on their journey to another life. By the richness and workmanship of jewelry found in tombs we know that women of the later Gallo-Roman province of Gaul were held in high esteem; that they had a love of beauty, that personal adornment was an important part of civilization.

It is probable that the crafting of jewelry was often the work of talented slaves who were sometimes given a portion of the profits from their work. Actually slaves supplied much of the Gallo-Roman work force. Slave artisans were not only organized to fabricate jewelry but were builders of houses, stone masons and woodworkers. From Rome came the philosophy of Epicurius. But this way of life, recommending the pursuit of pleasure, was never widely adopted in Gaul. More prevalent was the way of the Stoics who advocated that the good life could only be obtained through pure reason. The Gallo-Romans, for the most part, led an ordered life and looked forward to an ordered universe.

Literature, which included philosophy, humor and satire, played an important part in the Gallic culture. It was said that the language schools of Gaul surpassed even those of Rome. By the time the Roman empire had begun to crumble, Roman culture had formed the basis of a new civilization.

486 - 986 A.D.
FIRST CHRISTIAN KINGS

Franks unite under Clovis I but power shifts from later kings to Mayors of the Palace Charles Martel and Pépin the Short. Charlemagne, son of Pépin, founds the Empire of the West and leads the Carolingian Renaissance. The wheeled plow, horsecollar and horseshoe improve farming. Feudal laws and military and church reforms ameliorate peasant conditions. Viking and Saracen raids are repelled in the tenth century; monasteries are founded. Medieval art flourishes.

HISTORICAL CHRONOLOGY	
486	Last imperial governor of northern Gaul crushed by Clovis. Beginning of expansion of future Merovingian kingdom.
496	Franks become Christians with the conversion and baptism of Clovis.
613	Monarchical power shifts from Merovingian kings to the aristocracy.
732	Moslem invasion turned back at Poitiers by then mayor of the palace, Charles Martel. Beginning of use of mounted knights.
751	Overthrow of the Merovingian monarchy by Pépin the Short, mayor of the palace.
768—814	Charlemagne rules as king of the Franks.
786	Oath of loyalty sworn to Charlemagne by all Frankish subjects.
800	Charlemagne crowned emperor of the West on Christmas day.
810—911	Viking raids along the coast; Saracen pirates in the south.
843	Carolingian empire divided into three kingdoms at the Treaty of Verdun; one is France.
847	Beginning of decline of monarchical power and the rise of feudal lords: Treaty of Mersen orders all free men to commend themselves to lords.
848	Moslems invade Marseille.
c. 850	Bishops free themselves from the authority of the archbishops through the forgery of the Pseudo-Isidorian Decretal at Rheims.
877	Heritability of royal vassals' fiefs recognized by King Charles the Bald.
897	Boso creates the kingdom of Provence.
911	Viking leader Rollo recognized as duke of Normandy by King Charles the Simple.

ART CHRONOLOGY	
480 — 524	Boethius translates Plato and Aristotle into Latin.
573 — 94	History of the Franks written by Grégoire, bishop of Tours.
585—615	Celtic influence in Frankish Church occurs through Saint Colombanus, founder of monastery of Luxeuil.
629—36	Church of Saint Denis embellished by King Dagobert.
781	Alcuin of York meets Charlemagne.
789	Christian mission of Charlemagne defined in Admonitio Generalis.
790—800	Construction of Charlemagne's palace in Aachen.
791	Codex Carolinus, a collection of royal correspondence is compiled.
794	Synod of Frankfurt establishes the authority of Charlemagne concerning Church doctrine.
796	Carolingian court enriched by treasure of the conquered Avars.
797	Alcuin begins to call Charlemagne's power imperial. Center of manuscript production is located at his abbey of Saint Martin of Tours.
800's	Agricultural improvements: heavy-wheeled plow, horseshoe, three field crop rotation system.
817	Imposition of the Benedictine Rule upon all monasteries by Louis the Pious.
834—42	Bible of Tours.
842	Earliest record of French vernacular preserved in the Treaty of Strasbourg. History of the Sons of Louis the Pious written by Nithard.
892	Town wall of Troyes is rebuilt.
910	Benedictine monasticism begins with the foundation of Cluny by Duke Guillaume V of Aquitaine.

Baptism of Clovis in 481 as imagined by a fifteenth century artist. But the "fleur-de-lis" was not adopted as France's national symbol until 1368.

Clovis Expels
The Romans

Christianity did not begin in Gaul with the baptism of King Clovis I in 448, although he was the first major leader of the Saline Frankish people to become a Christian. His conversion was partly accomplished by his wife Clotilde, a princess of Burgundy. Clovis observed her from afar before deciding that she should be queen of the Franks. The contemporary historian Grégoire of Tours wrote that when Clovis asked for the hand of Clotilde, her father King Gundioc consented only because he was too frightened of Clovis to refuse him anything including his daughter. At first Clotilde tried to convert Clovis to Christianity with little success. However, when he faced defeat against the Alamanni army, he prayed to his wife's god for victory. After winning the battle, Clovis was convinced that God had shown him his power. Clovis took instruction from Saint Remigious, bishop of Rheims, then agreed to be baptized a Christian. Yet he was concerned about asking his army to forsake

their gods. A meeting was arranged but, Grégoire continues, "God had already interceded and the troops all shouted 'we will give up the worship of our mortal gods, pious king, and we are prepared to follow the immortal God about whom Remigious preaches.' "

The fame of King Clovis did not merely rest upon his acceptance of Christianity but upon his never ending battles, mostly successful, against the enemies of the Franks. It was his victory over the Romans at Soissons which heralded the end of Roman power in Gaul. After the victory, in the tradition of Julius Caesar, he executed the Roman General Syagrius.

Religion, as we have noted, came late to Clovis. Even after his coversion, he continued to be a brutal and bloody king. When he died in Paris in 511 at the age of forty-five, he had either personally killed or had executed most of his enemies. This included a considerable number of members of his own family.

In spite of his crimes, this early leader of the Franks remained a Christian. He was buried in the Church of the Holy Apostles in Paris, a church built by himself and Queen Clotilde. This church still exists renamed after Sainte Geneviève.

In these details from a ninth century ivory-carved book cover, the sacred oil (top) used to anoint kings is poured by the hand of God. (Below) Clovis is baptized and becomes the first Merovingian king of the Franks.

The sons and grandsons of King Clovis were neither wise nor powerful rulers; rather they proved to be lawless and dissolute. Interminable wars, inter-family murders, political assassinations and the torture of Christians marked their restless reigns. Within the anarchy that prevailed for the next 200 years, these inept rulers were ultimately reduced to puppet kings, manipulated by rich landowners and by their own inefficient bureaucracy. From the nobles a strong leader emerged known as the mayor of the Palace who became the real ruler of the medieval Franks.

Such a man was Carolus (Charles) Martel. The entire Carolingian period is known by the name of this remarkable man. In the year 732 he welded together a fighting force that succeeded in destroying the Moslems who had attacked Poitiers in force. This legendary leader became the father of Pépin le Bref (the Short), who successfully succeeded him as mayor of the Palace. And then came the political move that set the stage for the Carolingian Renaissance. In the year 751, Pépin the Short realized that the power of mayor of the Palace could be used more effectively if the crown went with it.

Fortunately he had a friend and ally in Bishop Boniface, a missionary and the official representative of the Pope.

The papacy needed all the help it could get at this time and Pépin needed the backing of the Pope. Within a year, Boniface confered the crown upon him. Shortly afterwards, Pope Steven II, traveling through Gaul stopped in Saint Denis, near Paris, where he officially repeated the ceremony. He crowned Pépin king of the Franks on July 28, 754 and with great prescience, he named Pépin's sons Charlemagne and Carloman as his heirs. This act effectively deposed King Childeric III. His long hair symbolic of kingship was cut, then he was banished to a remote monastery. Within two years, Pépin had repaid the Pope's favor by defeating the Lombards. He propped up the authority of Pope Steven with "the Donation of Pépin" when by force of arms he confirmed the Pope's authority over a broad strip of land that ran from Rome to Ravenna. Just before his death he divided his kingdom between his two young sons: Charles, who would become Charles the Great or Charlemagne, and Carloman his younger brother.

43

Charlemagne and his legitimate son Pépin whom he made king of Italy. His bastard son of the same name was tonsured and sent away to a monastery.

Charlemagne

To cope with the chaotic times, the fragmentation of tribal kingdoms and the instability of the Roman empire required a leader with a robust constitution, a quick intelligence and an enjoyment of power and glory. Such a man was Charlemagne, king of the Franks. He had the additional attributes of a love for women and family life, a positive belief in Christ and the institutions of the Church, and a passionate commitment to the improvement of the economic and cultural welfare of the vast number of people who looked to him for discipline and order. He kept in ready reserve the saving grace of a sense of humor.

Within a broad framework of incessant battles with the Saxons, the Lombards, the Moors, the Danes, the Avars and the Bavarians, the king lived a long, busy and — it would seem by the memoirs of his biographers — a happy life.

Charlemagne married four times. His first marriage,

arranged by his mother Bertrada, was to the daughter of Desiderius, king of the Lombards. But they were wedded only a year before he mysteriously sent this young princess away. She later caused him trouble when she joined his brother Carloman's widow and they moved into the court of her father. The young king quickly settled this dispute. He moved swiftly against Desiderius and defeated him in battle. Rather than executing his ex-father-in-law, he generously exiled the king to the monastery of Corbie for life.

He had more luck with his succeeding three wives. He outlived all three of them and three of his children as well, then began adding concubines to his bed. The legitimate queens bore him at least ten children. By four concubines he fathered another six or perhaps more.

Charlemagne's most important biographer, Einhard, was more than a friend and a scribe. For twenty-three years he was deeply involved in many of Charlemagne's exploits as trusted emissary and confidant. He wrote from first-hand observation that the king had personally directed the rearing of his sons and daughters, loved them all, and indeed "never sat down to eat without them and never went on a journey without them."

Believed to be Charlemagne, a Carolingian king rides with no stirrups which were unknown in France before the ninth century. Here he wears only a mustache but, after he became emperor, he is known to have grown a full beard.

45

One can imagine this imperial caravan traveling across the Roman built roads and *par monts et par vaux* of France, the king proudly riding with his sons on either side, his wives, daughters and concubines following.

The sons of the king were expected to study mathematics as their father had. For sport and survival experience, Charlemagne took the princes on the hunting forays which were a part of his weekly activities. Special attention was given to the use of arms in hunting and warfare. His daughters were taught reading and rhetoric, but emphasis was also placed on spinning and weaving. He must have had great plans for his daughters' futures for one of them, Rotrude, while a very small child became engaged to marry the young man who would become the Emperor Constantine VI. The marriage never took place. Charlemagne's affection for his daughters seems to have been excessive: although the royal princesses must have had many offers of marriage, the king never allowed them to leave his court. They lived with him until his death which did not come until his seventy-second year. This was an extraordinary age for any man to live to during the early Middle Ages. Such confinement of the young women to the court was not unusual. But at least two of them, Rotrude and Bertha, gave birth to illegitimate offspring. The king did, however, make provisions for these grandchildren. They were reared as royalty. And he later arranged lucrative and prestigious posts for them.

But we must leave this picturesque family scene to view the awesome power of this extraordinary ruler. First, we must go back to the pre-Christian kings to comprehend how that much authority came into being. The followers of the chosen leader had believed that he was imbued with sacred or magical faculties. This sacral power was hereditary, passing from king to king. By the time of Charlemagne, four generations of Frankish kings had accepted Christianity. Christ and the Holy Spirit had replaced the pagan gods, and the Frankish kings had become the direct representatives of Christ on earth. Even the touch of the king was believed to have a specific healing effect. Being Christ's representative gave the king even more actual spiritual authority than the Pope. His was in partnership with Christ whereas the Pope was considered only the representative of Saint Peter and the Catholic Church.

Charlemagne took his Christian responsibilities seriously. He attended mass every morning and whenever possible vespers at night. His thirst for religion was almost as great as his thirst for conquest and knowledge.

It is impossible to say whether Charlemagne actually ever learned to read. We know that he spoke the Frankish language and that he knew a considerable amount of Latin and a little Greek. His biographer at no time said that the king could not read but he was very clear about the fact that he could not write. Einhard wrote, "the king also tried to learn to write. He kept writing-tablets and notebooks under his pillow so that he could try his hand in forming letters during his leisure moments. Although he tried very hard he had begun too late in life and made little progress." Yet this inability to write did not prevent the king from having the important religious works of his time read aloud to him. His favorite author was Saint Augustine and he took special pleasure from readings from *The City of God*.

The king actively encouraged the revival and extension of Christian education. The Church under Charlemagne's prodding and support began what would become a cultural Christian renaissance. Then the right man arrived at the right time to visit the court at Aachen.

He was Alcuin, his surname Albinus, an Englishman who had directed the Cathedral School across the Channel in York. Like other learned men, including Einhard the Swabian (Charlemagne's biographer) and Warnefrid of Lombardy, (known as Paul the Deacon), Alcuin was impressed by the king's abiding interest in Christianity and culture. When they met later in Pavia, the king persuaded Alcuin to travel to Aachen and to head the Imperial Palace school. This Alcuin did with the result that Charlemagne, Einhard, the king's children, hundreds of clerics and other functionaries of his court all became Alcuin's pupils. It was Alcuin's dream and then Charlemagne's as well that a new and enlightened capital would rise in the Frankish kingdom and that it would be imbued with the fullness of the Holy Spirit. Surprisingly they succeeded amazingly well.

Without this revival of interest in the application of religion to education much of the stored knowledge, especially the literary works of the Romans and the Greeks, would have been lost. Alcuin put his pupils to work copying Latin poetry and prose, the literature of the Greeks and the tales and legends of the early Gauls. For the first time, Frankish culture was recorded in detail. Perhaps the greatest achievement of Charlemagne is not his ceaseless wars and the extension of territory to his empire but the preservation of the great literatures of the Greeks, Romans and Franks.

Not only did the Imperial Palace school furnish teachers to educate students hungry for learning, it also reached out, by order of the emperor, to the bishops and archbishops, commanding them to found new monastic orders and to extend studies and classes in the existing ones. Charlemagne himself ordered books from the other learning centers of Europe. His imperial library became among the richest in the medieval world. As important volumes were copied, they were widely distributed and read. Higher standards for the education of the clergy resulted in more and better teachers. The king had a passion for learning and he commanded *studium discendi*. He was obeyed: laziness and stupidity were severely punished; zeal was rewarded. Study could

Traditionally known as the talisman of Charlemagne, the center of this gold and jeweled pendant is believed to hold a relic of the Cross.

lead to being named bishop or abbot of a rich monastery. It was not enough simply to read and copy existing books. Errors in them were to be sought out and corrected. New editions of the Bible were edited and reproduced. So important was the work done at this time by Alcuin and his pupils that books created or copied by them carried the notation *x e x authentico libro*. And it was Alcuin who revised the apostles' creed and put it into the Frankish language in its current form. This form later was retranslated to become the standard one used in Rome.

It could have been the voluminous writings of Alcuin that influenced Pope Leo III and Charlemagne himself to think that the king could become emperor of the West. Yet other strong forces were at work to make this event inevitable. After the death of Charlemagne's father Pépin, the Lombards continued to threaten the papacy and Rome. At the request of Pope Hadrian, Charlemagne made two attacks on the Lombards and the second battle

effectively ended the Lombard kingdom. And then Pope Leo III, Hadrian's successor, was attacked by enemies within Rome who threatened to blind him and to cut out his tongue. He escaped and Charlemagne came to his rescue, occupying Rome and restoring Leo to the papal throne. The grateful Pope crowned Charlemagne on Christmas day of the year 800 in the Basilica of Saint Peter. The king was now "Charles, the most pious Augustus, crowned of God, to the great and peace given emperor be life and victory." Now he was emperor of the Romans and in fact emperor of the West. Charlemagne may have felt that such a title was not a good diplomatic move, but he accepted the honor and the title.

All was not always smooth sailing between the king and the head of his school. When Charlemagne forced baptism on the Saxons (after thirty-three years of incessant warfare), Alcuin protested telling the king that a man could be driven to baptism but not to a belief in God.

47

The scriptorium of the monastery of Saint Gall created this illustration of the biblical general Joab riding to war. But the battle standard his followers are carrying and their chain mail armor belong to the ninth century.

The Song Of Roland

As a great military leader, Charlemagne is not only remembered for the important battles that he won but for one unimportant battle that he lost. The Battle of Ronceveaux was fought high in the Pyrenees Mountains and was a skirmish with a band of Basque marauders bent on revenge for the Frankish assault on Pamplona. The Basques prepared an ambush in a narrow mountain pass. Charlemagne's army, which had invaded the Moorish-dominated Spanish peninsula on behalf of the Christians with moderate success, was returning to its headquarters at Aachen. His main force had filed through the pass and only the rear guard was exposed. The waiting Basques pounced upon them and, in the carnage that ensued, all of them were killed, including three or more of the notable knights of Charlemagne's court. They were Eggihard, *sénéchal* of the king's table; Anshelm, count of the Palace, and Roland, lord of the Breton Marches. With no survivors, there was no way for posterity to know the exact details of the conflict. However, this dramatic episode was transmitted as legend through the succeeding centuries, for more than 300 years later, the epic poem "La Chanson de Roland" appeared and quickly spread throughout France, England and Germany.

The simple historic account had undergone many changes. The raiding party of Basques became an

This book of psalms was made to be read or sung to the music of the psalter at bottom right. It was ordered by

Charlemagne who presented it as a gift to Pope Adrian I. Details on the cover show craftsmen making the book.

invading horde of Moslems intent upon destroying Christiandom. The three exemplary knights, Roland, Eggihard and Anshelm, had been joined by nine other heroes and a disloyal knight, Ganaleon, who betrayed them. Too late to save his heroes, Charlemagne, who is the central figure in the poem, turned back in time to avenge them. The theme of this medieval *chef-d'oeuvre* is the battle between good and evil as seen in the conflict

between Christianity and paganism. The secondary theme is the twelfth-century concept of chivalry and of death before dishonor. The "Chanson de Roland" was only one of some eighty such heroic poems that surfaced in the twelfth to fifteenth century. Most of these *Chansons de Gestes* (songs of deeds) celebrated the exploits of Charlemagne and of his heroic knights. We learn more about them in the twelfth and thirteenth centuries.

In a seminal painting of the Carolingian period, a talented artist from the Ebo monastery depicts an inspired Saint Matthew writing the Gospels.

The Carolingian Renaissance continued, although precariously, through the reign of Louis le Pieux (the Pious). Lacking his father's drive, Louis nonetheless continued to hold Charlemagne's empire together. New monasteries were founded; libraries protected collections of books and manuscripts and continued to create or copy them.

An important advisor to Louis was his illegitimate half-brother Drogo who, as archbishop of Metz, supported and directed the artists who created some of the most original and beautiful illuminated manuscripts of the entire Carolingian period.

Early in the reign of Louis came more raids by the Norsemen, which had started in Charlemagne's time. Sweeping along the coast and sailing up the rivers, they ransacked monasteries and plundered estates. Within the next thirty years they would penetrate the rivers of France as far as Amiens, Rouen and Paris. Longtime

traders with the Saxons, the marauders soon coveted not only the loot but the rich and pleasant countryside as well. While pirate bands continued to ravage and pillage, other raiders settled to become known as Normans (Northmen) and the region became Normandy. Within 100 years, the invaders had adopted Christianity and become defenders of French territory.

Because of the rules of succession Louis, at a relatively early age, divided his kingdom (which was considered his personal property) among his three sons, Pépin, Lothair and Ludwig. This he quickly regretted for he soon fell in love. He put aside the mother of his first sons, married Judith of Alemannia and fathered Charles, later known as Charles le Chauve (the Bald), who was then included in the partition.

Upon Louis's death, the kingdom was divided by four, later reduced to three by the death of Pépin. None of the brothers was content with the lands left to them.

REXREGUMDOMINUSMUNDUMDICIONEGUBERNANS
IMPERIIASCEPTRUMREGNANSQIIUREPERENNI
INMORTALTENESCUMCRIMINAMULTAPARENTUM
LAXASTRUGEIUSTITIAECUMFRENALOCARAS
OMNIBUSERGOTUISSERUISSUPERASTRABEATAM
SPERAREHINCUITATESCITOCHRISTEDEDISTI
DENIQUEETMODOEDEUSPATRISQETUIQE
NUNCNOMENDRITIAMUNCTASTUPEBANT
SAECULADUOUMENERTCEQOAGESTATURAMICA
SUMMIXPICOLEDUESONATRITEGERENDUMHOC
PERIUSTAMOTHREGNAYIDOQODTOLLERELEGEM
ATQDECERETOTUMAUGUSTUSNUTUEXCOLATORBEM
NAMHOCFANUSTANTOCIRANDOCARDINEPRODIT
ORBSSCIAUTCALEAMESULTUCAESARISORET
AUGUSTOPUREFERETALHINCLAUDECORONAM
NAMOPTIMDEXTRAMUTDIUINAPARETARTE
STIPSTESTUADETQTRIUMPOSCIMUSOMNES
IAMALMUMUSTOIUSTITIQUODREGNETUBIQE
HAECSILIEUDATATOUELIGATUGIRETAMICO
DUMADFERLORICAPLACITUMSICIPSAPARATUM
OPTEMUSNSEMPERAMIUMQUEMPIECHRISTUS
RETUTATURQUAMONILUSIALOPREMITASTFUR
FASUELINLLOATOTERATHOTISCRIMINEDIRO
DEFENSORRTESSEGIRMUMONSTRATAMANDUM
IUSORNATAMEATCAESARIOBTINETHAUSTUM
OMENFITQAMNOCTUTUMIMPERIUMMANETORBE
ENREGNAGALUOMNEPERAEUAMMUNERADONANT
ETPERSAUTOICREUISOBATELATUSAMBIT
GENSPLEBSLETAPROPAGOSUCINNAMPIEDONAT
MUSAMUIUTEOENSMANEATSCITSCUTUETAMARE
SPEMEXSULSCEPTRATENENDOOUMFIDEIDATUBIQ
REMHAUSTDONECSAECLASUADEPELLITABARTE
QAEFORMOELURATENEBUNTTELANEFASSINT
ETSEDAREIENTERRAESONDANDAFROTERUIAM
QUAMESTSOLISUSPERMANETEGITAUGUSTOUILE
TRANSFORATORBISCRISTICUMCLARATRIBUTA
IURECOLEDIDUMEMOREQTROPAPARANSDAT
QUAEHOCSINTUMENTIABIQMEANSDEOTUMABORE
NEMPETONATURGETQUEPROBEPECTUSDIUAMARI
SITTREMORESTQUEBONAEDIUINOMUNEREFAMAE
PROFICITINDEOQUEMADIDUMPRETUMINLICITAQ
SICABICITPORTUOCRUCEDATLAESUMSEQITURQ
HUNCTIBINIMINDODATUMOSEMPERCASTQPTUQ
CAESARLARGEMODOUISUTUCASTRAINIMICIAST
TERRESSPEMQETUMORALUINIMICATUGANSDAT
TUPIUSETCRATNIULUMPRONUMROGATHAECGENS
ADUENIAMREANTUUSNOBISADIUSSAPARENTIS
CONSCRIPSIDUDUONAMCRISTILAUDELIBELLUM
UERSIBUSETPROSATIBIQENUNCINDUPERATOR
OFFEROSANCTELIBENSCUIUSPRAECEDITIMAGO
STANSARMATAFIDEUICTOREMMONSTRATUBIQUE

Charlemagne's son, Louis the Pious, is pictured as a soldier of the cross in this unusual combination of text with illumination. A halo attests to the sacred status of kings and the letters read: "You Christ Crown Louis."

The splendor of Charles the Bald, last of the Carolingian kings, is revealed in a magnificent gold encrusted scene.

Above, the hand of God offers his blessing. This may indicate that the king's rule is under divine guidance.

The crowned Lothair tried to take over the country. Wars that had started between them before Louis's death continued. Charles and Ludwig joined forces, and in the Oath of Strasbourg agreed to defend and protect each another. This agreement divided France from Germany. Charles became king of the West, and Ludwig the East. Lothair settled for Italy at the Treaty of Verdun. Thus the empire of Charlemagne was split into France under Charles, Germany under Ludwig and Italy, including Rome, under Lothair. An historic oath was sworn at Strasbourg in Alsace. The followers of Ludwig spoke German, so Charles took the oath in that language. Ludwig repeated the oath in an interesting combination of early French and Latin. The oath was recorded by the historian Nitard, illegitimate son of Charlemagne's daughter Bertha. This is the first written evidence of the development of the French language. It read as follows: *ab Ludher nul plaid nunquam prindrai, qui, meon vol, cist meon fradre Karle in damno sit.* "I will make no agreement with my brother Lothair which shall, with my consent, be to the prejudice of my brother Charles."

A picture story from the Grandval Bible, made around 840 ▶
A.D., shows the creation, temptation, fall and punishment.

Some monks went on the crusades both for religious ideals and a wish to rid the Holy Land of the infidels. On his colorful robe is the insignia of the Order of the Knights Templars. Above him is his fighting helmet and shield.

54

THE CAROLINGIAN RENAISSANCE

Hugues Capet becomes king of France and establishes principal of primogeniture making eldest son hereditary ruler. First *Chanson de Gestes*, "Song of Roland," written and sung. Heavy-wheeled plows enable farmers to cultivate damp fertile soil. Guillaume, duke of Normandy, conquers England. The Abbey Church of Cluny is founded. Pope Urbain, a Cluniac monk, preaches the first Crusade at Clermont. Crusaders defeat Moslems and occupy Jerusalem for a year. Further forays into the East acquaint Europe with Saracen and Byzantine cultures affecting art, literature, science, philosophy, architecture and cuisine.

HISTORICAL CHRONOLOGY		ART CHRONOLOGY	
c. 10th C.	*The Church tries to limit violence with* The Peace of God *and later* The Truce of God. *The knight is defined as a soldier of Christ.*	*1070-1127*	*Guillaume, count of Poitou and duke of Aquitaine, said to be the "first troubadour."*
c. 11th C.	*Society becomes defined: those who pray, those who fight and those who labor.*	*1084-98*	*Cistercian Order, founded at Cîteaux, rejects wealth and ritual of Cluniac order.*
987	*Carolingian dynasty ends — Capetian dynasty begins with Hugues Capet.*	*12th C.*	*Rediscovery of Latin and classical culture. Romanesque and Gothic art and architecture.*
1035	*King Henry I performs his duty as feudal lord of Guillaume of Aquitaine.*	*1100-20*	Song of Roland *celebrates Charlemagne and the tragedy and defeat of Ronceveaux.*
1066	*Duke Guillaume of Normandy (William the Conqueror) invades England and becomes its king.*	*1119*	*Pierre Abelard (40), eminent teacher, is castrated for his love affair with his student Héloise (17). They both enter religious orders.*
1080	*Merchant and trade guilds are granted rights in Saint Quentin, Douai, Arras and Saint Omer.*	*1124*	*History of the first Crusade,* Deeds of God through the Franks, *by Abbot Guibert.*
1095	*The First Crusade — the People's Crusade — instigated by Pope Urbain II at Clermont.*	*c. 1126-45*	*Translation of Euclid's* Geometry *and Arabic works on algebra and trigonometry.*
1124	*The principle that the king can become the vassal of only the Pope places the former at the head of the feudal hierarchy.*	*1130*	*Walled city of Carcassonne.*
1128	*The religious knightly order of the Templars receives its authority.*	*c. 1130-80*	Chanson de Geste *Cycle of Guillaume of Orange celebrates Carolingian splendor and knights.*
1108—36	*Louis VI undermines the power of the nobility by granting independence to certain cities.*	*c. 1137*	*Biography of Louis VI written by his contemporary Abbot Suger of Saint Denis.*
1137	*Louis VII marries Eleanor, duchess of Aquitaine.*	*1141*	*Moslem Koran translated for Peter of Cluny.*
1147—49	*Second Crusade to the Holy land is led by Louis VII and Eleanor of Aquitaine.*	*c. 1154-86*	Romance of Mount Saint Michel *about pilgrims.*
1152—4	*Aquitaine is lost to France with the annulment of the marriage to Eleanor. She marries Henry of Anjou. He is crowned King Henry II of England.*	*c. 1168*	*Construction of Notre Dame of Paris begins.*
1170	*Henry II of England performs homage to his feudal lord Louis VII.*	*c. 1180*	The Conquest of Constantinople *by Crusader Villehardouin, the first great history in French.*
		1173-84	*Peter Waldo preaches absolute poverty and the purification of the Church.*

In 1066 a large comet (later called Halley's comet) was visible over England. King Harold is shown on this section of the Bayeux embroidery being informed of this ill-portent. The Saxons who are observing the comet are

The Norman Conquest

The rise of the knights, the spread of militant Christianity, the coming of age of feudalism and the development of a new style of warfare may all be seen in the life and exploits of a Norman duke, a vassal of the French King Henri I.

He may well have inherited his energy and daring from his father known both as Robert the Magnificent and Robert the Devil. Orphaned at the age of eight he was considered a bastard by Christian standards because his parents were not married in the Church. But this meant nothing at the time in Normandy, a region settled by Norsemen to whom the act of cohabitation constituted legitimate marriage. At the age of twenty, he ascended to the dukedom of Normandy. He was knighted by the king of France whose vassal he was. His name: Guillaume I.

A reckless fighter, Guillaume was also a diplomat. He skillfully used the new feudalism based on oaths of fidelity and mutual defense to create an invincible military organization. Guillaume of Normandy had a

clean-shaven although the majority of Saxons at this time were bearded. It has been conjectured that the Norman needleworkers at Bayeux (in Normandy) had never seen Saxons and so portrayed them beardless like the Normans.

vision of a new way to conquer the areas he planned to dominate. He first gathered together and trained a large number of mounted knights. The duke saw to it that they were supplied with well-schooled war horses. Then he set out to achieve his ambition to become king of England. After landing on the coast his mounted men showed their superiority over the English foot-soldiers at the battle of Hastings. Their use of the stirrup, recently adopted, made it possible for a horseman to keep his balance as he fought with long sword, battle-axe or lance. Horses of Guillaume's knights were iron-shod so that they could maneuver in rough country. Victory came quickly. He brought to history a new age based upon the use of armored cavalry.

Guillaume did indeed have a weak but legitimate claim to the crown. For his father's sister Emma had married the Anglo-Saxon King Ethelbert. When her husband died, Queen Emma married his successor. Their son became King Edward the Confessor. When he died without an heir, Duke Guillaume, his Norman first cousin, had an hereditary claim to the throne.

Guillaume's attack on England had the full support of Pope Alexander II. Indeed he supplied Guillaume with a banner emblazoned with the Cross of Christ. Guillaume I became conqueror of England. His weapons were his chevaliers (horsemen), the Church militant, the politics of feudalism and a new kind of mobile warfare. It was these developments that set the stage for the first Crusade.

The Crusades

France was at war with itself; terror in the form of murder, torture and rape was rampant. Philippe I, the king from 1060 to 1108, was said by Pope Gregory VII to be "the worst of plunderers." Knights were more likely to be predators than protectors.

Political and church reforms were overdue but they were not to come from the nobility, but the Church which held that monks must move out of their isolation, that they had a duty not only to God but to man. How near the country was to anarchy can be seen by two desperate measures put forward. The Truce of God asked that all refrain from fighting between sunset on Wednesday to sunrise on Monday. There was to be no fighting on holy days. A second proposal, The Peace of God, required that the lives of the clergy, merchants, farmers, women, children and pilgrims be spared. This proposal fared no better than the restriction on battle hours. As the king, dukes and vassals broke their vows, the clergy, using their feudal armies, began their own wars of defense and retaliation.

Then came a Cluniac monk who had advanced in the church to become the French Pope Urbain II. After receiving a call for help from the Byzantine Christians, then being attacked by the Seljuk Turks (who had already occupied much of the Holy Land), Pope Urban convoked the Council of Clermont (now Clermont-Ferrand). In a fiery sermon, the French nobles were urged to cease fighting among themselves, and to fight infidels instead. He exhorted them to become soldiers of Christ and free the Holy Land. The assembly is reported to have responded *Dieu le Veult* or "God wills it!" Urban promised remission of sins and a place in heaven to all crusaders. Immediate plans were made to rescue the Holy Land and to free Jerusalem.

A large unorganized horde composed of thousands of free men and women, thieves, brigands and pilgrims followed Peter the Hermit. He led most of them to disease, starvation or Moslem slavery.

The professional soldiers, with the help of the Byzantine Christians, conquered Jerusalem within a year—at a terrible cost for an occupation that lasted only twelve months. Out of the first and the following crusades came an ultimate victory for the Church and for France. But work not war occupied the artisans and laborers who remained at home to build the great cathedrals of Chartres, Rheims and Notre Dame. The country that had been ripped apart was mending. Crusaders brought back loot that included ancient books and works of art, but more importantly an expanded knowledge of the world.

Pope Urbain, a former Cluniac monk, now resplendent in gold and blue vestments, speaks at the dedication of the high altar

of the newly built church at Cluny. On the right is Abbot Hugues with monks surrounding him. In the left corner, a choir sings. The year is 1095 and Pope Urbain is en route to Clermont to preach the first Crusade.

The knights of the Crusade conquer and occupy Jerusalem in this fanciful painting by an anonymous artist of the twelfth century. The painting is imaginative in the spirit of the times. Christ appears among the knights.

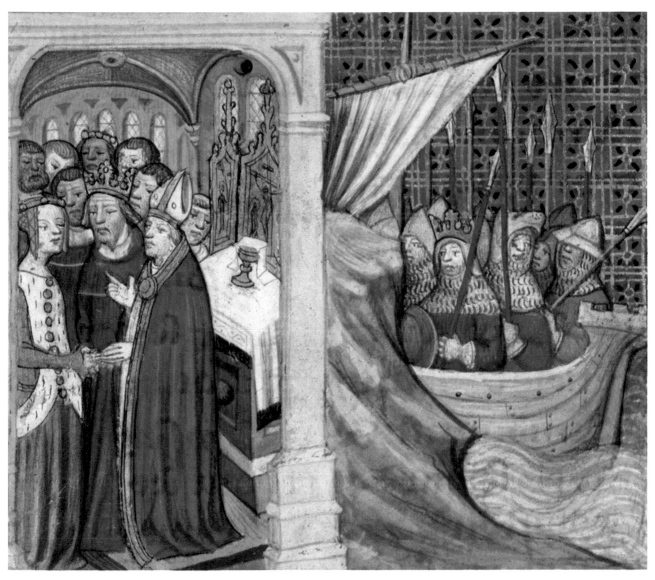

In a dramatic sequence Eleanor of Aquitaine and Louis VII are seen at their wedding (left). On the right they are *about to embark on the second Crusade. This miniature illumination is taken from the Great Chronicles of France.*

It was a provocative act for a just-married fifteen-year-old girl to insist on accompanying her husband Louis VII on a Crusade to the Holy Land even though he, as the king of France, was well guarded. Yet, Eleanor of Aquitaine made the dangerous pilgrimage and survived to become one of the greatest women in French and English history. Eleanor enjoyed the adventure but soon grew tired of Louis who had gone on the Crusade in penance for his attack on the town of Vitrey, where he had burned down a church with the congregation inside. As further penance, the Pope had him cut off his beard. The legend goes that although Eleanor had cared little for him before he shaved, she took a distinct aversion to him beardless and remarked that now he not only acted like a monk but also looked like one. Rumors about her behavior on the second

Crusade included talk of an affair with Raymond de Poitiers. The wildest rumor was that she was unfaithful with the Egyptian sultan Saladin who was, however, about thirteen years of age at the time. Eleanor and Louis lived together for fifteen years until in 1152 Louis divorced her on grounds of consanguinity although many thought that it should have been for rampant infidelity. Almost immediately after her divorce Eleanor married eighteen-year-old Henry of Anjou and took her property, the duchy of Aquitaine, with her. When combined with his provinces of Normandy, Tourraine, Anjou and Maine this meant that, two years later, when Henry II conquered England, he and his new wife controlled almost half of France. They soon increased their holdings by acquiring Brittany and the county of La Marche.

A farmer wearing belted tunic and hood, unyokes his oxen from a heavy-wheeled plow in this thirteenth-century *miniature. It illustrates a story of a peasant who was too stupid to learn more than half of his "Hail Mary's."*

A new agricultural prosperity came to France in the eleventh and twelfth centuries. The primary reason was that the adoption of the three-field rotation system of crops allowed farmers to keep less land fallow at one time, thus making more land available for cultivation. The introduction of the heavy-wheeled plow was an equally important development. Up until its invention, the light stick-plow could only scratch the surface of the soil. The two-wheeled plow, pulled by two or more oxen, could turn over the deep, rich earth allowing it to dry enough to be cultivated. Thousands of acres of soil that had been too damp and heavy were found to be almost miraculously fertile. Then the use of the newly invented horse-collar allowed teams of these faster-moving animals to be used for cultivation. Yet even though much more land could be plowed in a day,

the use of horses never became as widespread as oxen which were less expensive and hardier animals.

As a result of these new methods, the population of France increased not only among the peasants in the rural regions but in the rapidly growing villages and towns. It was, in spite of the almost continuous carnage among nobles, knights and mercenaries, a good period for the peasants. They had plenty to eat and a growing market for their surpluses. This relative prosperity allowed some peasants to make a payment to their lords in exchange for time off from labor to develop, for themselves, a trade or craft. By the end of the twelfth century, the largest landholders had begun to employ professional managers to operate their estates. These market-oriented enterprises led to more work for hired labor and more freedom for peasants.

The story illustrated tells of a young nun seduced by a nobleman who then marries her. Thirty years later the Virgin appears and asks the former nun to return to the the nunnery. She complies and her husband becomes a monk.

The impression that women in the Middle Ages were forced into convent life against their will is false.

In the eleventh century, nobles became increasingly concerned about the fragmentation of their hard-fought-for family estates. In an effort to preserve them they began to practice primogeniture, the inheritance of the entire estate by the eldest son. The problem was what to do about the younger sons and the daughters? The boys could remain in the household of their rich brother assisting him in defense and management. Or they could enter the service of another lord as an armed retainer, pursue a career in the ecclesiastical hierarchy or enter a monastery.

Women did not have this choice. Marriage meant the giving of a considerable dowry thereby diminishing the estate. It also meant a life of continuous child-bearing and quite likely an early death—for child-bearing was then the major cause of death among women. It was a time when marriages were economic, military or political devices. A woman could be bartered like a land parcel to a stranger. She, therefore, might find it more pleasant to enter a convent which might offer more freedom than she could find outside of it. Smaller convents were often supported by families and had no objection to breaches in discipline. Occasional investigations by the Church found that some nuns kept pets and servants, wore make-up and rich gowns. Even in the larger convents it was difficult to keep the discipline of silence among the women. Abbesses often complained that there was too much unseemly laughter and frivolity. There were exceptions, but all convents offered more security, education and companionship with other women than they could find in the outside world. Convents were especially attractive to widows. A noble heiress once widowed became a valuable article of trade. Her family or her liege lord could force her, with her personal holdings, into marriage to a person of his choice. Only when she entered a convent was she untouchable by man. She was then the bride of Christ.

63

Seen at sunset Carcassonne, France's southern medieval walled city, looks much as it did in the twelfth century.

The strategic hilltop was fortified by the Romans in the first century B.C. They also built the arched bridge

across the river. The next builders were the Visigoths in the sixth century. In the twelfth century, the city was extended by constructing new walls and towers. Inside were homes, shops, churches and military quarters.

The Justice Of God

Between the fifth century — after the Romans and their legal system had left Gaul — and the tenth century, the administration of justice often reverted to primitive customs. Instead of pagan gods, the Christian God became the judge. It was called justice by ordeal, and God's favor or punishment was witnessed by a representative of the Church. Trials by ordeal included duels and trials by heat (hot iron or hot water), cold water and oath.

The simplest was trial by sacred oath. An avowed Christian would swear to his innocence. The oath was taken before a cleric and it was believed that a person who swore falsely would be eternally damned.

Trial by water put the bound person into a large vat of water that had previously been blessed. It was assumed that the holy water would reject the guilty who would then float. Should the accused sink (being accepted by the water) he or she would be quickly fished out and freed.

In the hot water or hot iron ordeal the accused retrieved an item from the bottom of a pot of boiling water or carried a red-hot piece of iron for a specified distance, bare handed. The injured hand would be wrapped and later, when the bandages were removed, innocence was indicated if the wound had healed.

Of all ordeals, the duel was most favored by the Normans. The disputants would fight with sword and dagger with God awarding the victory to the innocent one. A major problem with the duel was that an extreme difference in age or physical condition could occur or that one disputant might be a woman. In such a case, the weaker person had the right to choose a champion to fight for him or her.

Two heavily armored disputants are seen in this form of judicial combat. Two bishops stand by as judges while the combatants in the center fight with daggers. God will then decide who is right by giving the survivor victory.

THE POPE IN FRANCE—
THE 100 YEAR WAR

Albigensian heresy crushed through violent crusade and Inquisition. Crusades end in failure. Papal court moves to Avignon. The 100 Year War begins but is interrupted by the "Black Death." Plague and war cause rural and urban revolts. Jeanne d'Arc defeats the English, Charles VII is anointed king of France and drives the English out. Louis XI forces Burgundy to end its separation from France. Dukes of Burgundy and Berry commission the illuminated "Books of Hours." Sorbon founds college in Paris. Froissart begins his chronicles and a printing press is established in Paris.

HISTORICAL CHRONOLOGY		ART CHRONOLOGY	
1186—1216	Philippe II establishes royal power over most of France and Flanders. He creates royal courts of justice.	1160—90	Tristan and Isolde and Perceval Arthurian romances by Chrétien de Troyes. Vengeance of Alexander romance of antiquity by Jean le Venlais
1199	Albigensian heresy threatens Church in the south. Simon de Montfort leads violent crusade against it.	1194—1280	Cathedral of Chartres is built in Gothic style.
1202 1270	Fourth crusade conquers Constantinople. Fifth and sixth crusades against Egypt. Louis IX dies on crusade.	1219	The Song of the Crusade of the Albigensians written in provençal verse by Guillaume de Tydèle.
1226	First truly hereditary and automatic succession of a Capetian king: accession of Louis VIII.	1230—75	Romance of the Rose begun by Guillaume de Loris and finished by Jean de Mung.
1280—1	Riots in Rouen and Provins against cloth merchants.	1243—6	Sainte Chapelle is built in Rayonnante Gothic style.
1295—1312	The Templar knights are tried for heresy, disbanded and expelled from France.	1256—7	Sorbon founds theological college in Paris. Thomas Aquinas, Master of Theology at the University of Paris.
1302	First Estates General called by Philippe IV the Fair.	1261—5	Theopilus play about the miracles of the Virgin, by troubadour Rutebeuf.
1305—8	Papal court moves from Rome to Avignon.	1298	Marco Polo writes account of his adventures in French.
1315	Serfs are freed on royal lands.		
1337—1453	100 Year War rages.	c. 1300	Passion of the Jugglers early passion play. Portrait of King Jean II, early easel painting.
1348—9	Plague epidemic kills up to half of the population.	1304—9	The Holy Words and Good Deeds of Saint Louis by Jean de Joinville.
1356—8	Jean II "the Good" is captured by the English. Great peasant rebellion: Jacquerie.	1357	Chronicles by Jean de Froissart, a history of the 100 Year War.
1374	Du Guesclin organizes permanent mercenary army. End of military feudalism.	c. 1389	Poems of the Rose and Letter to the God of Love by Christine de Pisan.
1378	Great Schism caused by election of one pope at Rome and one at Avignon.	c. 1410—6	Chantilly and Trés Riches Heures illuminated Books of Hours commissioned by Jean, duke of Berry.
1420	Charles VI "the Mad" recognizes Henry V of England as heir to the French crown at the Treaty of Troyes.	c. 1447—52	Mémoires a manual for princes and their advisors, by Philippe de Commines.
1429	Coronation of Charles VII at Rheims.	1453	Triumph of the Virgin painted by Charenton.
1430	Jeanne d'Arc is tried and burnt as a heretic in Rouen.	1461—83	Altarpiece of the Parliament of Paris shows Flemish influence in painting.
1438	Independence of French church from the papacy is formalized in the Pragmatic Sanction.		

A change in style appears in this Gothic stained-glass representing Saint Martin. He is shown on a horse with *sword in hand, pausing to give his cloak to an emaciated beggar. Such naturalism was not present in Romanesque art.*

Out Of
The Darkness

The quest for a way out of the darkness of the eleventh century began with an expansion of building that France had never seen before. It reached its peak in the Gothic period in art and architecture when a distinct French culture was born.

The Crusades had not been a patriotic effort but a movement of feudal lords and vassals whose interest was not in nationalism but in adventures and profits and the extension of Christianity and the destruction of "Paganism." But the seeds of French unity became apparent in the second half of the twelfth century as the monarchy, the nobility, the Church, the craftsmen and the serfs were caught up in a reaction against chaos and anarchy.

As the spires of the Gothic cathedrals rose into the heavens, the population of France, including the architects and artists, became no longer earthbound. The design of the Gothic cathedrals was revolutionary. Instead of the square look of the Romanesque, these unknown architectural geniuses created light, airy structures that extended ever upward. They seemed to

The warmth, humanism and lucidity of Gothic art is illustrated by these two earthy smiling angels outside of the Rheims cathedral. Their robes are Greco-Roman but their expressions reflect the joyous spirit of the times.

float between the sky and the ground. The slim high pillars were built close enough together to make high walls and many windows possible through the use of props called flying buttresses. The new vaulting allowed more windows, and therefore more light, without weakening the structure. On this vaulted framework, the slim pointed windows, rising from the ground level, hung like Christmas-tree decorations. The effect was like a fairy castle, but also like the arm and hand of God pointing ever upward. The interiors of the structures were even more impressive than the exteriors, if that is possible, for the soft-colored light filtering through the hundreds of stained-glass windows gave an atmosphere of unreality to the seemingly endless interior spaces. It was possible to be alone with one's prayer inside the Gothic cathedral even though hundreds of other people were there.

The early builders were men of genius who had learned their craft through trial and error. They were neither mathematicians nor engineers except in the most rudimentary way. Man had been building in stone for hundreds of years, yet here was a new concept and many of these magnificent structures dating back more than 800 years still stand as permanent monuments to their builders and to the industry and originality of twelfth-century France. The architects took risks but this was an era of risk taking. Some cathedrals collapsed; when that happened, the disaster was more likely to be blamed on the sinfulness of the congregation than on the builders.

Of Courtly Love

The evolution of knighthood and the rise of chivalry can be traced through the *Chansons de Gestes,* the songs of deeds that became a part of the education and entertainment of Frenchmen beginning in the early part of the twelfth century. Dramatic events of early history were narrated and sung by roving poets. The most famous, the "Chanson de Roland," reflected upon the ambush of Charlemagne's nephew 400 years earlier. A second important narrative recitation was the "Chanson de Guillaume," duke of Aquitaine. Both epics glorify victories over the Moors by the Christians. While many of the events are fictional, an historical base exists. Yet, like all good fiction, the authors added suspense and changed the few known facts to suit their plots. This epic poetry was, in fact, so believable that listeners accepted it as historically accurate. The themes were war, fidelity, bravery, cowardice and treachery, and reflected life in the eleventh century. Listeners knew enough of earlier events to be caught up in the adventures of familiar figures. Women played little part in the grim and bloody tales.

Attention to females was left to the next group of singers, poets and entertainers from the south—the troubadours. With the troubadours, the knight becomes more humane, even benevolent. A new and chivalrous knight was born. The agent of his creation was the beauty, charm and grace of noble women. The focus of the poetry of the troubadours was the unattainability of a lady be she married, widowed or single. It was her presence that enchanted the rough knights. In the courts of love, she became idolized. With her approval and encouragement he could become a better, a more perfect knight.

The poetry, melodies and fascination of romantic love of the troubadours—and in the north the trouvères—was a reaction against the brutality, heartlessness and cruelty that permeated the land. The Church allowed love to be given only to God, to Christ, to Mary and to itself. While such love of God could be confined to the monastery or to the nunnery, most men and women needed the comfort, warmth, tenderness and stimulation of romantic love.

The idea of courtly love and of its connection with chivalry grew out of a desperate need for human affection. The idea of paying homage to one's feudal

Two lovers prepare to kiss in a detail from a fourteenth-century fresco found near Avignon. A dove flies above.

lord had been well established, but in the courts of love, homage was now paid to the object of desire. Poems described the types of lovers and the kinds of love. The fickle, the constant, the shy and the brazen, were all delineated. A new music and song had swept away the chants and dirges and replaced them with imaginative, gay lyrics with melodies to match.

While the virtues of knightly behavior were expounded and that of his lady as well, the scope of their lyric poetry was wider. Intricate variations of courtship and love were explored. The troubadours expressed the themes, and the listeners practiced variations.

This trend lasted for over two centuries as increasing numbers of traveling minstrels, singing of the pleasures of love, wandered through France. As knights and their ladies adopted the idea of romantic love, colorful habits of dress added to the new types of conduct. Changing modes became so widespread that France assumed a cultural leadership that was quickly recognized throughout Europe.

While knights were being civilized by the troubadours and, more realistically, by the ladies of the court a new diversion appeared. This was the sport of jousting and the tournament. The art of warfare was played as a sport. The profession of the knight was that of a fighting man, so in addition to being in deadly combat, he needed a way to keep in training—the tournament supplied it. The early tournament had all of the elements of military action. They were in fact staged battles and competitors were sometimes seriously injured or even killed. At the later formal events, spectators were important, especially the ladies for whom the knights performed. Yet tournaments were not primarily held for entertainment or profit but were major sporting events testing the skilled use of arms and horsemanship. Called *conflictus gallicus*, the jousts and tourneys became a glorification of armed combat. The Church made futile efforts to ban them. But kings, counts, dukes and thousands of noble-knights continued to meet in contests of endurance and agility. The performance of contestants was graded, so far as possible, by a preliminary show of skill. The weapons that were used were blunted and were called *armes courtoises*. The lance had no point, the sword was dulled. Rules became strict, scoring was important, and national and local champions appeared. Instead of killing the enemy, one could win an event by breaking his opponent's lance or unhorsing him. The earlier tournaments, in which entire teams made efforts to capture the leaders of the opposing teams, were gradually replaced by man-to-man combat.

Qualifications for entry into these sporting events consisted of chivalrous behavior in the past, lack of a criminal record and the submission of credentials to prove the nobility of the knight. But the rules were often waived. If a knight came well recommended, was properly mounted and armored, he could usually enter the lists. The loser of a contest became the prisoner of his conqueror and was either forced to pay a ransom or to forfeit his horse and armor—his most valuable possessions.

The most highly respected knights were those who fought only for honor and prizes and the favor of their ladies. Yet the most popular ones were the winners of many horses, armor and ransom.

The violence of tournaments is depicted in this enlarged detail from "The Great Chronicles of France." Ladies including Queen Jeanne of Bourbon observe King Charles V breaking his lance against the visor of his adversary.

The Popes
In Avignon

A contest for power between the papacy and the monarchy of France started a chain of events that resulted in the removal of the papacy from Rome to Avignon in southern France. The aging pope in Rome, Boniface VIII (1294-1303), had censured the French King, Philippe for collecting taxes from the clerics without the permission of the Church. He further accused Philippe of misgovernment, and of not subordinating himself to the head of the Church. Philippe fought back — advising the pope that the throne of France was not subject to any papal whim and although backed by the States General, the Church refused to accept Philippe's criticism and stood firmly behind the pope. Philippe retaliated by sending a small group to kidnap the pope and imprison him. The plot failed but Pope Boniface died within a month of the attempt. French diplomacy then prevailed with the election of a new pope who was a Frenchman. Clément V began what he thought would be a sojourn in Avignon before going on to Rome. But instead the papacy, under considerable French influence — for the pope appointed several members of his family cardinals — remained officially in Avignon for sixty-nine years.

The popes prospered in France. Avignon was close to Italy and located in a province which belonged to the papal states. As the papacy settled into a countryside which was rich in produce, viticulture, stone quarries and excellent craftsmen, the French popes built magnificent palaces. Money poured into the Church until it was said that the papacy was richer than the monarchy and indeed the richest in Europe. This revenue was collected, in part, by selling "reservations," places on a waiting list for high religious offices, to ambitious ecclesiastics." Indulgences" were offered after "gifts" to the Church were made. Such indulgences, also granted by the pope for a fee, meant that guilt could be pardoned through the sacrament of penance. Sins for eternal punishment could be remitted and instead of hell, atonement in purgatory became possible.

Because of the literary and artistic propensities of a series of able and learned men, Avignon attracted artists from all over Europe. Surrounding the papacy itself, the cardinals built their own extensive palaces and ecclesiastic courts. The papal library in Avignon became renowned throughout Europe.

The court of Avignon was cosmopolitan in nature with artists of all kinds — easel painters, muralists and miniaturists, passing through en route to Italy or Spain. Many of the murals were executed by Sienese and Italian artists, yet the art of the school of Avignon was influenced by the variety of artists employed. In the Garderobe tower were frescoes illustrating outdoor life, hunting, grape-picking and bathing. The French popes encouraged easel painting. Almost 100 years later, a second school of Avignon flourished. The fortress city was occupied by the papal legates who continued to act as patrons for French and Italian painters. Interesting forms developed out of the Gothic naturalism wedded to Italian and Spanish formalism. Most notable of the French artists of this school was Enguerrand Charenton.

The popes made a distinct effort to mediate the 100 Year War but their efforts bore little fruit. Mercenaries roamed the countryside during a time of truce and made a direct attack on Avignon to partake of its riches. Yet the Avignon popes prevailed until 1378 when pressure from Italy and clerics everywhere demanded that the Holy See be returned to Rome. Grégoire XI complied. There the cardinals, under the influence of the government and the congregation in Rome, named an ascetic Italian archbishop as Pope Urbain VI, a choice they soon regretted. Urbain so insulted and berated the pampered cardinals, especially the French ones, that he was soon denounced as a devotee of the Devil, an anti-Christ, and his election declared invalid. A faction of the cardinals then elected another Frenchman, who took the name of Clément VII. However, Clément and his cardinals were unable to dislodge the unwanted but legitimate Urbain and were forced to return to the fortress in Avignon. Now there were two popes and two colleges of cardinals. Each excommunicated the other amid some violence and a great deal of ecclesiastical confusion.

The theologians of the University of Paris worked diligently to correct the situation. However the schism remained for thirty-nine years and it contributed to the rise of reform movements of the Church of Rome — and to the progress of Protestantism.

The last pretender to the papacy, Jean XXIII, was condemned after a trial wherein he was accused of fornication, adultery, incest and sodomy. When his sins were considered proved, he was deposed and was lucky to get off with his life. Shortly afterwards Grégoire II (who at one time had been elected) abdicated. Only one of the popes was left, Bénédicte XIII. He was still ensconced in Avignon and refused to give up his office. However, after his cardinals were pressured by representatives from Rome, he was deposed by the Council as a heretic and as an incorrigible promoter of schism. The Church was reunited with the election of Pope Martin V. The schism was over. God was in heaven and his Church was back in Rome.

In a painting from the School of Avignon, the blessed ▶
Pierre, a young cardinal, kneels in the papal Palace.

Extending her cloak, the Virgin Mary offers mercy to commoners and kings. Kneeling, left, is Jean Cadard, *physician to the children of Charles VI. His wife at right introduces him to Mary in this Avignon painting.*

The Cult Of The Virgin

For Christianity to become widely accepted, missionaries were specifically instructed by Pope Gregory the Great in 590 to "not interfere with any traditional belief or religious observance that can be harmonized with Christianity." The cult of the Virgin Mary is an example of the assimilation of pagan gods into Christianity. She took over the duties of countless pagan goddesses to become the sole "Queen of the Universe."

That is not to say that theologians did not differ on the role of Mary. Was she impregnated by God—and if so, how? Another question was whether she was only the Mother of Christ or was she also the Mother of God? And what about her mother? Was Mary immaculately conceived? In 1389, a Dominican monk, Jean de Montson propagated the view that the Virgin was conceived in original sin. He was condemned by the University of Paris that upheld the position of her immaculate conception as well as that of her son.

Before the high Middle Ages, the image of Christ was that of a divine king, a holy warrior battling Satan. The medieval mind saw Christ sitting next to God in judgment of mankind. Pessimism was, therefore, a normal state in the early Middle Ages because all humans were destined to be doomed. Only through attainment of individual perfection could salvation be

assured so that on the Day of Judgment, the sentence handed down would not be purgatory or hell. This thought instilled such fear for their souls that everyone searched for an intermediary to approach Christ on their behalf—and who could intercede better than his mother. She became the mother not only of Christ but of all men and women, not judging but forgiving those who implored her regardless of their merits or sins. In the "Miracles of Notre Dame," a cycle of popular plays performed in the towns throughout France, the Virgin redeems every kind of malefactor who reaches out for her intercession through the act of repentance.

From the twelfth century on, her cult became the most important aspect of popular Christianity. She was the most often represented subject in art whether it was in sculpture, stained-glass or painting. She was shown either in the episodes of her life as the mother of Jesus, or as a protector of the people. As her influence grew, the title "Our Lady" came into general use. The rosary was introduced. Knights fought in her name. She became the patron of numerous religious orders. The Virgin was so admired and worshipped that it was believed that she helped women deliver babies painlessly, and even took the place of women in their beds to keep husbands from discovering their adultery.

More churches were dedicated to *Notre Dame* (Our Lady) than to all saints combined. Every church had a Mary chapel, located in the center of the apse, directly behind the altar. She was as prominent as the crucifix and her importance in the Church became second only to Christ.

The circumcision of Christ is dramatically depicted in this School of Avignon painting. Halos surround the heads of the Virgin and the child, the priest performing the ritual operation and Joseph who cannot help weeping.

The Day
Of The Devil

A demon is exorcised and flees from the mouth of his victim in a detail from a fifteenth-century miniature.

To the people of the Middle Ages, the Devil was a resourceful and clever adversary; an ever-present threat to those who believed in Christianity. He had taken over many of the early pagan qualities and so could do much more than merely tempt man. He had become not only the enemy of God, as his earlier role had been, but the enemy of man as well.

At his side were a horde of sub-demons. The Church estimated that the exact number of these were 7,405,926. The Devil had become, by the fourteenth century, a mirror image of God except that all of God's motives were good and all of those of the Devil were bad. His Mass was black, his home was not heaven, but hell where he ruled, his churches practiced black-magic and witchcraft and his twelve disciples were evil. But in spite of all his experience and his cunning, he could be outwitted by man and by God. While the opposite force to Christ was the Devil, the opposing figure to the Virgin was the witch. She was as impure in thought as the Virgin was pure. Witches were believed to have intercourse with the Devil. They also were suspected of having sexual relations with men to make them impotent. While there were male witches, the medieval Church seems to have decided that sorcery was almost entirely practiced by women. They were *une beste imparfaicte sans foy, sans loy, sans craincte, sans constance,* an imperfect beast without faith, without law, without fear, without constancy. It was often pointed out that it was a woman, Eve, who had yielded to the blandishments of the serpent and convinced Adam to eat of the tree of knowledge. No woman except the Virgin Mary had been immaculately conceived and immaculately impregnated. Men who sinned were considered products of their environment while women had been born sinful. It was believed that women were willful and unstable because their "mother," (a word used to describe their uterus) moved about.

Witches were tolerated in the early Middle Ages and the Church, as early as the eighth century, passed laws that said putting a witch to death should be punished by death. John of Salisbury, bishop of Chartres in 1176, took a reasonable view saying, "some falsely believed what they suffered in imagination. . . because (of) their own fault was real and eternal." He continued, "we must not forget that those to whom this happens are poor women or simple and credulous people."

But this insightful view did not develop or prevail. For more than 100 years, an intense hunt for witches continued. By the end of the fifteenth century, witches were being persecuted primarily in the area of sexuality. They were accused of preventing women from becoming pregnant and of causing male impotence. It even became heresy to deny the reality of witchcraft. It was in this atmosphere that two devout sects challenged the Church of Rome in the middle of the twelfth century. Both had flourished in southern France—the Albigenses from the region near Albi and the Waldenses from the region of Lyon. The Albigenses held that the papacy was corrupt in that the clergy did not, like Christ, sell what they owned and live a life of poverty and celibacy. The sect did not accept the Catholic doctrine of purgatory nor hell, believing that the soul was reborn over and over again, each time striving for perfection. The Church adjudged them to be heretics and disciples of the Devil.

Pope Innocent III called for a crusade to totally destroy the Albigenses. Not only would these heretics be extirpated but their lands would be taken over by the crusaders. The duke of Burgundy and the French barons of the north who coveted the rich southern lands

Gloating demons hold sinners underwater, boil them in a caldron and feed others to the flames in a detail from the illuminated manuscript of Vincent de Beauvais. The visitors were probably inspired by Dante's "Divine Comedy."

raised an army and spread destruction over the *Midi*. Their leader was the notorious Simon de Montfort who arranged the massacre of thousands. In the minds of many he was inspired by the Devil. Yet he was made Viscount of Béziers and Carcassonne with the papal legate present.

The religious crusade provided an excellent excuse for the several wars that followed. Louis VIII demolished the walls of Avignon and the countryside was in ruins when he issued a royal ordinance condemning all heretics to be burned. It was the first time French law (not only the Church) sanctioned fire as a punishment for heretics. Many so-called heretics made peace with the monarchy but many more were burned. To ensure that the heretics did not rise again, the Inquisition — operated by Dominican monks — was established in Toulouse. The Albigensian heresy was finally rooted out but it had taken thousands of lives and destroyed a thriving civilization. Then the power of the Inquisition moved on to attack sorcery and witchcraft. Even the knights of the Temple were accused of sorcery and their riches confiscated.

Superstition was a part of daily life. Unseen forces, under the influence of demons, fairies and witches, practiced two kinds of magic: white-magic, or useful magic, and black-magic. White-witches were helpful; they healed the sick by countering the Devil's magic, told fortunes, found lost articles, concocted herb-medicines and read fortunes. Witches who were devotees of the Devil performed harmful magic. Saints were also believed to practice white-magic, effecting miraculous cures. It was believed by many that the manner of a saint's death foretold the type of illness he or she could cure. Saint Agatha whose breasts were cut off when she was martyred, was believed to cure diseases of the breast. Not only credulous or ignorant peasants but the nobility, the monarchy and the religious institutions believed in both black and white magic. Saint Thomas Aquinas seriously considered whether witchcraft could cause impotence — he decided it could. Guilbert of Nogent testified that his father had been rendered impotent in the marriage bed — but, with the Devil's help, could still copulate with women.

Homosexuals and sodomites were branded heretics although both were common among the clergy. By the time *Maleus Malificarum*, (the Witch's Hammer) was published in 1486, even mid-wives who were often local healers, were being accused of killing new-born babies to use their bodies in sorcery and cannibalistic rites. It was generally believed by the Church that women were more likely to become witches because "they could reach the absolute heights of good and goodness or the absolute depths of evil." And again "all witchcraft comes from carnal lust, which is in women insatiable . . . wherefore for the sake of fulfilling their lust, they consort even with the devils."

That witches were believed to leave their bodies and ride away, is shown by flying "Vaudoises" on their brooms.

78

It was believed by both the nobles and peasants that satanism was a real and ever-present danger, that great harm was done when witches met in secret groves at midnight to worship and pay homage to Malin, the Devil.

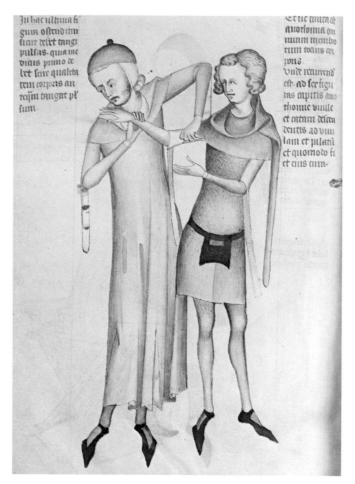

The taking of the pulse had been known since Hippocrates and was often used as a preliminary to blood-letting.

Physicians, Surgeons, Barbers And Midwives

The profession of healing the sick and treating the wounded in the Middle Ages was beset with problems. The first problem was the Church. Even though medicine was taught at the universities which were religious institutions, it was a time when all healers, except God, were suspect. All innovations and new approaches were discouraged.

Yet people wanted to keep on living and so the traditions of healing that had come down from Hippocrates and Galen were respected. In Paris, Lyon and Montpellier, students of medicine concentrated on learning from earlier textbooks. Few student doctors ever laid a hand on a living body — or even a dead one.

Early texts taught that the four humours of man were moist and dry, cool and warm. It was believed that an imbalance of the humours caused illness. Cures for most illnesses included blood-letting (or leeching), induced vomiting and enemas. Of these, blood-letting was the most popular. It indicated to the anxious patient that something was actually being done. After the patient's blood had run into a vial and set for a few minutes, it would be seen that the top layer took on a yellowish-brown tinge. When clotting began, the second layer showed a different pale-yellow color. On the next level, the red blood-cells would be deep red, on the bottom, the sediment would be almost black. So the theory was that the four humours of the body were reflected by the condition of the blood. Yellow represented heat, on the next level (cold) phlegm, then red blood — activity or energy. At the bottom, black represented melancholy. Our phrases "good humor" and "bad humor" come from this early attempt to classify illness. In France patients were bled from the same side as that of the pain, although Arabian physicians drew blood from the opposite side. In the seventeenth century, Guy Patin, dean of medicine at the Faculty of Medicine in Paris, bled his patients at every opportunity. They included his eighty-year-old father (eight times), his mother (four times for pleurisy) and himself many times for a variety of ailments — including toothache.

A nobleman goes hawking while peasants are shown doing seasonal tasks during various months of the year. This is a detail from the calendar year from the "Rustican," an illuminated book ordered by King Charles IV, circa 1370.

Physicians did not generally see their patients or, if they did see them, they rarely touched them. They would observe the patient and send a surgeon or a barber to actually draw blood. Their clientele was usually among the wealthy — who could afford them. Surgeons were a different matter entirely. They received some medical training, but did not get a degree from the university. Warfare taught surgeons much about wounds. From treating thousands of wounded knights, they became expert at bone-setting, amputations and sutures. One of them, Ambroise Paré, who is considered the father of modern surgery in France, discovered that the traditional method of treating gunshot wounds — putting boiling oil or pitch into the wound — was worse than useless. After a battle he ran out of oil and was forced to put a simple dressing on the wounds. He felt sure the patients would not survive. Instead, he discovered that "those whom I had not put the oil (on were) feeling little pain. . . the others, to whom I had applied the boiling oil I found feverish with great pain

and swelling from their wounds. Then I resolved with myself never more to burn thus cruelly poor men wounded with gunshot."

Charlatans, quacks and alchemists all practiced healing. But there were also many sincere, hard-working physicians and surgeons. Guy de Chauliac continued to work with the plague-ridden people of Avignon during the "Black Death," but he realized ultimately he had no cure. He died with his patients.

At the bottom of the list of medical practitioners were midwives. Their medical knowledge was questionable but more often than not, they were useful for difficult deliveries. Obstetrics were not studied by the physicians — for men were forbidden to observe childbirth. Louise Bourges was midwife to the family of Henri VI and wrote a fascinating book about her profession. In it she expressed the idea that she knew more about medicine, using herbs and potions, than all of the physicians and surgeons combined. There are many reasons to believe that she was right.

81

With the French in pursuit, the English led by the duke of Lancaster flee the blood-soaked battlefield. This scene from the 100 Year War is an illumination from Jean Froissart's chronicles, written in the fifteenth century.

The 116 Year War

By the fourteenth century, the French and their neighbors in England had much in common. To both countries the Celts had brought their legends, skills at sword-making and horsemanship. Both had been occupied by the Romans and profited from their laws, literature, arts and the introduction of Christianity. They had shared rebellious Saxon tribes and Viking invasions. Then Guillaume (or William) brought the French language and the elaborate French feudal system to England where both were adopted. So the wars of the French and English did, in fact, have the elements of a family feud.

The 116 Year War occurred because much of France had come under the control of English kings. In 1337 England owned the provinces of Gascony and Guyenne. But Philippe VI, reclaiming these lands, declared war and dispatched the French fleet against England. Edward III retaliated by claiming the throne of France. Edward, with his warrior son the Black Prince (named for the armor he wore), took a well-trained army to invade France. After English victories at Crécy and Calais came a tragic break in the fighting.

A more powerful force than any army attacked England, France and most of Europe. The "Black Death" killed more people than all the wars of the Middle Ages. It has been estimated that this plague, a virus transmitted by fleas and spread by rats, was responsible for the death of at least one-third and possibly one-half of the population of Europe.

The war resumed as soon as the countries began to recover. The French king, Jean le Bon, planned a major battle at Poitiers which would drive the English out of the country permanently. Instead, his huge army was defeated and the king was captured.

The second phase of the war began nine years later, but this time the French, under the inspired leadership of Bertrand du Guesclin, were victorious. To seal the peace, the English King Henry V married Catherine, daughter of the French king.

In the third stage from 1415 to 1420, England's Henry V claimed the throne of France. With the internal assistance of the powerful duke of Burgundy, his army swept over France. The French King Charles VI sued for peace. The resulting treaty ceded most of France to England and it provided that upon the death of Charles VI, England would also inherit the throne of France. When the French and the English kings died, Henry's infant son, Henry VI was proclaimed king of England and France.

The French immediately rose in rebellion and the English suppressed them brutally. The Dauphin was not an inspiring leader and his army was repeatedly defeated. In all of France, only Orléans acknowledged his rule.

The work of an artisan-painter, this is considered the earliest royal portrait in Europe. The subject is Jean the Good, father of King Charles V, Louis of Orléans and of Dukes Jean of Berry and Philippe the Bold of Burgundy.

The Maid
Of Orléans

At this dramatic stage of the conflict came an unexpected interruption or, as many believed, a miracle occurred. *La Pucelle d'Orléans*, (the maid of Orléans), Jeanne d' Arc, arrived on the scene. She came from Domrémy in the province of Lorraine which did not become a part of France until almost 350 years after the death of Jeanne. She had learned about war when, at the approximate age of thirteen, she saw her village burnt and plundered by Anglo-Burgundians. In that same year, 1425, she began to hear voices and reported seeing the archangel Michael who told her to "go to France, if you must." She traveled to Vaucouleurs where she convinced the army commandant that she should be taken to the Dauphin. Jeanne then convinced Charles that, clad in armor, she could lead his faltering armies to victory.

Jeanne must have been completely credible to the Dauphin for the idea of a woman dressed as a man was on the thin edge of being both illegal and heretical. Yet she was given a horse, white armor and a banner which read "Jhesus Maria." She raised the siege of Orléans and after that victory persuaded Charles to proceed with his coronation at the Rheims cathedral, where all French kings had been anointed with the Holy Oil of God. This act, making the Dauphin officially King Charles VII, helped to rally the French.

The victories of Jeanne d' Arc charged the French army with energy. She joined the king's men in a series of successful engagements. Then in May 1430, only two years after coming to France, she was captured by a Burgundian at Compiègne. She was held for six months in captivity when, now some eighteen years of age, she was sold to the English for 10,000 pounds. Jeanne was tried for heresy and witchcraft by a tribunal of French ecclesiastics. She first confessed her errors because, she said two days later, she had been afraid of being burnt. But while in meditation, she concluded that her fear had been inspired by Satan. She finally realized, she said, that her visions, her beliefs and her actions had been inspired only by God. The judges had little choice but to act according to Canon Law of that time. As a confessed heretic, Jeanne would have been imprisoned but as a "relapsed" or "unrepentant" heretic, the only punishment was death by burning. The articles convicting her of sorcery and heresy were approved by the University of Paris theological faculty. On May 30, 1431, the sentence was carried out. Charles VII went on to win over the English. But Jeanne was forgotten during the next twenty-four years. Then the Church, in 1455, admitted to its error. She was finally canonized as Sainte Jeanne in 1920, almost 500 years after her death.

Jeanne d'Arc arrived from her home in Lorraine just in time to save the Dauphin, later Charles VII, from defeat

by the English. Here she is shown in armor meeting the Dauphin who greets her at a palace drawbridge. This contradicts the historical texts that claim that she recognized him standing among a large group indoors.

One of the greatest portrait artists of all time, Jean
Fouquet painted this revealing likeness of the weak king
Charles VII. With the financial aid of the wealthy
merchant Jacques Coeur, Charles built a victorious army.

The Burgundians
Saints And Sinners

Wearing a brilliant red robe trimmed with ermine, Duke Jean of Berry kneels as he is presented to the Virgin.

Two brothers, who together became rich and powerful, expressed extreme behaviors from violence and self-interest to an unselfish love for paintings, sculpture, literature and poetry in fourteenth-century France. Forceful, sensitive and able, their actions were not always in the interest of France.

Philippe and Jean were the two youngest sons of Jean le Bon (the Good), king of France. At the battle of Poitiers, both fought bravely and well against the invading English. So valiantly did fourteen-year-old Philippe fight that, for the rest of his life, he was known as Philippe le Hardi (the Bold). The battle of Poitiers was lost, but out of this defeat ultimately came the wealthy and influential dukedom of Burgundy. The captured princes were ransomed and the English allowed the king to return to France temporarily to raise his own ransom. While he was in France, the duke of Burgundy died leaving no heirs except a twelve-year-old widow, Marguerite of Flanders. In an altruistic gesture, the king invested Philippe and his heirs with the duchy of Burgundy. He then created him duke of Burgundy and First Peer of France. Then the king returned to England. Upon his death, his oldest son, Charles V, older brother of Philippe, became king of France. It was he who started building the Louvre palace.

The younger brothers, Philippe of Burgundy and Jean of Berry, were inseparable. Over the years Philippe, by marriage, inheritance and purchase, increased the duchy in size and influence. His brother, the duke of Berry whose interest was primarily in riches and art, governed the southern lands while Philippe managed the northern reaches of their semi-independent state. As the brothers grew older, they ranked among the most important rulers of Europe. Their influence, through their own efforts and those of Philippe's son, Jean sans Peur (the Fearless), his grandson Philippe le Bon (the Good) and great-grandson, Charles le Téméraire (the Daring) greatly influenced the history of France for 104 years.

The marriage of Philippe the Bold to the young Marguerite of Flanders offers an insight into the affairs of royalty in the fourteenth century. The most advantageous marriage that Philippe could possibly make was to the child-widow Marguerite of Flanders and Burgundy. But her father, the Count of Flanders, instead made an agreement with Edward III of England to allow his daughter to marry Edward's son, Edmund Langley, in return for the towns of Calais and Pontaieu plus 175,000 livres in cash. The deal was made and all seemed settled except for an impending dispensation for consanguinity from the pope, for the couple was related. Pope Urban V, however, was a Frenchman. Realizing this was not a good marriage for France, he refused permission and ordered the archbishops of Canterbury and Rheims not to perform the wedding ceremony.

But three months later, at the request of Charles V, he granted such a dispensation to Philippe allowing him to marry. This cleared the way for Philippe's marriage to Marguerite but it took two years of bargaining with her father to get him to agree to accept three French towns and 200,000 livres in return for his daughter.

The dukes of Burgundy rapidly made their holdings relatively independent from France. Their interests were often in opposition to the political aims of the king. However, Philippe the Bold and his brother Jean of Berry served France by becoming, upon the death of Charles V, regents for the eleven-year-old Dauphin. As guardians of the king, Philippe and Jean often used their influence at court and the riches of the monarchy in their own interests. Under Philippe and his brother Jean, duke of Berry, Burgundy prospered. By the mid-fourteenth century, the annual revenues to the dukes were at least one million ducats—nearly twice as much as the income of the papacy.

If the dukes used their money for their own advancement, they also used it generously in their support of French culture. Artists, mural painters, sculptors and especially illuminators of manuscripts were invited to the court of the dukes and given princely retainers. Not merely collectors but true art patrons, the brothers Philippe and Jean competed with one another for the most talented artists and book creators of the time. The "Books of Hours" of Philippe the Bold and the duke of Berry were considered the most brillant in France. The duke of Berry owned at least 100 major manuscripts. Ninety-three were illuminated and he personally supervised the art work in many of them. His interest and his ego had taken him so far that he had himself painted into a number of his own "Books of Hours." One magnificent work Les Grandes Heures shows the duke entering heaven with Saint Peter greeting him.

As the fame of the illuminators work spread so did new techniques, styles and themes. The School of Paris introduced what became known as the international Gothic style as illuminations were influenced by Flemish and Italian miniaturists. Genre scenes reflected life about them even in prayer books. Castles rose and sometimes floated in the backgrounds, sheep grazed, birds flew about while painted streams and brooks flowed through the pictures.

The brothers spent time and money in their search for artists. Under their patronage, the Limbourg brothers, Pol, Jean and Herman, became the most popular artists in all of France. The wide range of illuminations they produced shows in sensitive and revealing detail how the life of the nobility was lived in Burgundy—with many revealing glimpses of the peasants at work. Another great artist, Jacquemart de Hesdin, created masterful illuminations for the brothers.

A very special culture with a humanist base was slowly growing among the intellectuals and the nobility. The reading and writing of poetry played an important part in court life. Literature generated at the Burgundian courts helped to establish the northern French dialect as the literary language of France. The patronage of the Burgundians was not merely limited to paintings and manuscripts. Tapestries were imported and others were woven within Burgundy, especially in Flanders. The

years 1363 to 1377 are well-known as the early period of the Burgundian school of art, yet it was also an extension of the Flemish school—Flanders being one of Europe's artistic centers. The dukes patronized, among other Flemish masters, the Van Eycks and the sculptor Claus Sluter.

The dukes and especially the duke of Berry gave impetus and support to the humanistic works of such outstanding men as Jean de Montreuil and Gontier Col. These men and their colleagues, who included Pierre d'Ally and other teachers at the University of Paris, were among the avant-garde thinkers of their time. It was the beginning of the end of the age of chivalry. The way was open for a new type of literature in France.

It came, surprisingly enough, from a young woman, Christine de Pisan, the first professional woman writer in France. Christine's father, an Italian astrologer, migrated to France and was employed by Charles V when she was four years old. She married at the age of fifteen and bore three children. Then at twenty-five, her husband and father died. With no professions open to women, Christine determined to make her way as an author and poet. She succeeded so well that she (with Honoré Bonet and the poet Eustache Deschamps) became the most widely known writer in France. In her allegorical-fictional work, the *Epic of Othea* she included included a large cast of characters, with parts taken by ancient Greek and Roman gods as she imagined them. Christine wrote out of her own moral convictions and was widely accepted. Among her first patrons were the Duke Philippe and Jean of Berry. She dedicated an early work to each of them which they found worthy. She considered them generous patrons.

A dedicated feminist, Christine had her admirers and detractors, and even in the masculine world in which she lived, she was a huge success. Her poems and prose exalted the worthiness of the female sex at a time when the Church fathers still held that God had created man but not woman. She wittily wrote that women had not only been created by God but they were made, not from lowly dust as man was, but from Adam's rib.

Not only a prolific author, Christine was also the first woman publisher in France and probably in all Europe. With an eye for excellence in art, she selected illuminators of great talent. A woman of energy, intelligence and wit, Christine can be credited with writing a famous early biography, that of king Charles V at the request and under the patronage of the duke of Burgundy. As newly-invented printing techniques evolved in Paris at the end of the fifteenth century, Christine's masterpiece *Epic of Othea* was printed. Many editions later, it had been translated into English three times.

Musicians with trumpets and the banner of Burgundy herald the ▶
wedding of Philippe the Good with Isabelle of Portugal.

At the center of his court of justice in Dijon, Charles the Daring of Burgundy sits high on a throne wearing *resplendent ceremonial garments over his battle armor. Standing on the left, four nobles address the assembly.*

Chivalry
And Decadence

Court life can only be described as extraordinarily extravagant, sometimes sublime, often ridiculous. Philippe the Bold prided himself on being the best-dressed man in France and sometimes traveled with a large black pet leopard. At some ducal banquets, as many as forty-eight courses were served by liveried retainers. Their chefs were among the first to realize the taste potential of serving various kinds of wild game with the Burgundy wines of Volnay and Pommard.

Music was a favored art. Composers were welcomed and endowed. Individual musicians were well-rewarded. The brothers' competition was avid not only in the field of art, but also in music. Jean the Fearless, the son of Philippe the Bold, once kidnapped the best choir-masters and boy- singers from his uncle's, the duke of Berry's, court. Jean forced the choir to entertain at his father's chapel. One of the great advances in music, polyphonic sound, in which several lines are blended harmoniously into one melody is said to have begun at the Burgundian court. It is much like the harmony we hear today.

The age of chivalry reached its peak and went beyond it into decadence in the Burgundian courts. Duels were fought over such minor points of honor as who wrote the best love poetry or whether a man was impotent.

In 1430 Philippe the Good, son of Jean the Fearless, created the Order of the Golden Fleece. Its purpose, like other orders before it, was to free the Holy Land. Membership in this exclusive society was open only to men of proven military skill and valor. Members of the Order of the Golden Fleece vowed never to retreat even

Note that all sixty-nine people portrayed are almost all clean shaven and all have distinctive expressions. The lettering clearly gives the function and the name of each of the officials. In the foreground are the petitioners.

when confronted by clearly superior forces.

Burgundy was never a simple geographical place. It became an extended, fragmented state held together by the leadership of the first dukes and their equally forceful and often violent descendents. It included the duchy of Burgundy with the capital at Dijon and the adjoining county of Burgundy (Franche-Comté) which in theory belonged to the Holy Roman Empire but was governed by the dukes. These two formed one unit. In the north, even richer territories became part of Burgundy by purchase, inheritance or by marriage. At their zenith, the dukes of Burgundy were rulers of Flanders, Artois, Brabant, Limburg and Luxembourg

and, further north, Holland, Friesland and Zeeland. It was a remarkably rich combination of territories, yet it was not the land but rather the spirit of the Burgundians that made them great.

The Burgundians have been widely criticized for their continuing independence from the rest of France. Yet what was good for France was not necessarily good for the Burgundians. When it was not, they did not hesitate to make an alliance with England or anyone else. It was vital for them to make alliances with England because Flanders, the most profitable part of Burgundy, depended upon English wool for its cloth exports. Such exports were an economic factor in the continuing

The martyrdom of Saint Denis, first bishop of Paris, is shown in this narrative painting by Bellechose, believed to be the first easel painting. Left, St. Denis takes the ▶ last communion from Christ; at right, he is decapitated.

This magnificent tomb from the Chartreuse of Champmol shows Jean the Fearless, father of Charles the Daring *with Marguerite of Bavaria. Golden-winged angels hold a replica of his war helmet and the Burgundian coat of arms.*

wealth of Burgundy. So although they were vassals of the French monarchy, they opposed actions that might weaken their semi-independent status.

The Burgundians have never been completely forgiven for their capture of Jeanne d' Arc and for selling her to the English. Burgundy did not become a part of France entirely by choice. Louis XI, an exceptional diplomat, out-maneuvered Charles the Daring, the last

of the great dukes. A series of alliances arranged by Louis XI caused Charles to be defeated in three major battles. With Charles, his head split open, dead on the battlefield, Burgundian hopes for a separate independent Burgundian kingdom ended. Burgundy at last became completely integrated into France. One of the first acts of King Louis XI was to ship the entire vintage of Volnay 1477 Burgundy wine to his chateau at Plessis-les-Tours.

1494 - 1661
FRENCH RENAISSANCE

The Reformation brings about the Wars of Religion between Catholics and Huguenots. Revolts at all levels are generated by increased taxation to support foreign adventurism. Gunpowder and arquebuses alter military tactics. Richelieu and Mazarin expand monarchy toward absolutism. Introduction of the printing press increases literacy and speeds up exchange of ideas. In art, while classical themes echo the work of the Italian Baroque artists, a French Eclectic School emerges.

HISTORICAL CHRONOLOGY	ART CHRONOLOGY
1494 *France invades Italy.*	*1528—31* *Italian artists Rosso and Primaticcio decorate Fontainebleau and form first school of painting.*
1509 *Birth of Calvin, the great Protestant theologian.*	
1539 *Trials of Protestants are shifted from church courts to government courts.*	*1534* *Gargantua by Rabelais proposes educational scheme.*
	1536 *First Bible published in French by Lefèvre D'Etaples.*
1540's *Peasant rebellions and violence against royal tax collectors.*	*c. 1545* Nymph of Fontainebleau *by Italian sculptor Cellini.*
1557—9 *Regency of Catherine de Medici after the death of Henri II. France renounces ambitions in Italy.*	*1549* Defense and Illustration of the French Language *by Joachim du Bellay exalts its cultural potential.*
1572 *Massacre of Saint Bartholomew's Day.*	*1552* Captive Cleopatra *by Etienne Jodelle is the first French tragedy to recreate Greek drama.*
1584—5 *Widespread Catholic rebellion forces Henri III to renounce all concessions to the Protestants.*	*1559* Heptameron *by Marguerite d'Angoulême, sister of François I, shows Italian and religious reform influences.*
1589 *Assassination of Henri III. Henri de Navarre becomes king.*	*c. 1610* Astrée *by Urf popularizes romance novels.*
1593 *King Henri IV gives up his Protestant faith.*	*1618* *Marquise de Rambouillet opens her famous salon.*
1598 *"Edict of Nantes" allows Protestant worship and grants rights to Protestants in designated areas.*	*1631* *French Gazette, the first French newspaper, is founded by Théophraste Renaudot.*
1604 *The "Paulette" system makes government offices hereditary for a yearly payment to the Crown.*	*1634* *Witchcraft trials are examined after the priest Urbain Grandier is burnt for witchcraft.*
1610 *Assassination of Henri IV. Marie de Medici serves as regent during Louis XIII's minority.*	*1635—6* *Académie Française is founded.* The Cid *is written by Corneille.*
1624 *Cardinal de Richelieu admitted to the Royal Council.*	*1637* Discourse on the Method *by Descartes.*
1629—39 *Peasant unrest: Nu Pieds (barefoot) rebellion.*	*1648* *Royal Academy of Painting and Sculpture is founded. Romance literature reaches its highest form in the novels of Mademoiselle de Scudéry.*
1635 *French invasion of Lorraine: Thirty Years War.*	
1642—3 *Death of Cardinal de Richelieu and Louis XIII. Anne of Austria serves as regent with Cardinal Mazarin.*	*1658* Les Précieuses Ridicules *by Molière criticizes salon society.*
1648—52 *Noble revolts: the Fronde. Louis XIV appoints Mazarin as his primary advisor.*	*1658—62* Pensées *by Pascal, a collection of notes written to himself during his final illness.*
1659 *France defeats Spain and receives Artois and Roussillon.*	*1661* Entry of Louis XIV and Marie Thérèse into Paris, *baroque painting by Charles Lebrun.*
1661 *Death of Cardinal Mazarin.*	

A nobleman returns from the hunt and hands over a plump hare and his javelin to his velvet-gowned lady.

The French Renaissance

"Now it is that the minds of men are qualified with all manner of discipline, and the old sciences revived, for which many ages were extinct. Now it is, that the learned languages are to their pristine purity restored."

These are the words of François Rabelais, a French satirist, humorist and humanist. Believed to have been born around 1494, Rabelais lived wisely and well during more than half of the sixteenth century. As a monk, he studied and practiced medicine and traveled widely over Europe. But his great fame rests on his two outrageous and intemperate novels *Pantagruel* and *Gargantua*. Both portray people of the sixteenth century and their appetites, often exaggerated to afford a belly laugh

— for nothing but God was sacred to Rabelais. Below his surface humor he revealed the facts, foibles and follies of human nature.

In the sixteenth century the spirit of the Italian Renaissance was, in France, marked not only by a renewed concern for the values of the ancient world but by an intense interest in the arts, the sciences and classical and contemporary literature. It was a time of absolutism demonstrated by the monarchy of François I, of the exquisite poetry of Ronsard, of the ideas brilliantly expressed in the "Essays" of Montaigne and of the mathematical genius of Blaise Pascal.

In this inspiring period the graphic arts were equally exciting. Jean Fouquet, Jean Clouet and soon his son François limned the nobility in revealing paintings. Primaticcio, artist, sculptor and designer, was kept busy for almost forty years at Fontainebleau by François I.

The secular life began to lead rather than follow the traditional religious life. This opened up new vistas in

In this tapestry from Flanders dated 1520, labeled "Arithmetic," one can see that some noblewomen could and did receive educations in more than spinning, reading and writing. Yet no women were admitted to the universities.

Court entertainment, often with noblemen and their ladies participating, became a popular diversion. In this sixteenth-century Flemish tapestry, the lady strokes the zither while her companion plays a Renaissance-style conical flute.

On the left is Giohargius, said to be the inventor of the art of weighing while on the right is Tubalcain, inventor *of the art of iron-working. These respected crafts had been formed into powerful workers' guilds by the year 1500.*

the areas of education, religion, medicine and even courtship and marriage. In this time of French intellectual brilliance, even the conflicts arising from the progress of Protestantism stimulated reforms within the Catholic and the Protestant churches and also brought about religious wars. The entire period was one of rapid changes in the authority of the nobility and the swift rise of the middle class.

Even the status of women changed. Limited educational advantages were extended to girls throughout Europe. Juan Luis Vives wrote: "The woman, even as the man, is a reasonable creature and hath a flexible wit both to good and evil . . . all lewd and evil women are unlearned and they which be learned are most desirous of honesty, nor can I remember that ever I saw any woman of learning or knowledge, dishonest." A woman's education was styled to make her a good wife and mother, and a helpmate as well: "Nor shalt thou have her as a servant, or as a companion of thy thoughts and prosperity only, but also as a faithful secretary of thy cares and thoughts, and in doubtful matters a wise and hearty counsellor."

The Wine
Of France

Wine was drunk as if it was water in the sixteenth century and was definitely healthier. Carefully tended vineyards, each one competing both in quality and quantity, spread over the country. At the time of the grape harvest, whole villages turned out to pick and tread the grapes to render the juice.

Wine was shipped in barrels. It has been estimated that at least 100,000 barrels, the entire 1698 wine vintage of Orléans, were consumed in Paris alone. All wine that was shipped was new wine and was best drunk within a year or less for it soon turned to vinegar. It was in the seventeenth century that the process of clarifying, bottling and corking made long-time storage possible. Yet before this, hundreds of thousands of barrels of new French wine went out to Italy, Holland and Spain. The wines of France became internationally known as early as the time of François I.

It all started with a romance. An ancient Greek legend tells how Dionysus, the god of wine, visited the king Oeneus and found the queen desirable. When the king learned that Dionysus wished to make love to his wife, he graciously arranged a brief journey for himself. He returned to find his wife happily with child — by the god. The daughter was called Decaneira. Dionysus rewarded the king for his generosity by making him a gift of many vines with which the king began a vineyard that grew succulent grapes.

The Greeks introduced viticulture into their trading post at Massilia, later to become Marseille. The Gauls made wine long before their conquest by the Romans. After the conquest, the wine of the Gauls was so much in demand by Rome that the Emperor Domitian in the first century A. D. prohibited its import. By the time the Roman Emperor Julian resided in Paris, the entire nearby hill of Sainte Geneviève had been planted in wine grapes.

Saint Rémi, the bishop of Rheims and patron saint of that city, was himself a great wine lover. It was he who crowned Clovis king. A legend relates that when Clovis went out to defend Paris from the Huns, Saint Rémi blessed a goblet of wine so that no matter how much the king and his men drank from it, it never became empty. Over the centuries, monasteries took great pride in their vineyards and produced excellent vintages including the justly celebrated *Clos de Vougeot*.

When Henri IV was born in 1553, it is said that his father Antoine de Bourbon sprinkled a few drops of wine on his lips before he had even tasted his mother's milk. The child licked his lips and smiled. His father exclaimed: "What a true Béarnais!" The wine was a *Jurançon of Ay*.

Men carry hampers of freshly picked grapes, putting some into a hand-operated wine press. In the center, grapes

are treaded using fool power. The "maître," at upper right, pours a sample of the juice for the approval of the richly dressed lord while his lady is sampling a grape. Note the bright red underskirt of the young woman on the right.

101

In spite of a long nose, François I was vain about his looks. Here at age thirty, he is painted by Jean Clouet.

François I

He wrestled with his friend, King Henry VIII of England, and won the first and only fall. He rode on the hunt so recklessly that he frightened his companions and the game as well. He gathered the greatest artists and sculptors of his time to decorate his most extravagant palace at Fontainebleau. He jousted against champions. He won and lost great battles, often fighting hand-to-hand in the forefront of the French army — and he was very fond of women. Women as mothers, women as wives, women as sisters and women as mistresses. Women, he said, "are works of art."

His mother was Louise of Savoie, who at the age of twelve was married to Charles d'Angoulême. At fifteen, she had a daughter, Marguerite, and at eighteen, she gave birth to her only other child, François. As Queen Mother, she outlived her husband by thirty-four years and throughout her life was François's closest friend and confidante.

François loved and respected his brilliant and beautiful sister, Marguerite, who became Queen of Navarre. As children they played chess together. Later, he sought her advice, for she supported the humanist movement that was working toward the French reformation of the Church. Marguerite was a gentlewoman of character, a writer of poetry and of the lusty *Heptameron.* She was tolerant of Protestantism and tried to temper the fury directed against it.

François I's wife, Claude, was a patient and understanding woman. Tolerant of his mistresses, she bore him seven children in the ten years before she died in 1524. After her death, François confided to his sister that if he could buy back her life with his, he would do so — "with all his heart."

A man of many mistresses, his favorite, after the death of his wife, had been selected by his mother Louise and his sister Marguerite. She was the blond, intelligent eighteen-year-old Anne d'Heilly. Other mistresses fought over him but none ever replaced Anne.

Six years went by before François married again. His new queen was the quiet and colorless Eleanor of Austria, sister of his old enemy Charles V. But Anne

Henri II — possibly painted by Jean Clouet, c.1523 — second ▶
son of François I, became king in 1547 at age twenty-eight.

102

A symbolic many-breasted statue "La Nature" was created by Le Tribolo in 1527 at Fontainebleau. It is still there.

remained his mistress and was made lady-in-waiting to his new wife. At Fontainebleau, Anne had her own ornate bedroom. In an effort to make their relationship appear respectable, François found for her an understanding husband who had no objection to sharing his wife with his king. François made them Duke and Duchess d' Estampes.

With France between wars, François began to build his reputation as a patron of the arts. He worked diligently to create a court where art and letters would be of paramount importance.

Only a year after becoming king, he had convinced the aging, yet still active, Leonardo da Vinci to grace his court. The great artist brought with him his notebooks and drawings. In France, Leonardo had the title of *Premier Peintre, Ingénieur et Architecte du Roi.* In the three years that Leonardo spent with François, he made sketches of the palace, designed a canal to connect the Saône river to the Loire and created a marvelous mechanical lion that walked forward and whose breast sprang open revealing a cluster of golden fleur-de-lis. Leonardo died in May 1519, leaving a priceless legacy to France in his paintings: *the Virgin of the Rocks, The Virgin and Child with St Ann, The Portrait of St John* and the priceless *Mona Lisa.*

While da Vinci was still alive, the king added Andrea del Sarto, the Florentine master to his court. This artist painted the new-born Dauphin, François and the famous *Caritas.* Intent upon searching out only the best talent, François approached Michelangelo, who refused to leave his home in Rome. But François could not be denied; he added Bellini and the brothers Giusti as respectively court painter and sculptor. The master goldsmith, Benvenuto Cellini, had been jailed by Pope Paul III for insults to the Church and the papacy. Through the influence of François he was allowed to go to Fontainebleau. François paid him the same amount as he had paid Leonardo da Vinci, 700 crowns a year plus his own petit château.

In his third year in residence, Cellini created the celebrated golden-salt cellar. For the "Nymph" of Fontainebleau that was used as a bronze panel on the front gate, he sculpted a nude woman modeled by his own mistress.

For Fontainebleau, François sought out French painters as eagerly as he had Italians. By 1515, he had found and employed Jean Clouet (or Janet) and given him the honorable title of Gentleman-in-Waiting. Two outstanding French artists of his court, Jean Perreal and Jean Bourdichon, were excellent illuminators who sometimes painted portraits. But it was Clouet, a marvelous observer of the robust society around him, who recorded for all time the style, ceremony and costume of François I's court.

The founders of the first School of Fontainebleau

were Rosso Fiorentino and Francisco Primaticcio who, upon Rosso's death succeeded him. François had spirited Primaticcio away from the duke of Mantua, made him a chamberlain, and as a reward for his excellent frescoes and stuccos, appointed him the abbot of St. Martin. It was Primaticcio who created the manner of figure drawing that was to become one of the most recognizable characteristics of French-mannerist painting. Primaticcio's women were tall and delicate with great elegance of form. The artists who worked at Fontainebleau created a new style which was neither in the French tradition nor the Italian.

François was always a restless king; in his youth he roamed the taverns at night. He owned palaces, hunting lodges and châteaux and never stayed long in any of them. He found a home at Fontainebleau — he called it "Chez Moi" — and what a home it was! Originally a manor house deep in the thick forest of Compiégne, he made it into one of the most beautiful palaces in Europe. Around him was fine hunting, and within his palace, he had a huge library and his enviable art collection which by this time included works by the most sought after painters and sculptors.

François I was a man of letters, a diplomat, a courageous and resourceful Renaissance man — and the father of the French Renaissance. He read, laughed and commented on the ribald stories of Rabelais. He even went so far as to give him a title, Master of Request, and no doubt identified with him when he called the writer "a merry devil."

Elongated nude figures identify this frieze at Fontainebleau as the work of Primaticcio. The oval painting is classic voyeurism. The Greek artist Apelles, in love with Campaspe, has been ordered to paint Alexander who makes love to her.

Diana is being prepared for her bath in this pastoral scene by François Clouet. It includes two satyrs, three attendants and a knight out hunting.

Cleanliness And Godliness

Viewing the sensuous paintings, tapestries and illuminations showing nude and semi-nude women bathing, one could easily get the impression that cleanliness was customary in the fifteenth and sixteenth centuries. However, the exact opposite was true. Bathing was an expensive luxury indulged in only by the very rich. Some castles, châteaux and manor houses had wooden tubs bound with iron rings usually kept in their basements. But even these crude bathrooms were the exception rather than the rule.

Artists in residence found it expedient to paint the kind of pictures that François I, Henri II and IV and Louis XIII and XIV enjoyed. That the monarchs were partial to nudes was clearly visible at Fontainebleau. Artists painted the kings' mistresses as goddesses (Diana was most popular) or took the opportunity to show them bathing indoors or outdoors.

Only mistresses, never queens, were portrayed nude or in the bath. While French queens bore from four to twelve children and even more, mistresses seldom became pregnant. Could it be that the mistresses knew something the wives did not?

The painters of ladies in their baths were not invading their privacy. For privacy was neither desired nor possible even in the royal court. Kings, queens and mistresses lived out their not-so-private lives attended by ladies-in-waiting, knights and ladies of the bed chamber, chamberlains and a host of bodyguards and servants. Everyone wanted to stay as close as possible, hoping to influence the king, queen or favorite. The nobleman d' Aubigné saved the life of Henri IV by being with him when, in 1575, the king was relieving himself and would have been killed by a scythe-wielding woman had not d'Aubigné intervened. The Duke de Saint Simon wrote that both Madame de Maintenon and the minister Louvois accompanied Louis XIV to the "toilette."

Private toilets or water closets did not appear in France until the seventeenth century, when the water closet, which had been invented at the end of the sixteenth century by Sir John Harrington, began to be used by some of the affluent families of France. Until then, the "pot de chambre" served both kings and commoners.

Public bath houses, an idea brought back by the crusaders from the East, were well established and widely used in the fifteenth and sixteenth centuries.

106

"La Vie Seigneuriale" or "the noble life," shows the lack of privacy and the special attention given to a high-born lady in her bath. Her ladies and gentlemen-in-waiting offer music, food and jewels in this imaginative tapestry.

There was also the earlier example of the Roman baths in Gaul. Men and women met at these baths where individual tubs were available at a price, but both sexes usually soaked in the communal heated pool. When people started using the baths for prostitution and homosexual contacts, and venereal diseases became prevalent, most were shut down by the beginning of the seventeenth century. Those few that stayed open posed as barber-surgeon health spas, which some of them really were.

107

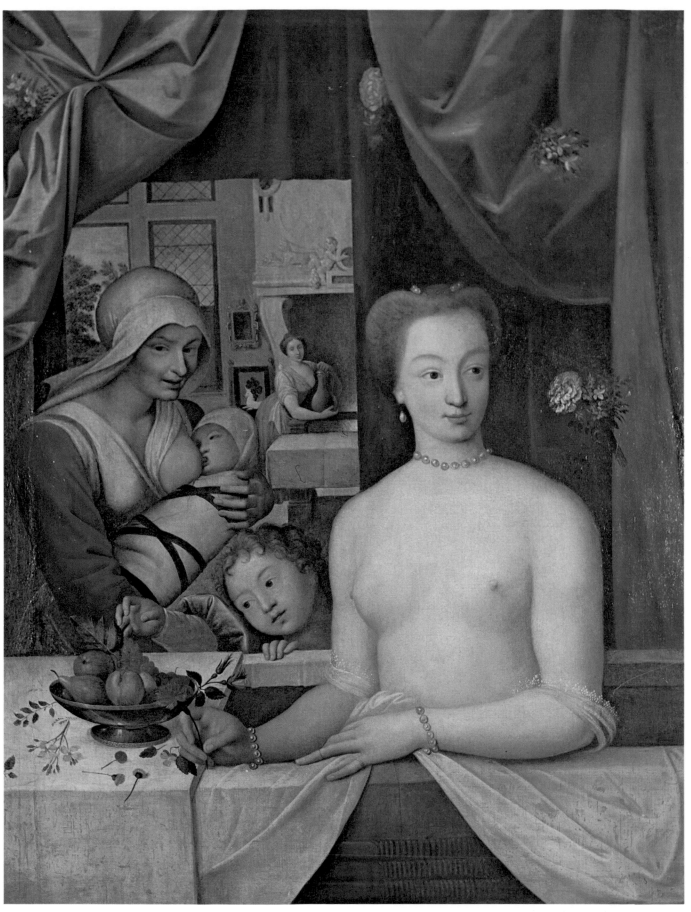

Clouet painted Diane de Poitiers, mistress of Henri II in her bath in 1571. Some thirty years later, an unknown artist replaced Diane with Gabrielle d'Estrées, mistress of Henri IV; the children, nurse and decor are the same.

Diane de Poitiers became the mistress of the future Henri II when he was twelve or thirteen years old. She was twenty years older. At the age of fourteen, he married Catherine de Medici, but Diane remained his favorite until his death.

In this equestrian portrait of Henri II his head is copied from a portrait by François Clouet. On the caparison, the intertwined two D's for Diane create an H for Henri.

The Reformation

At the time that Henri II was born in 1519, Martin Luther's books dealing with the reformation of the Catholic church were selling well in France. As Henri grew up, books banned by the Sorbonne were being printed secretly.

Few educated people doubted that the Catholic church needed major reforms. Some of these changes were voluntary. Others were forced by the rise of a native French Protestant leader, Jean Calvin (or Cauvin), born in Noyon, educated in Orléans, Bourges and Paris. His preaching and writing were a major factor in the rise of the Huguenots, French Catholics who had turned to Protestantism. By the time of Henri II's death in 1547, there were some 2,150 Protestant churches in France. Calvin became firmly established in Geneva and from there dispatched missionaries to further the Huguenot cause. Many nobles joined the cause, perhaps as much for political protest as for piety, while others joined together in the "Catholic League" to fight the rising Huguenot forces.

The regent, Catherine de Medici, made sporadic efforts toward tolerance in the interest of avoiding civil

Catherine de Medici, wife of Henri II, was the mother of three French kings. She and Charles IX ordered the massacre of the Huguenots on St Bartholomew's Day in 1572.

war. Under her Edict of January, the Calvinists were to be accepted as the *religion prétendue réformée* — RPR, or the "religion calling itself reformed." It pleased no one. Over the next thirty-three years, sporadic but devastating religious wars continued.

When Henri III's son, the duke of Anjou died, Henri of Navarre, his cousin, became heir apparent. Yet, as a Huguenot leader and with Henri III on the throne, it seemed unlikely that he would ever be king. Then a young Dominican monk bearing messages to Henri III drew a knife and gave him a fatal wound. The dying king pleaded with his cousin Henri of Navarre, now King Henri IV, to convert. Henri IV overcame the resistance of the Catholic League and its Spanish supporters. Saying "Paris is worth a Mass," he converted

to Catholicism and issued a manifesto promising to maintain and preserve the Roman Catholic and Apostolic religion in its entirety. This alleviated the fears of some Catholics, but it did not end the Catholic-Huguenot strife. As each year passed, he became more accepted by the people of France. Then on April 15, 1598, he offered the Edict of Nantes.

The edict did not give Protestants full equality, but among its provisions it gave them the right to worship with freedom of conscience in their own churches and to control the education of their children.

Over the next twenty years, Henri IV would show that he was strong enough to mediate between the Catholic and Protestant leadership and preserve the unity of France.

The grandeur of a ball shows the emphasis on extravagance and elegance at the court of Henri III. On the right side, the musicians are the king's "mignons" or "pretty boys" who dyed their hair and wore make-up. On the left are the

newlyweds, Marguerite of Lorraine and the Duke of Joyeuse.
Under the canopy, wearing a small crown is Henri III with
his mother Catherine de Medici. Behind her is the Duke of
Guise, known as "Scarface," leader of the Catholic League.

An aristocrat, magistrate and skeptic, Michel de Montaigne originated the essay form and wrote ninety-six essays exploring the mores of the sixteenth century.

The Art
Of Thinking

Two writers born in the sixteenth century offered new ways of reasoning that became the foundation of modern thought not only in France but throughout the world. The first was Michel Eyquem, seigneur de Montaigne, born in 1533 in the family château near Bordeaux. The other was René Descartes, born in La Haye in Touraine sixty-three years later. Both men came from aristocratic families, both traveled extensively and both saw active service in the French army. More importantly, they were men whose minds were free to think in new directions. They ventured beyond the limits imposed by prejudice and custom. Their mission in life was to question everything.

Montaigne's father was a Catholic, his mother a Protestant of Portuguese-Jewish ancestry. Up to the age of

six years, Michel was required by his father to speak and hear only Latin. Therefore, his mother and the house servants learned enough Latin to communicate with him. He learned Latin, he later wrote: *sans art, sans livre, sans grammaire ou précepte, sans fouet et sans larme* (without art, without book, without grammar or rule, without punishment and without tears).

Montaigne received a classical education and grew up to be a courtier and latter-day knight. At Rouen he fought under Henri II and later served as mayor of Bordeaux. At the age of thirty-eight — after traveling widely throughout Europe, sampling the food, wine and women — Montaigne said that a life of pleasure was too hard on his health and retired to his château to write.

From his war experiences, he observed that not only nobles but *roturiers* (commoners), tradesmen, justices and artisans held their own in military knowledge and in fighting for France. His own simple coat of arms bore the legend *Que sais je* (What do I know).

A knowledgeable and honest commentator on his

life and times, Montaigne was not a philosopher in the scientific sense. While he observed the chaos around him and analyzed it, he looked for reasons for the bigotry, depravity and bloodshed that were so prevalent. Out of this introspection he developed a new writing style, the essay. In his *Essays*, he dissected, criticized and probed every facet of the life of his time. Montaigne never stopped questioning. He used his skepticism as a thoughful man's way of coming to a rational conclusion. He believed in the supremacy of reason and the art of thinking.

The questions he raised in his *Essays* were provocative and even radical and he was often accused of heretical statements. He wondered if we are not prizing our own opinions too highly when "we roast people alive" because they do not agree with us, and also asked, "Is not the record of human beliefs contradictory and absurd?" Yet Montaigne was not a moralist, but rather a skeptical man who believed reasoning led to rationality. His was a free mind, perhaps the freest of its time.

Like Montaigne, René Descartes chose thinking as his foremost activity. Unlike him, Descartes was both a philosopher and a scientist. While his curiosity was no greater, for that would be impossible, Descartes wrote not for the sake of distraction or commentary, but for the advancement of his scientific method. Descartes doubted everything that he could not prove while Montaigne doubted because of his will to doubt. That Descartes, a soldier of fortune who joined armies because they afforded him a way to travel safely wherever he wished and paid him well besides, became the first scientist-philosopher of modern times may be surprising, but to follow his logical thoughts even for a short time is to become convinced of his genius.

In his earliest publication, which bore the title *Rules for the Direction of the Mind*, he reduced the rules of logic from thirty-six — which he originally contemplated — to only four which can be summarized as: (1) do not accept as true anything that is not known by evidence to be true; (2) break down problems in as many parts as possible and consider each part in turn; (3) organize your thinking in an orderly fashion, passing from the simple to the more complex or from what is easiest to the most difficult, and (4) make sure that nothing is omitted but cover the whole ground.

Descartes believed that the basic conflicts in man and woman reside in the brain where the physical being comes into conflict with the soul. He wrote: "the two are in conflict with one another and the stronger dominates the weaker." Man doubts — therefore he thinks, he wrote: he thinks — therefore he is.

The Flemish influence on French painting, including the work of Roger Van der Wyden, was very strong in the mid- *sixteenth century. This tavern or brothel scene is in Paris, with the spires of Notre Dame in the background.*

The Catholic League, called "La Ligue," organizes a procession on February 4, 1593 in Paris to demonstrate against the Protestant King Henri IV. Ranging from nobility in armor — carrying pikes and swords — to armed, robed monks and

GLADIO. BIPENNI ET CRUCIS SIMULACRO...

clergy, they march through the central Ile de la Cité. At the center are onlookers; probably a prominent Huguenot has been shot by a fanatic. Note the masked woman at right. Henri IV gives up his Protestant faith, and becomes a Catholic in 1593.

The Nobility
In Jeopardy

The nobility, who ruled France with the king, was in serious difficulties by the mid-sixteenth century. Revolts, massacres, assassinations and the pressure of the religious wars all added to the existing problems of the aristocracy.

New ideas of reform were carried through the spread of printing. The previously inviolate rules and privileges of the nobility were being questioned. Change was very slow, for the nobility was not only deeply entrenched,

it was also widespread. It was not simply a matter of a few nobles with large estates but thousands of nobles of various kinds, from those who came close to having their own kingdoms to the aspiring newly-rich families who were willing and often able to purchase titles and land for themselves.

As the cost of living rose, landowners made efforts to increase their incomes, resulting in more work hours for the peasants. Revolts in various sections of the country had a direct effect on the aristocracy, especially in those areas like Brittany where many were attacked and killed. In retaliation, peasants were prohibited from bearing arms and their houses were searched for weapons. Neither the slowly rising middle-class nor the peasants could help but resent the power and weapons in "noble hands" that were often undisciplined, greedy and frightened of the rural population. A petition to the Estates General early in the seventeenth century complained that although the country was at peace, peasants were being unjustly imprisoned, tortured and killed by nobles.

In the Alps near Grenoble, Henri IV battles the combined forces of the Duke of Savoie and the Catholic League *supported by Spain. His hat is adorned with his famous "panache blanc" as he surveys the siege of Montmélian.*

The opulence and decadence of the reign of the effete Louis XIII is strikingly revealed in this copy of a painting by Simon Vouet now at Versailles. The two women are not his mistresses but symbols of France and Navarre.

"The Cheat With the Ace of Spades" shows the mastery of dramatic lighting of Georges de La Tour. The intensity of the gamblers and the ostentation of their dress give us insight into high life at the royal court. De La Tour is

The Gamblers

notable for his skills at naturalistic detail. He worked for the city of Luneville and became peintre ordinaire du roi.

Large fortunes sometimes changed hands at the gaming tables of the courts of the nobility and of the king. Both men and women threw dice, played cards and roulette by candlelight long into the nights. Versailles was disparagingly called *ce tripot* (a sordid gaming house), and the *Grand Appartement* of Louis XIV were reported to resemble a casino. Card playing for high stakes was a regular form of entertainment but Louis did not like to sit, so he usually played roulette. In addition to great sums of money, even tracts of land — including the peasants who lived on them — were won and lost by high-stake gamblers. The queen, Marie Thérèse, played regularly. Her card games were important to her, as they had been to her predecessor, Queen Anne of Austria. A few noblemen played shrewdly and made fortunes. Madame de Sévigné wrote in her diary: "I looked at Dangean playing and I realized how stupid we are. He only thinks about his game and wins while others lose; he misses nothing and takes advantage of every opportunity. He is never distracted. In one word, his skill defies luck; thus 200,000 francs in ten days, 100,000 écus in one month are added to his winnings." One nobleman of note, the Marquis de Sassic, was caught in the act of cheating at the king's table after winning 50,000 écus by using marked cards. He was immediately banished from the court.

La Bruyère, author of *Les Caractères,* wrote: "A thousand people ruin themselves by gambling and tell you coldly that they can't help it. What an excuse! Is there any passion, however vile and shameful, about which you could not give the same excuse? Can one say that one cannot help stealing or killing? A terrible game without end, without moderation, without any limit, where one sees the total ruin of his opponent, where one is carried away by the desire of gain and desperate over the losses . . . where one bets on one card or the luck of the dice one's own future as well as that of one's wife and children; is that something that is permissible?"

La Bruyère was critical of both the ignorance and the neglect of the nobility regarding the affairs of state and even their own affairs. They even made a virtue of it: "They let themselves be ripped off and directed by major domos and are satisfied to be merely connoisseurs of food and wine. Meanwhile citizens learn, study government and become astute. They know the strengths and weaknesses of the state, figure out how to rise in power and to help the prince in his public duties. The nobles who used to be disdainful of the citizens now revere them and are only too happy should one of them become their son-in-law."

121

As the powerful prime minister of Louis XIII, Cardinal de Richelieu favored a policy of expansion by conquest. He encouraged the settlement of Quebec.

Richelieu

Few political leaders have been so hated and loved as Armand Jean du Plessis, Cardinal and Duke de Richelieu. Beginning as a priest, he was a bishop by the age of twenty-two. He became a cardinal and chief of the royal council of France before he was thirty.

Richelieu's rapid rise to the most prestigious post in the kingdom, below the king, was due to a series of other people's misfortunes. One was the assassination of King Henri IV which left his second wife, Marie de Medici, regent for her nine-year-old son, who became Louis XIII at the age of fourteen. Another was the expulsion from France of Marie de Medici when her unpopular minister Concini was killed.

With the queen's banishment came Richelieu's greatest gamble. He accompanied the queen into exile. When she escaped and provoked a revolt (two revolts, in fact), he arranged the peace with her son. A good friend of the queen, he managed to be readmitted to the royal council when she moved back to Louis's court. Marie showed her gratitude by obtaining a cardinal's hat for Richelieu and persuaded her son Louis to make him chief minister.

An expert at intrigue and diplomacy, Richelieu first attacked the French Huguenots — winning over them in La Rochelle, then he infuriated Marie by breaking her alliance with Spain and weakening the Catholic nobility by allying France with the Protestant powers. On one fateful day, still refered to as the "Day of the Dupes," Marie tried to force Louis to dismiss Richelieu. The king turned the tables by sending his mother into lifelong exile and retaining Richelieu.

Cardinal Jules Mazarin succeeded Richelieu as prime minister during nineteen years. He ordered this life-sized portrait to match the one of Richelieu.

Mazarin

To carry on after the death of Richelieu, France was fortunate in having the services of Jules Mazarin, a close friend and colleague of Richelieu who had left the papal court to become a French citizen. Three years before Richelieu's death in 1642, he came to the French court and succeeded him as France's chief minister.

After sorting out France's huge debts and paying most of them, over the succeeding years he brought the Thirty Years War and the war against Spain to an end. When the deeply entrenched noblemen began to attack the growing absolutism of the monarchy and threats also came from the over-taxed middle class, he found himself faced with the Fronde, France's first civil war.

Standards of living which had dropped considerably for both groups were the underlying causes of the Fronde. The civil war lasted for five years before Mazarin, with hard deeds and reassuring words, demonstrated to both the nobles and the French people that the monarchy was supreme and would survive.

The second civil war was more serious for the monarchy. The center of the new revolt was the "nobility of the sword" with the Prince de Condé leading a well-equipped and large army. But Mazarin's talent for intrigue, in a time when power and money changed hands quickly, brought him and his adolescent King Louis XIV a complete victory.

In the next eight years, before his death in 1661, Cardinal Mazarin not only achieved great power for himself, but also helped to finally establish the absolute monarchy of Louis XIV. In those final years, the queen mother, Anne of Austria, as she had earlier, left the affairs of state entirely to his judgment. It was even rumored that he and the queen were secretly married.

A robust baby, Louis XIV was born with two well-developed teeth. This rare portrait of the Dauphin, with his wet nurse, was painted by the brothers Beaubrun. He wears the blue ribbon and medal of the Order of the Saint Esprit.

A devout Catholic and a generous patron of the arts, Anne of Austria is shown praying to Saint Benoît with her oldest son Louis and his brother Philippe. At the time of this painting, she was Queen Mother, Regent of France.

Trial And Triumph Of Anne of Austria

The most remarkable fact about Anne of Austria is that she was tolerated by Louis XIII and his court for twenty childless years. Queens who did not promptly deliver an heir, preferably male, usually were divorced or had their marriages annulled and were sent back in disgrace to their families.

To say that Anne was unpopular would be a distinct understatement. Some members of the court suspected her of being a spy for her father, the king of Spain. She and Cardinal de Richelieu became antagonists with the odds weighted heavily against her. Then, one might say overnight, all of her burdens were lifted — when she announced that she was pregnant. With the birth of a handsome, healthy boy she found herself, at least temporarily, the most popular woman in France. A gold medal was struck in commemoration of the fortuitous birth. The Latin inscription said: "Thus Rises the Sun over France."

The king called his son *Dieudonné* (gift of God). Louis XIII had never shown much interest in women and his display of potency, after all those uneventful years, seemed to him a miracle. But the court whispered that the "miracle" happened one stormy night when the king was stranded in Anne's wing of the palace by a heavy rain, and rather than brave the cloudburst, he retired to her apartments where she wined, dined and seduced him during his overnight stay.

Impressed by Anne's ability to provide heirs — she subsequently bore him a second son, Philippe — and as a belated recognition of her personal resourcefulness, the king, before he died, made her the regent to rule for the "Dauphin" until he reached his majority. This she did for eighteen years — although she delegated most of the actual governing to Cardinal Mazarin. Anne, the gossips said, "hated work and loved Mazarin."

Three singers with their accompanists and their song books illustrate the sense of "hearing." This is one of five such paintings — the others being sight, touch, smell and taste — made from lithographs by Abraham Bosse of Tours circa 1635.

Toward Modern Music

The musical Renaissance, like that of art, began in Italy and moved speedily to France. The new sound was in the "baroque" style. It employed a more personal approach than earlier religious music and developed from natural speech rather than from chants. Song books and music scores became part of every household with musical tastes that could afford them. In the late fifteenth century, the master composer Monteverdi completed his first of many books of madrigals. These lyrical songs, often love songs, were accompanied by string instruments. They were arranged for three or four voices and soon all of France was singing them.

As early as 1638, the French theorist Marin Mersenne wrote a most important volume entitled *Harmonie Universelle.* In it he described new trends in musical knowledge and listed most of the instruments in use: the lute, tenor, violin and bass viola, cello, recorder, flute, clarion (a type of bugle), trumpet, oboe (or hautboy), cromone (a reed wind instrument with a curved base), clavicord, harpsichord and the organ. At mid-century a musical form, the overture, was developed in the French style — and the French horn was added to the instruments of the orchestra.

From these and related developments in modern harmony came the Italian opera, which was greeted with great enthusiasm in France. Mazarin, a devotee of music, imported a complete Venetian opera company to play in Paris shortly after he became first minister. In 1645, Jean-Baptiste Lully, virtuoso instrumentalist, director, dancer, ballet-master and libertine, received his first important post as the director of *Les Petits Violons du Roi.*

From his newly built palace at Versailles, Louis XIV reigns as an absolute monarch. His extravagant court life stimulates painting, music, theater, ballet, architecture and gives rise to the Baroque style. The Protestants are alienated. In spite of a serious financial situation, Louis XV continues his constant wars of conquest. The new Rococo style evolves around his mistress Madame de Pompadour. Voltaire, Rousseau and the Encyclopedists usher in the Age of Enlightenment.

HISTORICAL CHRONOLOGY	
1664—7	Louis XIV names Colbert minister of state. Royal investigation of the titles and privileges of the nobility. Standardization of civil and criminal laws.
1673	Parliament loses its right to protest the promulgation of an edict by the king.
1667—1679	War of Devolution over the Spanish Netherlands ends with French predominance over Europe.
1680—4	Annexation of Luxembourg, Strasbourg and parts of Alsace; invasion of northern Italy.
1682	Court leaves Paris to reside in Versailles.
1685	Protestants lose all rights in the revocation of the Edict of Nantes. Permanent embassies established abroad.
1689—97	Nine Years War begins with French invasion of the Palatinate.
1692	Louis XIV claims independence from the pope in temporal matters. Also claims ownership of all property, with his subjects having right of use. Louisiana claimed as a French colony by La Salle.
1695	Beginning of general taxation (including nobles) during wartime.
1700—13	War of the Spanish Succession.
1712—14	Decline of French power in Europe.
1715	Louis XIV dies. Court returns to Paris. Duke d' Orléans is regent for Louis XV.
1722	Court returns to Versailles.
1740—63	All colonies, except for Louisiana and Sainte Dominique, are lost to England. The Seven Years War ends.
1768	Corsica purchased from Genoa.
1771	Parliament of Paris loses jurisdictional functions to royally appointed, salaried judges.
1781	Officers' commissions reserved for men with at least four generations of noble blood.
1787—8	Government bankruptcy enables the Assembly of Notables to force Louis XVI to call an Estates General.

ART CHRONOLOGY	
1664	First fête at Versailles, The Pleasures of the Enchanted Isles.
1664—70	Molière criticizes bigotry in his play Tartuffe. With Lully, he produces ballet-comedies.
1666	Academy of Science founded by Colbert. Salon of Mademoiselle de Scudéry begins.
1668	Construction of the Palace at Versailles begins. Fables by Jean de la Fontaine.
1669—72	Astronomical observatory established by Colbert. Academy of Music founded by Lully.
1674	Boileau writes Poetic Art.
1677—8	Racine becomes historian to the king. Madame de Lafayette writes The Princess of Clèves.
1686	First girl's boarding school founded at Saint Cyr by Abbot of Fénelon and Madame de Maintenon.
1697	Tales of Mother Goose by Charles Perrault.
1714	French spoken at the Congress of Rastadt.
1716—20	The Embarkation for Cythere by Watteau.
1722	Rameau introduces an harmonic system for classical music in his Treatise on Harmony.
1731—5	Marianne and Upstart Peasant, psychological novels by Marivaux. Philosophical Letters by Voltaire praises England and indirectly criticizes France.
1748	Spirit of the Law by Montesquieu calls for reform of the legal system and equality under the law.
1750	First Discourse on Inequality by Rousseau.
1750—77	Encyclopedia compiled by Diderot and D'Alembert.
1763—86	La Charlotais proposes national education.
1770	Theater built at Versailles for the wedding of Louis XVI and Marie-Antoinette.
1775—84	Barber of Seville and Marriage of Figaro, both by Beaumarchais, are produced. Chemist Lavoisier suggests that oxygen is used in breathing. First balloon launched by Montgolfier.

The Sun King

With no confidence in royalty other than himself, no trust in the nobility around him—including his family—and no faith in the clergy, Louis XIV stood alone. He thought of himself not as a representative of God in France, but as *the* god in France. He, the Sun King, gave every sign of believing that he was a "visible divinity."

On the day after the death of Cardinal Mazarin, Louis ordered a meeting of his cabinet. He curtly informed them that henceforth the country would be governed by no one but himself. No decisions, no matter how minor, were to be made without his approval. He said little more, except to remark that things would be done differently from the way they had been done.

At the time Louis was twenty-three years old, well educated and athletic. He had watched and waited while first his mother, then Richelieu and finally Mazarin dominated his life. Then he had stepped forward. When the Archbishop of Rouen asked Louis whom he should address regarding affairs of the clergy, the king replied shortly *"Moi."*

Shortly after Louis had taken over the government, his homosexual brother, "Monsieur," asked to be appointed governor of Languedoc. Replied Louis: "It would show a lack of foresight and judgment to place the high governing functions in the hands of the sons of France, who, in the interest of the State, must never have any other retreat than the court—nor any other secure position than in the heart of their brother."

This was the policy that he used with his family and the nobility. He kept them distracted at court and gave them no part in government. For advisors, he looked primarily to the "bourgeois." He could control them—the middle-class citizens—because they were entirely dependent upon his largesse. These appointees were selected because they had no other interest than that of the crown, which was not true of the nobility.

His first minister, Jean-Baptiste Colbert, was not an aristocrat, but a former war secretary employed by Cardinal Mazarin. Four years after his first assignment, Colbert became the king's minister of finance after Louis had dismissed Nicolas Fouquet, his larcenous finance minister. Fouquet was found guilty of stealing millions over a period of years, secretly planning a coup, building a fortress complete with cannon and—adding insult to injury—competing with Louis for the finest artists of France. The council of State sentenced Fouquet to exile and confiscated his estate. Louis increased the sentence to life imprisonment in France.

In a commemorative painting of two important events—the founding of the Science Academy in 1666 and the Observatory

in 1667—Louis XIV poses with his minister Colbert at his right. Behind the king, his brother "Monsieur" wears a red coat; next to him is the architect Charles Perrault. With Colbert, Louis XIV created a number of notable institutions.

In 1682, Louis XIV officially moved the government of France to Versailles. He was forty-four years old. Some courtiers protested leaving Paris because there was no town nearby. Louis remarked that wherever he lived, a town would soon rise.

A detail from the large painting (overleaf) shows a coach waiting to take the victims of an altercation and of an accident through the palace gates. At bottom right, two courtiers fight while another is being helped from his chair.

130

In a spiral pattern, members of the king's cavalry ride through the front gates of Versailles. Lined up on either *side is the famous Swiss Guard. State carriages drawn by white horses wait to transport Louis XIV and his entourage.*

The king wanted a place to play. As a child, he had often stayed at his father's hunting lodge near the village of Versailles. So this dedicated outdoorsman, who hated Paris, made a decision. He resolved to build a spacious palace near Versailles that would contain his hunting lodge, large stables for his horses and kennels for his many hounds, thus giving him the opportunity to lead, at least part of the time, the outdoor life.

A fortuitous series of events brought his grand plan to fruition. First, he and his minister Colbert arranged a rehearsal. Changes were desperately needed at the Louvre, at Fontainebleau and the Tuileries. As they were being made, the king became impressed with Vaux-le Vicomte, the palace of his disgraced minister Fouquet. These events all contributed to his plans for Versailles. The spaciousness became reflected in the endless gardens, the lake and the woods, and this grand design was Louis's contribution. But the magnificent ornamentation, the excellent paintings and the incredible

details were in the hands of Charles Lebrun — the most prominent painter of the time who acted as artist, designer and director. Also contributing were the master landscape gardener Le Nôtre and the architect Le Vau who supervised the building of the palace.

The plans first considered had been drawn by the Italian artist Bernini. They were discarded and Claude Perrault and his brother Charles's architectural plans were adopted. By eliminating most of the Italian Baroque, Versailles became a simpler, more open and more typically French palace.

From his windows in the centrally located hunting lodge, Louis could watch the stream of life go by. He succeeded in his two aims: to give himself the open spaces he missed, and to create a magnificent showcase displaying the splendor of France to the world.

Entering Versailles under escort, Louis XIV is in a coach ▶ *drawn by six horses. The queen is in the second carriage.*

131

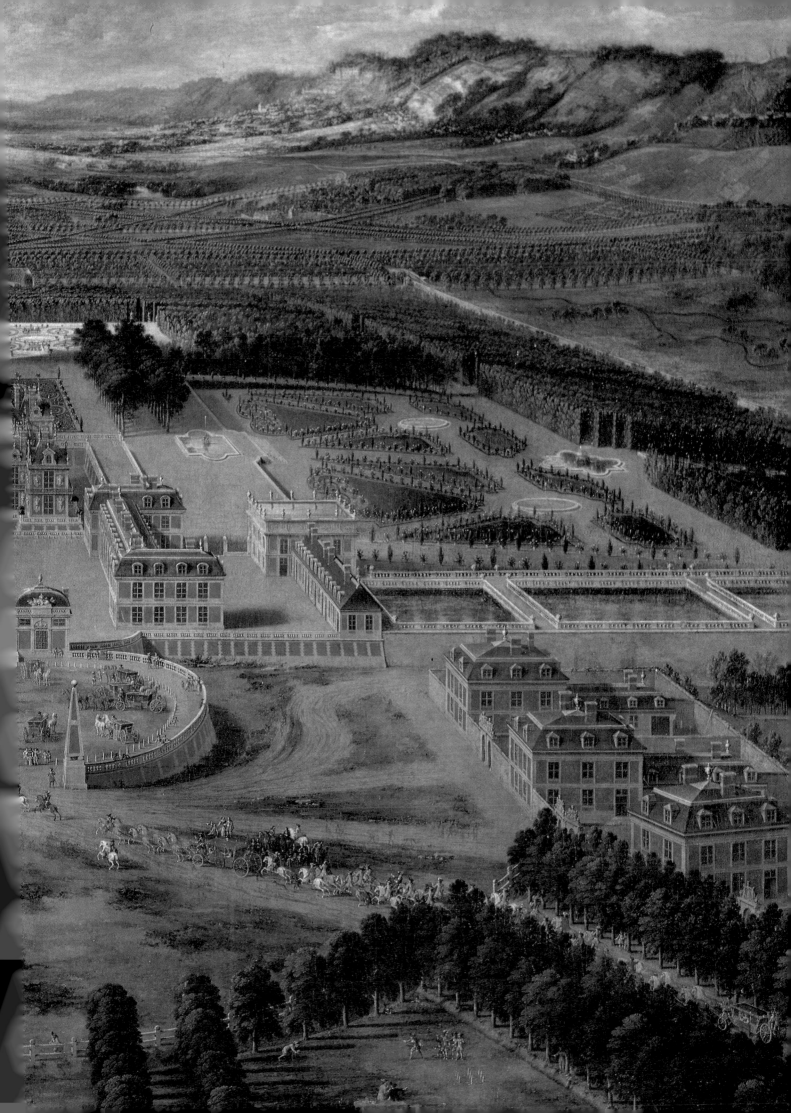

During a royal hunt, hounds feast on a dead stag. In the late sixteenth century, George Turbevill wrote: "They take *a delight to cut off his head with their woodknives, skaynes or swords." The severed head is visible in the foreground.*

The Hunt

In the sixteenth century, neither the pursuit of women nor the pursuit of money compared with the pursuit of game. For centuries, hunting had been the sport of kings and nobles. To Louis XIV and his court, it was a way of life. The king himself spent as much time hunting as he did on affairs of state. In good weather, nearly every day was a hunting day. Each morning after Mass, with the hunt master and his hounds, he would set out through the woods, not returning until dinner time at two in the afternoon. He often missed dinner.

As the Dauphin, Louis had hunted not only deer and small game but wolves as well. One of the outstanding days of his life, he later remembered, came when he killed six wolves while hunting in the Ile de France. When his long-time mistress Madame de Montespan died, the king was told about it as he was on his way to the hunt. He continued the hunt but, after killing a stag, took a long walk through the woods — alone.

By the latter part of the sixteenth century, much of the larger game had vanished from the countryside. To bring back the deer, thousands of acres of arable farm land were put aside for the king and the nobles as exclusive hunting preserves. These preserves were so well stocked with deer that the huntsmen could always be sure of a good day of sport.

Through the years, the nobility had overrun the peasants' tilled fields following their legal right to pursue an animal wherever it might go. But strict laws prohibited the peasants from killing game even though the animals were consuming their crops. A peasant could, for killing a rabbit, lose his hand or even his head.

While one party of hunters untangles the hounds, another closes in on a bounding stag. A special "great knife" for hunting was developed in Bayonne, and later was known as the bayonet. It was subsequently attached to army muskets.

A favorite mistress for nineteen years, the Marquise de Montespan is painted with four of her children by Louis XIV.

With one hand at her breast and the other pointing to the falling flowers, she may be pregnant with another child.

Wives And Mistresses

There was one official wife: Marie Thérèse of Spain who was short, fat and good-humored. With her, it was said, the king exercised his conjugal duties twice a month. She bore him eight children of whom five survived. Then into the court came Athénaïs de Montespan, a reckless, witty and ambitious beauty. It was customary in the time of Louis XIV for the king to have a favorite—an acknowledged mistress whose status was one step below the queen. His first choice was Louise, duchess of La Vallière, a gentle, fragile, blue-eyed blond of seventeen. She and de Montespan became close friends.

Of the four children who were born to him by La Vallière, only one Marie Anne was legitimized. Six years after Marie Anne's birth, the court buzzed with the gossip that Madame de Montespan was pregnant by the king. She was married and her husband strongly objected to her remaining at court, but arrangements were made by the king and she had soon obtained a legal separation. Louis continued to see La Vallière, but their passionate romance was over. At the age of thirty she left the court and became a Carmelite nun.

Then Madame de Montespan introduced her friend Madame Scarron, widow of a well-known but impecunious poet to the court. She had discreetly cared for Madame de Montespan's and the king's first-born

◀ Posing as Diana, this is Louise de La Vallière, mistress at seventeen of Louis XIV. At age thirty she became a nun.

Madame de Maintenon secretly married Louis XIV. Behind her ▶ niece is the House of Saint Cyr, founded to educate women.

137

child when it was important that the birth be kept a secret. Madame Scarron was a devout, quiet, unobtrusive, but not unattractive woman. At first, the king ignored her. Later, noticing that she was an excellent governess and educator of de Montespan's seven children, he began referring to her respectfully as Madame de Maintenon, her family name. Although she never competed with de Montespan for the physical affections of the king, she did let him know that she was interested — in saving his soul.

Always sexually predatory, the king now turned to a series of minor mistresses. He developed a passion for the young and nubile Mademoiselle de Fontagues. When the king made her a duchess, Madame de Montespan was consumed with jealousy and consulted an old and wise friend, Madame Voisin.

At that time, there was a widespread fear of poisoning. Fortunetellers and dabblers in the art of sorcery were suspect. Voisin was arrested. She confessed to performing abortions and also admitted that she did fortunetelling and sold love-potions. Under torture, she gave the police many names but never mentioned that of de Montespan. Along with another convicted witch, Voisin was burnt alive. When it looked as though de Montespan might be questioned, the king issued a *lettre de cachet* directing that only prisoners named in the letter should be imprisoned and that all others should be released. The affair of the poisons was over. The king was completely convinced of his mistress's innocence and they lived together at Versailles for the next ten years.

At the age of forty-five, Louis seemed ready for a more placid companion. He secretly married, probably at Versailles, the ex-governess, Madame de Maintenon, who was now forty-eight. The marriage was morganatic — he gave her his left hand — and she forfeited all rights and inheritance claims. Louis went on with his wars, his building and his hunting. He and the woman who was determined to save his soul lived together until his death at seventy-seven.

Marie Adelaide was eleven and Louis de France thirteen when they were married in 1697. Two years later the marriage was consummated. Louis XIV is at left in orange costume. Both Marie and Louis died in a measles epidemic twelve years later.

Hyacinthe Rigaud painted this small canvas when Louis XIV was sixty-three years old. From it he made the life-sized one.

The fine art objects and the frantic craftsmen are life-sized in this huge Gobelin tapestry commemorating the state visit

Rigaud made this self-portrait and also painted such artists as Lebrun, Mignard and Coysevox and the fabulist La Fontaine.

Gobelin— Art For The Glory of France

Louis XIV's primary concerns were war, hunting, power and glory. His finance minister Colbert's concerns were the French economy, trade, taxes and—glory. Fortunately

of Louis XIV and finance minister Colbert to the Manufacture des Gobelins *located near Paris. Entering the room on the left is the king looking to black-clad Colbert on his right. Besides tapestries, a variety of luxury items were made here.*

for France and the world of art, the two men conceived the Gobelin project.

In a huge workshop near Paris, craftsmen produced inlaid classic furniture, luxurious rugs, fine laces, paintings, ornate silverware and resplendent tapestries. To direct the enterprise, the king and Colbert selected the multi-talented artist Charles Lebrun who moved into the workshop. There he drew cartoons that were worked by master weavers into tapestries. With sensitivity, good taste and good judgment, Lebrun set high standards for the Gobelin workshop. Colbert's faith in the ability of French artists and craftsmen to produce works for the international luxury market was justified. Versailles was furnished splendidly with art works from Gobelin fit for a king and dedicated to the permanent glory of France.

141

Mignard has portrayed the playwright Molière as a hero of classical tragedy.

Corneille, Racine and Molière

Actors performed poetic tragedies and Italian comedies on tennis courts and within the enclosed courtyards of urban and country inns, for Paris had no permanent theater before 1629. Most acting troupes were Italian, though occasionally strolling English and Spanish players appeared. Mime was a popular art and was often combined with singing. Gestures were broad and often vulgar; there was much slapstick comedy, burlesque and swordplay.

The Palais Cardinal theater was built in 1629, mostly because of the interest of Cardinal de Richelieu. Shortly

A troupe of French and Italian actors, wearing splendid costumes and false noses, appears on the stage of the Théâtre Royal in a slapstick comedy. Crystal chandeliers and a row of candles in the foreground are the only set illumination.

Molière and the actress Madeleine Béjart, his leading-lady in life and on the stage, may have posed for Pierre Mignard when he painted this Roman love scene between Venus and Mars. The heroes of Racine's tragedies often lived in ancient Rome.

afterwards, to avoid the disrespect some actors were showing the Church and royalty, Richelieu made himself responsible for the censorship of its plays. Generally, by the time Louis XIV took an interest, the theater was considered so respectable that there was even a bench set aside for bishops. But respectability did not extend to the "pit." Serious theatergoers never occupied the pit where prostitutes made their contacts, pickpockets were busy pilfering from the playgoers and fights over favorites often broke out.

A brilliant young poet, Pierre Corneille formed a theatrical company, *Le Marais*, in 1629. His first successful play, *Mélite*, opened that year in Paris. Valuing his creative freedom, he did not actively seek patrons, yet he was glad to form a tenuous relationship with Cardinal de Richelieu who expressed admiration for certain of his works. It was the cardinal (an amateur playwright himself) who convinced Corneille that he should try a more tragic style. The result of this advice was Corneille's *Le Cid*, based upon the larger-than-life Spanish hero. The play had a triumphant première before an élite audience at Richelieu's palace and was often repeated over the years throughout France.

At the funeral of Corneille who died in 1684, the younger playwright Racine spoke of how Corneille had added to the taste and beauty of the theater: "He put reason on the stage, accompanied by all the pomp and all the ornaments of which our language is capable."

Like Corneille, Jean-Baptiste Racine was a student of Greek and Roman drama. Both were intrigued by the "rules" for drama laid down by Greek and Roman playwrights. But both were also willing occasionally to bend and even break the rules to obtain a new dramatic effect. In his elegantly written plays, Racine

143

projected the human condition always poetically but usually pessimistically. To him love was the ultimate obsession. His heroes and heroines were destined to suffer tragic endings because of their great love.

Jean-Baptiste Poquelin, who called himself Molière, arrived on the Paris stage twenty-eight years after Corneille's first première. He was a manager, leading actor and playwright.

Molière was, from the beginning of his career, destined to change the way the seventeenth century viewed itself. Out of the mores of his time, he found ideas for comedies. He drew his material directly from the life around him. In his plays the audience recognized themselves, their leaders and their acquaintances—and they found the portraits highly amusing.

Yet within the framework of his comedies, Molière did not neglect ancient myths and legends. He wove them into his dramas as only a master-playwright could. His themes depicted the morality and immorality of seventeenth-century society. For example, *Tartuffe* dealt with religious hypocrisy, *Le Bourgeois Gentilhomme* with social pretensions, *L'Avare* (the miser) with the excessive love of money and *Le Malade Imaginaire* with hypochondria.

For thirty years, as playwright, director and leading-actor, Molière made an ever larger theater-going public laugh and applaud his satiric insights.

Before joining a group of amateur actors at the age of twenty-three, he had briefly studied law. But the lures of the theater and the voluptuous beauty of a talented auburn-haired actress, Madeleine Béjart—who became his leading lady and his mistress—were so strong that Molière abandoned the law and toured the provinces for thirteen years. He won his first success in Paris in 1658 with *Les Précieuses Ridicules*. In that comedy, he ridiculed, among other respectable institutions, the intellectual pretensions of the new "salons." He was then fifty-six and at the height of his powers. His troupe became the "King's Comedians." He was considered supreme in his field.

For the next seventeen years, Molière wrote such successes as *L' Ecole des Femmes* (the school for wives), *Le Marriage Forcé* (the forced marriage), *Le Misanthrope, Amphitryon* and *Les Fourberies de Scapin* (the cheating of Scapin). In 1673, he wrote one of his greatest successes, *Le Malade Imaginaire* and died while playing the leading character.

Louis XIV enjoyed Molière's satires so much that he gave him his Palais Royal theater rent-free.

La Fontaine, a friend of Racine and Corneille, wrote eleven books of witty fables inspired by Aesop, the Greek fabulist.

Lancret illustrated Les Lunettes, *a fable about a man who got caught spying on the nuns in a convent—with binoculars.*

Leading his army against the Austrians in 1744, Louis XV fell so seriously ill that, convinced he was about to die, *he confessed his sins in public. Marshall Saxe took command, won the victory at Fontenoy (above) and occupied Flanders.*

Of Louis XV

Louis XIV died leaving almost insurmountable problems for his grandson, the five-year-old Louis XV, and the boy's regent, the Duke d'Orléans. The most difficult was the result of Louis XIV's revocation of the Edict of Nantes in 1685. Ever since the edict had been promulgated by Henri IV, Jesuits and other militant Catholic groups had chipped away at this guarantee of Protestant rights — with the king's approval. Protestant schools and churches were closed and many burnt. Catholic soldiers had been quartered in the homes of leading Protestants. By the time Louis XIV revoked the edict, he had convinced himself that the Protestants had become so discouraged, they no longer were of major consequence in France.

He was very wrong. Within the next fifty years, throughout the reign of Louis XV, hundreds of thousands of talented Protestants — artists, writers, craftsmen, sailors, soldiers and educators — fled from France to seek religious freedom in Holland, Germany, Switzerland, England and the American colonies. Nonetheless, Catholicism remained the state religion of France.

Another problem inherited by Louis XV and his regent was the lack of financial stability caused by the unsuccessful wars of Louis XIV. Then too, there was general criticism of the policy of royal absolutism which was carried to extremes by the adult Louis XV. People were beginning to find their voices but Louis was not interested in hearing them. During his entire reign, he was less interested in governing properly than in hunting game and pursuing women. For only a few years did he actively work as the head of state.

The youth, who had been called "the well-beloved" by some of his subjects, became greatly disliked and even hated. His popularity was limited primarily to his docile court, his ministers, a few wealthy landowners and his many mistresses — including Madame du Barry and Louise O'Murphy, a model for Boucher. He also kept a côterie of courtesans on call in a special set of apartments at Versailles.

145

Even though Jupiter is uncovering the nude Antiope, Watteau has succeeded in giving the scene a feeling of innocence.

Watteau's World

Jean Antoine Watteau was the ultimate painter-psychologist of the fantasies of court life. His was an innocent, lyrical sensitivity. He painted a fairyland inhabited by gossamer figures, somewhere between the pastoral and the theatrical. Many of his backgrounds have the airy, soft quality of the later impressionists. And Watteau's women were never of mere flesh and blood like those of Boucher or Fragonard. His was a world of charming goddesses playing at love.

He filled volumes of notebooks with his sketches. When he went to paint, he carried costumes for actors and cavaliers and, if they consented, he dressed his models in them. A devotee of music and poetry, most of Watteau's paintings included one or more musicians.

In 1712, he was admitted to the Royal Academy as a painter of *fêtes galantes* — a new genre invented to describe his work. Watteau died of tuberculosis at the age of thirty-seven. With more time, he might well have gained the patronage of the king.

Italian comedians were deported for a fancied insult to de ▶ Maintenon. Watteau painted Gilles *upon their return in 1716.*

Jeanne Antoinette Poisson, born into a wealthy banking family, had intelligence, charm and beauty. Her friends included *Voltaire and Montesquieu. She became the mistress and confidant of Louis XV who made her Marquise de Pompadour.*

Pomp
And Pompadour

Whether the new Rococo style in the decorative arts and painting was created for the Marquise de Pompadour or whether she was created for it, is unimportant. The two went together like champagne and oysters or wine and cheese.

Pompadour was as bright and gay as Madame de Maintenon had been dull and prim. The new Rococo style was as light and ornate as the Baroque had been heavy and pompous. Almost from the time of her romantic meeting with Louis XV at a masked ball at Versailles — she costumed as Diana and he as a yew tree — Pompadour was the king's mistress and more. She became his confidant and often his advisor. For her he had the formal apartments built by Louis XIV

A love of the sensuous life is mirrored in this painting by Fragonard, with the suggestive title, Le Feu aux Poudres.

147

en amour et en peinture
L'on cherche toujours le
...ait de la nature

Porcelain gained in popularity and in quality under the patronage of Madame de Pompadour. This faience plate was produced in Rouen c. 1739. The inscription reads: "In love as in painting, one always looks for the touch of nature."

redecorated in the new, extravagant and spritely Rococo style. Such painters as Watteau greatly influenced Rococo decor as did Fragonard, Nattier, Lancret and Boucher. Pompadour, a patron of the arts, was painted by Boucher, Vigée Lebrun (the noted woman artist who had been admitted to the Academy) and Quentin de La Tour, who surprised her by removing his garters, collar and wig and then asking the king to leave the room while she posed—explaining that he never worked with an onlooker present.

While Pompadour did not officially have a salon of her own, she promoted gatherings of important men, both artists and writers, who met in small groups in her boudoir. She used the power of her relationship with the king to promote the manufacture of the lesser arts of the period—like tapestry and porcelain—and with her brother, the Marquis de Marginy, she worked at

improving the output and the artistic quality of the workshops of Gobelin, Aubusson, Sèvres and Beauvais. These "factories" of the arts had continued operating since their founding by Louis XIV, but enjoyed a new life with the attentions of Pompadour and her brother. She was influential in assisting the artist Boucher to become the director at Gobelin and also to have him work with the sculptor Falconet at the porcelain factory at Sèvres. Pompadour owned a château at Sèvres and the factory was already noted for its porcelain. Through her patronage and influence, much of the white porcelain produced in Limoges was shipped to Sèvres. There, Falconet and Boucher collaborated on designing and producing figures in porcelain (influenced by the Rococo) which had the flowing lines and colorings of these master artists. Their shepherdesses, nymphs, cupids and vases were celebrated throughout Europe.

148

The Salons

In the eighteenth century, the social influence of the salons increased immeasurably. No longer did the court and the academy furnish the only forums for exchange of ideas and conversation. By 1720, there were salons on various social levels that catered to different tastes. At the center of each salon was an interesting and attractive woman.

Such a woman was Madame de Tencin, a former nun who before settling into respectability had had a series of love affairs including one with the Regent. She and her brother had made a great deal of money in *Affaire Le Mississipi* investments in John Laws' bank. Rich and attractive, Madame de Tencin became a gracious hostess and her early sins were forgotten. Her cuisine became so famous that one member of the clergy remarked "if she offered poison, she would see that it was well sweetened."

Not all salon hostesses were rich and famous. One of the most popular, Madame Geoffrin, came from a bourgeois family. She became internationally renowned for the good company that met at her salon. Popular writers and philosophers such as Diderot and Voltaire graced her gatherings. She arranged her salon so that on one day artists would be invited, on another musicians and on a third, philosophers and authors. Among these artists were such outstanding talents as Boucher and La Tour. When young Mozart came to Paris, he visited her salon.

Without a claim to nobility, Madame Geoffrin could not be presented at court. But she counted foreign royalty among her good friends. Neither witty nor beautiful, she possessed a gift for listening and had infinite tact. Her guests called her *Maman* (mother).

Madame Geoffrin had been married at the age of fourteen to a businessman thirty years her senior. When she became thirty, with the help of her good friend, the ex-nun Madame de Tencin, she began her social ascendancy. Her salons were strictly social; no card playing was allowed and when arguments grew too hot or one guest spoke too long, Madame Geoffrin would gently but firmly say *Voilà qui est bien* (Very well now).

A group of artists and writers listens to the first reading of a play by Voltaire in 1755 at the salon of Madame Geoffrin (she sits fifth from right in yellow). This imaginary scene was painted sixty years later for Joséphine de Beauharnais.

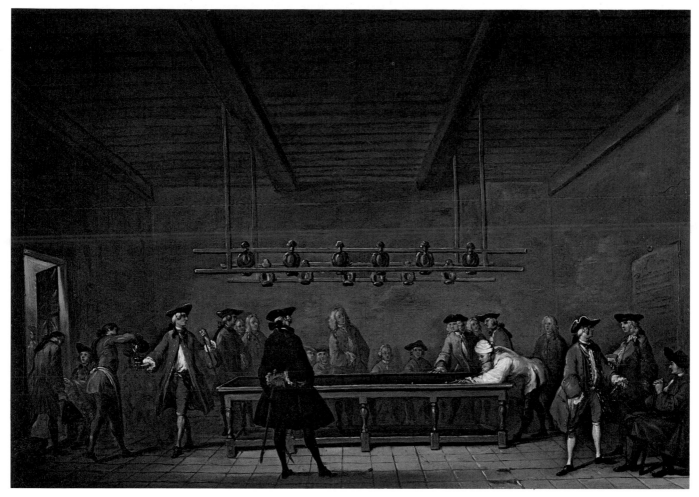

This scene, attributed to Jean-Baptiste Chardin, shows a public billiard room in Paris circa 1725. Billiards was a popular gambling game in France. The players belong mainly to the bourgeoisie. Note the billiard table has no pockets.

In Royal Kitchens

Cookbooks, such as *La Ménagère de Paris*, had appeared in France by the fourteenth century. Catherine de Medici, wife of King Henri II, brought to France some of her favorite Italian recipes and her own chefs as well. She introduced the *apéritif* which quickly became a standard before-dinner drink in court circles. Even before Catherine's arrival, François I had introduced Italian cuisine at Fontainebleau. As bakers learned to make bread softer and whiter, Marie de Medici, wife of Henri IV, came to love the light French loaves made with white flour, salt, brewer's yeast and milk that became known as the "queen's bread." Later, white flour became so much in demand that for a time it was forbidden to use it for cosmetics or to powder wigs.

La haute cuisine evolved on the stoves of peasants, from

◀ *A champagne party is pictured in "The Oyster Lunch," which decorated Louis XV's apartments. Note the cork in mid air.*

la cuisine bourgeoise and *la cuisine régionale*. Such favorites as *marmite perpétuelle*, the soup that cooks forever on the back of the stove, *poulet à la bonne femme* and *pot au feu* are some examples. And the spur-of-the-moment decisions made by imaginative chefs, *la cuisine impromptue*, added to the reputation of French cuisine.

Besides pleasing the senses of taste and of smell, French chefs insisted that their creations also look beautiful. It was not enough merely to broil a pheasant — the entree must look as though the bird was about to spread its wings and fly from the table.

Such a grand chef was Vatel who was in the service of the Prince of Condé. At the height of the brilliance of Versailles, Condé invited Louis XIV and his retinue of some 200 to visit and dine at his Chantilly palace. This was a great honor for Vatel. An elaborate *souper* was arranged for the evening meal — but all did not go as smoothly as Vatel had planned: some of the tables were short of meat. The major meal was scheduled for the next day, Friday, and fresh fish was to be served. But on that morning, only a small amount of fish was delivered. Already disappointed by his previous failure, Vatel could see only one way out. He went up to his room and committed suicide with a carving knife.

151

The Notre Dame bridge in 1756 afforded a marvelous view to those Parisians who lived in apartments built on the bridge foundations. At the left is a water-pumping station and through the arches a wheat-loading dock can be seen. From

their windows, residents watch the annual water tournament of bargemen and one bargewoman, in the foreground. The object is for each team to tumble members of the opposing team into the Seine, using long poles. Note the man falling.

153

Five remarkable men whose adult lives spanned the period between 1628 and 1778 changed the history of France. They were Pascal, Montesquieu, Diderot, Rousseau and Voltaire. Here are a few brief glimpses of them at work:

PASCAL

Blaise Pascal, who was born in 1606 to a *petite noblesse* family, was a devoutly religious man, a Jansenist who nonetheless found gambling fascinating. He studied the mathematics of gambling and made wagers himself to test his theory of probability, which is still studied today. His most famous words on betting were: "What will you wager that God is or is not? Which side shall we bet on? Reason cannot help us." His decision was that one should bet on God: "For if He exists, you win all; and if He does not, you lose nothing."

Pascal and Descartes, both using skepticism as a starting point, came to completely different conclusions regarding man. While Descartes believed that man, by observation and questioning, could understand everything, Pascal wrote: "Man is altogether incomprehensible by man."

MONTESQUIEU

Of the philosophers, Montesquieu was easiest to read for he wrote short, lucid prose. His ideas were provocative and original and he had a sense of humor. In addition to being a prolific writer, he was an historian, political philosopher and lawyer.

His first and most popular book was a satire and critique of French society. It was called *The Persians' Letters*. It sold out eight editions in the year that it appeared, 1721. The light style of Montesquieu was perfectly adapted to the mocking attitude he took toward the memory of Louis XIV and prominent religious and political figures. The book took the form of letters to and from two Persian travelers in France. This form afforded the author an opportunity to satirize French culture.

In one of the letters, Montesquieu invented the fable of the Troglodytes, a civilization where each individual's credo is *"I will be happy."* But by being concerned only with their own interests rather than all of society, they destroy themselves. In other letters, Montesquieu traces the fortunes and misfortunes of his invented civilization. Through them he shows that the good life is not a selfish, individual existence, but is that of the caring, responsible and virtuous citizen. In his later works *Considérations*, a comparative study of ancient Greece and Rome, and his master work, *The Spirit of the Laws*, he expresses his dominant themes—virtue and liberty.

DIDEROT

When *Chamber's Encyclopedia* appeared in Britain in 1728, it had a marked effect on the French writer, mathematician and art critic Denis Diderot who decided to translate the book into French. As he reflected on the task, he realized that he wanted to produce not merely an encyclopedia, but a cultural as well as scientific work that would (he wrote) not only offer information, but change the usual way of thinking (*pour changer la façon commune de penser*).

Between the time Diderot and his distinguished collaborators began in 1751, and the publication of the encyclopedia almost twenty years later, the work was continually threatened by censorship. When it did appear, it reflected much of his own philosophy.

A daring thinker, Diderot considered the possibility that life on earth might have originated without a creator. In an earlier age, he would have been burnt alive for heresy. His search for meaning in religion and his questioning of the existence of God kept him in trouble with the authorities during most of his life.

ROUSSEAU

"I am different from anyone I have ever met—I will even say that I am like no one in the whole world." And indeed, Jean-Jacques Rousseau was a unique revolutionary. In his *Confessions*, the reader is jolted and often astonished by the intimate revelations he makes of his emotional and intellectual processes. Rousseau mounted a blistering attack on the accepted rationalist views of his free-thinking colleagues. To put it as bluntly as he did, he was opposed to the idea that progress in civilization comes from progress in science and the arts. He held that they were corrupt instruments that served only the rich.

Rousseau was deeply affected by his concept of the "noble savage" which came from his studies of the discoveries in the New World. To him the savage was a man who, depending on his emotions and rejecting his intellectual powers, had achieved a perfect life which civilization then destroyed.

It was Rousseau's belief that modern man must bring about a *détente* with emotion and reason, with science and morality—and out of this create a new and balanced society.

VOLTAIRE

Voltaire was in bad repute with the authorities for some of his early satiric writing. After an altercation with the powerful Chevalier de Rohan, he found himself in the Bastille, where he wrote his first tragedy *Oedipe*.

Diderot's spirit and vitality come to life under Fragonard's brush strokes in red and gold harmonies. Diderot, the force behind the encyclopedia, wrote of Fragonard, "The ideas of this artist are sublime." In 1806, Fragonard died in poverty.

Voltaire gets out of bed at his home in Ferney, near Geneva. The master of satire was sent to the Bastille and banished from France. He lived first in England, then in Lorraine and finally in Prussia for a year as guest of Frederick the Great.

Exiled from France in 1726, he chose to go to England. There he came into contact with many of the political, social and scientific ideas that greatly influenced his later life and works. He was impressed by the great esteem in which Isaac Newton, father of modern science, was held, and praised the effective coequality in government enjoyed by the English people. His *Philosophical Letters Concerning the English* was, as he no doubt expected, burnt as "a scandalous work, contrary to religion and morals" by the French government. He was the author of five plays, three philosophical works, innumerable essays and poems and two novels, *Zadig* and *Candide*.

A master of satire, Voltaire challenged the accepted ideas of current social, political and scientific mores in ways that showed how ridiculous they were. In *Candide*, he singled out three great evils in the world — vice, boredom and need — and expressed his conviction that only through work could they be overcome. He wrote: "Let us cultivate our garden."

1789 - 1815

REVOLUTION, NAPOLÉON

American War for Independence and record inflation of food prices and land rents force royal government into bankruptcy and hurl France into Revolution. Louis XVI and Marie Antoinette are executed for treason. The Terror follows. With Napoléon's rise, France changes from a republic to an empire. Public education advances. Classical forms in art, architecture and dress recall the Roman Republic and the Roman Empire. A new appreciation for popular culture and Romanticism appears.

HISTORICAL CHRONOLOGY	ART CHRONOLOGY
1789 *National Assembly formed from Third Estate. Fall of the Bastille. Declaration of the Rights of Man and Citizen. Church lands are sold.*	1789 *Sieyès writes "What is the Third Estate?" First political journal,* Journal of Debates, *founded.*
1791 *Louis XVI attempts to flee France. Constitution of 1791 is adopted.*	1792 *National anthem, the* Marseillaise, *is composed.*
1792 *September Massacres. Radical Convention replaces Legislative Assembly. Monarchy is abolished.*	1793 *Louvre declared a public museum by the Convention. Dechristianization attempt; religion of the Supreme Being, new calendar based on the Revolution.* Condorcet *writes* Progress of the Human Mind *while in hiding.*
1793 *Executions of Louis XVI and Marie-Antoinette followed by mass executions (the Terror). Universal male suffrage and abolition of slavery.*	
1794 *Executions of Danton and Robespierre.*	1794 *Camille Desmoulins, two days before his execution, writes "the gods are thirsty." Condorcet and the chemist Lavoisier are executed. The Convention founds the Polytechnical School and the Institute of France.*
1795 *The Directory replaces the Convention. Bonaparte puts down insurrection of the National Guard in Paris.*	
1797 *Republican coup d'état of Fructidore. Bonaparte suppresses uprisings in Paris.*	1802 The Genius of Christianity *by Chateaubriand marks the appearance of Romanticism.*
1798—9 *Bonaparte departs on Egyptian expedition and seizes control of the government after becoming First Consul.*	1805—7 Coronation of Napoléon in Notre Dame *painted by Jacques-Louis David.*
1802—3 *Napoléon Bonaparte is elected Consul for Life and sells Louisiana to the United States.*	1805—10 Colonne Vendôme *by Gondoin and Lepère shows classical influence in architecture.*
1804 *Bonaparte crowns himself Emperor Napoléon I. Civil Code is established.*	1806—36 *Construction of the Arc de Triomphe.*
1806 *Napoléon I creates the Confederation of the Rhine and tries to exclude England from the continental economy.*	1808—9 *Géricault's* Raft of the Medusa *painted in Naturalist style. Du Maître writes* Du Pape.
1809—10 *Papal states are annexed and Pope Pius VII is imprisoned. Napoléon divorces Joséphine and marries Marie Louise, Hapsburg princess.*	1810 Germany *by Madame de Stael criticizes French literature and praises those of Germany and England.*
1812 *Destruction of the* Grande Armée *in Russia.*	1811 *Bases of atomic and molecular theories laid down by Avogadro and Ampère.*
1814 *After Napoléon's abdication and exile to the island of Elba, Louis XVIII becomes king of France.*	1812 *Fourier, noted physicist and utopian socialist, recognized by Academy of Science.*
1815 *Napoléon escapes from Elba, is defeated at Waterloo and exiled to the island of Saint Helena. Monarchy is reestablished.*	pre—1815 *Antoine-Jean Gros appointed Battle Painter of the Empire. Pierre Prud'hon paints Joséphine. Madame Tussaud's wax-works opens.*

In this highly symbolic naïve painting, Louis XVI and his minister Necker are in the ship of France. With them are Goodness and Truth, who holds a mirror to illuminate paintings of the past, present and future. Louis is safe from the devil.

Louis XVI
And The USA

The United States owes much to the France of Louis XVI. Thanks in part to French contributions of men and materiel and to the cooperation of the king and his ministers, the Americans were able to achieve victory over the English in their Revolutionary War.

When Benjamin Franklin was dispatched by the rebellious colonies to purchase munitions from France, offering in exchange the doubtful collateral of Virginia tobacco, he was received graciously by Louis even though he appeared at court in a plain suit and unpowdered hair. His newly-made wig had not been finished in time for the reception. But he found the king and all of France sympathetic to Americans and their revolutionary government. Voltaire admired the Quakers, Rousseau the Indians, while Turgot, Louis's finance minister, wrote that America was "the hope of the world."

The Americans owed much to French siege guns and French troops commanded by Rochambeau, Saint Simon and Lafayette. They also were aided by the magnificent seamanship of Admiral de Grasse.

Although Louis XVI occasionally vacillated in making important decisions which, according to his great-grandfather Louis XIV, a king should never do, he accomplished much during the years 1774 and 1792. His opposition was formidable: a reactionary *Parlement* and a powerful conservative clergy that tried to stop every reform measure put forward by Louis and his ministers. His queen, Marie Antoinette, made no secret of her loyalty to Austria and refused to limit her huge expenditures. Nonetheless, there was progress. Corsica was acquired; the last traces of serfdom were abolished. Huguenots received more rights, trade was improved and Papin invented the steamboat. Steam engines were built and Montgolfier invented the hydrogen balloon.

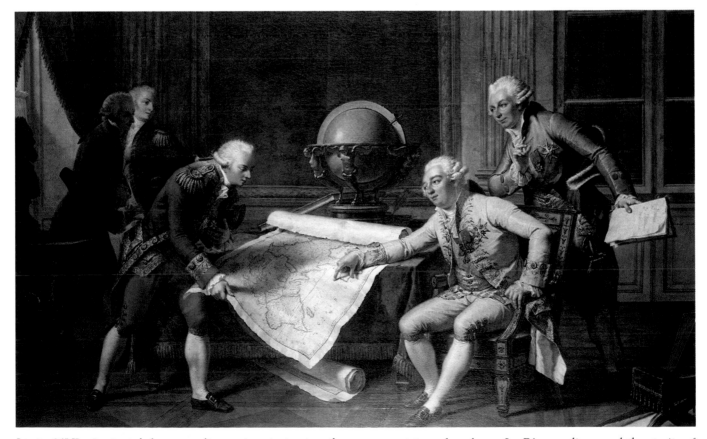

Louis XVI, fascinated by new discoveries, is tracing the route to be followed around the world in 1785 by La Pérouse, sea captain and explorer. La Pérouse discovered the straits of northern Japan, which were named after him. He was lost at sea.

Thought
For Food

The French possessed the marvelous ability to convert and flavor meats, fish and vegetables by using herbs and condiments so as to create a distinctive cuisine. Most of the great chefs came from humble backgrounds — their cooking schools were their mothers, or their fathers or their aunts — people who knew their way around a kitchen.

Even a king could cook. At the court of Louis XV, the king gave intimate suppers and at one of them he created an asparagus omelette in honor of Madame du Barry. Both Pompadour and du Barry were themselves capable cooks although limited to a few specialties. The French could choose among hams from Bayonne; oysters, crabs and lobsters from Bretagne; *foie gras* and truffles from Gascogne; honey from the Dauphiné; pigeons from Picardie; vegetables from the Ile de France (and almost everywhere else); sole and turbot from Dieppe; beef from Franche-Comté; duck from Normandie and cheeses from Bourgogne. These were but a few of the regions where French cooks learned to perform culinary magic, inventing such succulent dishes as *cassoulet, escargots* in garlic butter, *bouillabaisse, poulet de Bresse, carottes à la Vichy* and *canard farci façon du Limousin.*

By the 1770's, ordinary taverns began to expand their food service. Cafés, where only a cup of coffee and a roll had been available, now began to serve light meals. The bourgeoisie (and occasionally the nobility) in Paris began to patronize primitive restaurants like the *Procope* which catered to men of letters including Diderot and other encyclopedists.

The first true restaurant in France was probably the one opened by Beaubillères, who had been the chef of Monsieur, the count of Provence. He called it *La Grande Taverne de Londres* and, in addition to French dishes, he featured such English delicacies as *wouelche rabette* (Welsh rabbit), *mach potetesse* (mashed potatoes) and *plumbuting* (plum pudding).

Not satisfied with preparing great cuisine, some French chefs wrote voluminously about it. Perhaps because of the French penchant for scientific appraisal, they wrote in exhaustive detail of their techniques and philosophies, and of the art and poetry of cooking. Antonin Carême, possibly the greatest of all chefs, wrote a twelve- volume work in which he equated the art of

cooking with those of music, painting and architecture. "Pastry," he wrote, "is a principal branch of architecture." And "the gourmet's palate and olfactory sense respond to sensations like those of lovers of painting and music."

Another recorder of culinary science was the philosopher Brillat-Savarin whose meditations on transcendental gastronomy included chapters on the senses, his theory of frying, and on women as *gourmands.* He recommended that women follow "a succulent, delicate and well-chosen diet. . . this keeps away the external appearances of old age." Among his aphorisms are "the invention of a new recipe does more for man's happiness than the discovery of a new star;" "animals feed, man eats, wise men dine;" "he who invites guests and is not attentive to the repast offered them is not worthy to have friends;" "to wait too long for a late guest is an insult to those present," and "dessert without cheese is like a pretty girl with only one eye."

And then there was Grimod de la Reymière, the huge man with a gargantuan appetite who wrote the *Almanac des Gourmands* — an eight-year task. It was said of him that he had the kind of faith that raises pie crust. And with a great appreciation of seasoning, he once said: "With this sauce — I could eat my father."

An outdoor sign showing a portly gourmand *dining, advertises that this shop sells such* comestibles *as seafood (lobsters and mussels are shown), wine, bread and paté. It was painted c. 1800 by Debucourt and is now in Paris in the Musée Cluny.*

This wine merchant's sign informs potential clients that he caters to all classes of society. A priest drinks with a soldier while a bourgeois, wearing the tricolor republican cockade on his hat, gives his lady-friend a ride on a swing.

During the troubles of 1790, the National Guard commanded by General Lafayette was charged with keeping law and order.

Above, an officer reads a proclamation ordering citizens back to work. On the right, a man swallows a last-minute drink.

The Revolution Begins

There are no simple explanations for the French Revolution. Some of its causes originated during the reign of Louis XVI (but the revolution was not a movement to depose him), others sprang up in the years before his rule and still others had their roots in the traditions of feudalism and a privileged nobility that had existed for centuries in France.

The revolution arose not from immediate causes nor even from those that were the most visible. A shortage of crops and the resulting rise in the prices of commodities were factors, but in the past there had been many food riots and particularly bread riots that did not explode into revolution. Nor did the writings of the philosophers Voltaire and Rousseau have much to do with inspiring the revolt, even though the National Assembly subsequently gave them credit by moving their coffins to the memorial church of Sainte Geneviève.

They contributed, and so did the successful American Revolution with its emphasis on life, liberty and the pursuit of happiness, the new democratic constitution of the United States and the political and social philosophies of Thomas Jefferson, Benjamin Franklin and Samuel Adams.

Another cause was simply the lack of money to keep the old institutions going. England was destroying French shipping and crippling its foreign trade. The clergy and the nobility paid little or no taxes. A series of finance ministers came and went and none of them found a solution. Meanwhile, the monarchy would not curb its extravagance. Finally the *Parlement* was forced to call a session of the Estates General, representing all of France: the First Estate was the clergy, the Second the nobility and the Third the people.

At the meeting, the Third Estate, claiming to represent most of the nation, harangued, raged and ultimately took control of the Assembly. Led by bourgeois landowners, businessmen, minor officials and soldiers, its interests were those of the upper middle class. But because they also thought they had much to gain, it was reinforced by women's groups, political clubs, members of the crafts guilds, deserters from the army, shopkeepers and even servants and peasants — the proletariat who would do most of the actual fighting in the revolution.

It was never a question of what the people wanted. Rather, it was what the people did not want. They did not want the nobility, the reactionary clergy and the landowners who did not themselves work. They were willing to let the king remain, controlled by a people's assembly.

In December 1788, the Royal Council doubled the number of representatives in the Third Estate, making it the most influential of the three. Six months later, it had seized the initiative and power from the nobles and the clergy and proclaimed itself the National Assembly. Shortly afterward, the king ordered the clergy and the nobility to join.

The new National Assembly had expected leadership from the king and was disappointed by his support of the nobility. Some of its members became panicky when a meeting hall, being prepared for a joint session of the entire Estates General, was temporarily closed by soldiers — who actually had arrived to protect the king. Believing that the soldiers had come so that the king could dissolve the Assembly by force, the delegates marched to a nearby tennis court where they took an oath (only one dissented) never to separate and to meet whenever necessary until the new constitution of the kingdom had been established. As the news of these meetings spread throughout Paris, there were wild rumors of what might come next. Workmen, shopkeepers and housewives took to the streets. They no longer wanted to wait for reform, they wanted to make it happen.

On July 14, 1789, a mob of 20,000 marched on the Bastille, which had become a minor prison for rowdy noblemen where inmates with money could live in comparative luxury. Pets and visitors were allowed; food was excellent. Prisoners were allowed three bottles of wine (including champagne) a day. It was in this unlikely place that the revolution started. The storming of the Bastille freed only seven prisoners: two men who had been imprisoned for insanity, four forgers and one aristocrat who had been locked up — at the request of his father — for debauchery. There were no starving peasants, no ill-treated bourgeois to release. However, it was a royal fortress.

In frustration and rage, the mob killed the governor of the Bastille and three of his officers, hanged three men of the garrison and destroyed the prison. The slaughter in the Bastille was not a reprisal for any wrongs committed there, but a violent expression of people's fears that a possible military coup by the nobles and the king would destroy any hope of reform. By their act, the people of Paris demonstrated to the nobility and the king that they would be adamant in seeking representation in the government.

Within weeks of the destruction of the Bastille came *La Grande Peur* (the Great Fear) which began with a grain shortage and then grew into a general peasant uprising. Again rumors played a part; the peasants in rural areas of Normandie, Franche-Comté and Alsace heard that noblemen were plotting to send brigands to attack them. Although there was probably no such plot, the peasants ransacked castles and manor houses, stopped paying rents and began trapping game illegally. When the rumors stopped, so did the uprisings. Frightened by these incidents, the National Assembly passed decrees that finally abolished the feudal rights of the nobility and ended their privileges.

Less than two months later, on October 5, 1789, a delegation of women — inspired by a popular pamphlet charging that the authorities, not the bakers, were to blame for the bread shortage — met in the National Guard headquarters at the Hôtel de Ville in Paris. They hoped to convince the National Guard to accompany them on a twelve-mile march to Versailles to present their grievances to the king. While the women were importuning the guards to march with them, General Lafayette, who had become the head of the National Guard, received orders from the Municipal Council to escort the women and to bring the king back to Paris.

As the group set out, more and more sympathizers joined the procession. The delegation, grown much larger, arrived in the early afternoon at Versailles. Louis had just returned from his usual hunt. He quickly received them. More bread, he promised, would soon be available in Paris and prices would no longer increase. Some of the delegates were satisfied and left but others arrived during the evening. By the next morning, a huge mob was on hand — the critical mass required for a confrontation. Shooting began and some of the royal guards were killed. The king and queen, realizing that they could not hold out indefinitely against the thousands of rioters, decided to accept Lafayette's offer to escort them to the Tuileries Palace in Paris.

The procession got under way with Lafayette riding alongside the carriage in which the king's family was traveling. Wagons from the king's storehouse carrying flour and grain followed behind. The National Guard came next, trailed by the mob which was led by men carrying the severed heads of two of the king's guardsmen on their pikes. The mob's urge for action had been appeased. It happily marched back to Paris satisfied by what it had accomplished.

The plaque under Louis XVI's bust reads "The Hope of The Golden Age." He took an oath to obey the Constitution in 1791.

Last Days Of The Monarchy

As in the United States, the French constituent assembly adopted a bill of rights. It began with the statement that all men were free and equal in their rights. The guarantees followed: Freedom from arbitrary arrest and imprisonment; freedom of religion; freedom of speech or opinion, and freedom from taxation except with the people's consent. Property rights were inalienable and inviolable. Law would be based upon the will of the people expressed through their elected representatives.

At this time, Louis XVI and Marie Antoinette were alive and well and he, within limits, was still the king. A decree of the assembly said that "Louis XVI, by the grace of God and the constitutional law of the state" was still "king of the French." The wording made it plain that Louis was no longer king by absolute and divine right, for the Declaration of Rights stated that "the source of all sovereignty resides essentially in the nation." The implication was that France hoped to have a government of the people and for the people headed by a constitutional monarchy. Although the safety of the king and his family was not threatened, he was convinced after the death of his friend, Count of Mirabeau, that they should flee to Metz where, if necessary, they could escape across the northeastern frontier.

The escape of the king, queen and the two royal children from Paris was made in darkness late on the night of June 20. Their journey was relatively uneventful; more than once, they were recognized, yet were allowed to continue on. Bad luck befell them at the town of Varennes where a revolutionary recognized and stopped them. They had become separated from their bodyguard and soon they were surrounded by armed peasants. The National Guard was summoned. The royal family was taken back to the Tuileries Palace and put under surveillance by both the National Guard and the king's own Swiss bodyguards.

On the night of August 9, crowds gathered around the Hôtel de Ville where a revolutionary committee was working. After listening to inflammatory speeches, the crowd marched over to the Tuileries Palace. There its leaders called for Louis and tried to storm the palace doors. Shots were exchanged by the guards and the attackers. The king ordered his Swiss guards to cease fire. As a result, they were massacred when the revolutionists brought up reserve riflemen and a cannon. The attacking group lost some 373 men; the Swiss Guard and the nobles about 800. The king was spirited away to the Legislative Assembly Hall.

The Assembly, however, was still intent upon having a constitutional monarchy. When a petition was drawn up by some of the anti-monarchists to force his abdication — even though a riot ensued, with fifty of the enemies of the king killed — the king was not involved and on September 14, 1791, he signed the constitution.

After Louis XVI's attempt to escape from France, he was mistrusted by almost everyone — and for good reason. He rejected the new government rather than agreeing to become a part of it. Letters found at the Tuileries clearly showed that Louis had intrigued with Austria against the revolutionary government. It was his hope to be rescued by the Austrians and Prussians. Once France declared war against Austria, the king actually had some genuine hope of deliverance. Few observers expected the revolutionary forces to be victorious. Yet the French army was successful, defeating the Austrians and occupying Belgium. The conquering army carried with it a proclamation to assist all people who wanted to revolt against tyranny in their countries and it promised to abolish all feudal dues in the countries it conquered. It said that these countries could elect their own leaders and be recognized by France.

Then the Convention turned to the trial of the king. He was sentenced to death by a majority of three votes.

On the eve of his execution in 1793, Louis XVI bids farewell
to Marie Antoinette and his children, the Dauphin Louis XVII
and Marie Thérèse. The royal family was imprisoned in the
Tower of the Temple where the dauphin probably died in 1795.

165

Found guilty of treason, Louis XVI was publicly guillotined in the Place de la Concorde on January 21, 1793. The use of the guillotine had been decreed by the National Assembly in 1789. This painting was made by an anonymous Danish eyewitness.

Saint Guillotine

Doctor Joseph Ignace Guillotin was a man who happened to have the right idea at the right time. In October 1789, the Legislative Assembly was in session looking for ways to improve the lives of French citizens. The Bastille had fallen and the king was under house arrest in the Tuileries awaiting his execution.

Dr. Guillotin, a humanitarian, told the Assembly he had been thinking about the death sentence, and had decided that all of the methods of execution being used were too gruesome to continue. Beheading with the axe or the sword was too hit-or-miss, the good doctor said; the executioner often missed the neck altogether and then had to take as many as three or four strokes to get the job done. In fact, there had been occasions when

he finally had to use a knife and stab the victim to death. The doctor also criticized the rack — the pulling apart of people by horses and that ancient French favorite, burning victims alive. Then, as the assembly listened attentively, he announced that he had thought of something new: a machine for putting people to death that would be quick, painless and infallible. It would consist of a heavy, sharp blade mounted between two long vertical guides on a wooden platform. The victim would be strapped to the platform with his head extended over the edge. A basket would be placed below the edge. The executioner would release the blade, and it would drop swiftly and unerringly, severing the victim's head which would drop neatly into the basket.

The assembly approved of the doctor's idea for an effortless decapitation machine, and turned the details of its manufacture over to another doctor, Antoine Louis, who was secretary of the French surgical

Queen Marie Antoinette, disparagingly called L'Autrichienne (the Austrian woman), was guillotined nine months after the king. Unpopular for her extravagance and indifference to the people, she could not be rescued by the Austrian Emperor.

Academy. Working from Dr Guillotin's sketch, Louis designed the mechanism (many people think it should have been named after *him*) and then a German piano-maker, Tobias Schmidt, took on the job of constructing a prototype. Soon there was a neat and glistening guillotine standing in each of the largest cities and in many of the towns of France.

At the time of the Terror, when Robespierre raised himself up to be a dictator over the bodies of earlier patriots, the guillotine was used daily. It also was used indiscriminately. A conservative estimate would be that at least 40,000 persons lost their heads, of whom possibly half had been denied the trials guaranteed them by the Constitution.

Executions became a bureaucratic routine, dismissed as necessary for the protection of the Republic. In a letter to her parents, a Parisian working-girl said that each day, cart-loads of prisoners being taken to the guillotine rumbled past her work place and returned late that evening with the bodies. It became such an ordinary sight, she said, that "people just went on working in the shops, often not even bothering to raise their heads." At one time, there arose what was almost a religion of the guillotine. George Sand wrote that "during the Terror, the men who spilled the most blood were those who had the strongest desire to lead their followers to the dreamed of golden age and who had the greatest sympathy for human misery."

There were even songs extolling the instrument of death and referring to the act of execution as the Red Mass. One song went:

Saint Guillotine, protectoress of patriots, pray for us.
Saint Guillotine, the dread of aristocrats, protect us.
Gracious machine, have mercy upon us.
Admirable machine, have mercy upon us.
Saint Guillotine, deliver us from our enemies.

167

The mayor of Rouen, Fontenay, wearing the tricolor ribbon symbolizing his function, blocks the entrance to the Hôtel de Ville during a bread riot in August 1793. These frequent bread riots were based on the widespread belief that

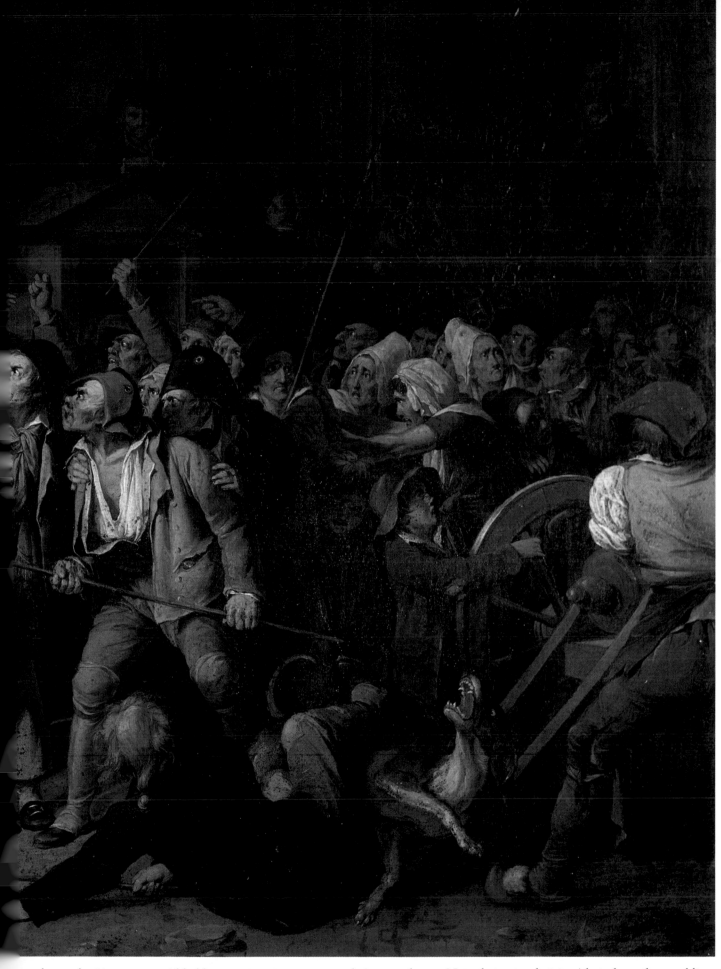

the authorities were withholding grain in a pacte de
famine to force prices up and punish the peasants and
workmen. Note that several rioters' hats bear the republican
cockade. This event was painted by Boilly forty years later.

Marat, a radical Jacobin, was stabbed to death in his bath by Charlotte Corday, a Girondist sympathizer who had been angered by his role in overthrowing the Girondists in the National Convention. He had long espoused public violence.

The End
Of The Revolution

Three unusual men — idealistic, eloquent, patriotic and intelligent — were major leaders of the French Revolution. They were Marat, Danton and Robespierre. Their efforts to bring about desperately needed reforms were relatively successful, but the methods they used cost the lives of thousands of citizens.

Jean Paul Marat was a physician and a scientist. But after his work had been rejected by the Academy of Sciences, he became a political revolutionary. His enemies: the intellectual elite, the nobility and the monarchy. "I believe in the Revolution at last," he wrote after the king's execution. His neurotic, suspicious nature saw spies, enemies and treachery hiding in every shadow. The young woman who assassinated him was able to make an appointment only because she promised in a note to disclose his enemies' plans against him.

To Georges Jacques Danton, it was neither an urban nor an intellectuals' revolution. He saw it as a provincial uprising and put his faith in the *sans culottes*, the men of the street — shopkeepers, former peasants and farmers. He represented these people through their organizations, the *Girondins* named for the area near Bordeaux from whence he came, the Gironde.

A rational radical, Danton had hoped to keep the king and queen alive to use their influence to avoid war with Austria. But in this instance, as in later efforts to unite the opposing revolutionary parties, his motives were suspected. Every effort that Danton made compromised his own radical position. Robespierre, who would become the dictatorial leader of the Committee of Public Safety, had him arrested and guillotined.

The third of these sincere Revolutionists, Robespierre, was a brilliant advocate of political democracy and, like Danton, once a supporter of a constitutional monarchy. But after the execution of the king, Robespierre who (like Marat) had had a secret wish for a dictatorship, became one — for a time. An austere moralist, Robespierre wrote: "Under a revolutionary regime, the State must protect itself against all who attack it." Under the aegis of his infamous Committee of Public Safety, he drew up a list of suspects that included most nobles and wealthy businessmen. Convinced that he was killing in a noble effort, he felt justified. But he lost the support of the bourgeoisie as he had that of the provincials by executing Danton, and the politicians around him so feared for their own lives that the Directory issued an order for his arrest. When his time came, his head dropped silently into the basket under the guillotine.

"The incorruptible patriot," Robespierre was a revolutionary leader who had hundreds guillotined until his own turn came.

The fall of the revolutionary government began when Danton was executed. Within four months, Robespierre followed him.

171

The Louvre

The Louvre, built on the right bank of the Seine, began as a repository for the preservation and protection of the royal treasury, the State Archives, the fine furniture and other treasures of the twelfth century. Eight hundred years later, it had become one of the great museums in the world.

It was the resplendent François I who so loved the ancient location that he commissioned Pierre Lescaut and Jean Goujon to build the Louvre palace. François then encouraged such major talents as Leonardo, Cellini and Primaticcio to come to his court, and as a result, priceless paintings like the *Mona Lisa* became part of the Louvre collection.

Benefiting from the gifts of subsequent kings, the Louvre continued to grow. Henri IV extended and completed the long gallery and passageway begun by Catherine de Medici. Beneath this upper passage, he left space for shops, small apartments and the Royal Mint.

Louis XIV at the age of twenty-one converted this space into studios, workshops and living quarters for artists, sculptors and other craftsmen. Such well-known artists as Le Moyne, Boucher, Chardin, Greuze, Fragonard and David all lived and worked there. Some quickly grew rich as they had few living expenses — as well as the most prestigious address in Paris.

When Versailles was built, Louis XIV moved out of the Louvre. For the next thirty years it housed the academies of art, architecture, science and sculpture. Louis XIV's bourgeois minister Colbert added to the king's collection. From the banker Jabach, Colbert bought 5,532 drawings of the masters and most of the art collection of Charles I of England. Colbert followed this coup by acquiring the collection of his predecessor, Cardinal Mazarin.

From 1726, the Louvre began its rise to fame as a museum. It became the setting of the annual exhibition of the *Académie des Beaux Arts*. In 1793, the Revolutionary government opened the museum, displaying to the public for the first time its magnificent collections.

When Napoléon III made Paris "the city of light," the Louvre became one of its brightest gems. The first stone of the new and finally completed Louvre was laid in 1852.

This is the interior of the Louvre as seen by Hubert Robert ▶
who was named curator of the museum after it opened in 1793.

172

During a tumultuous session of the Convention in 1795, the head of Deputy Féraud, assassinated during a Jacobin riot outside the chamber, is displayed to the president, Boissy d'Anglas. Féraud received a State funeral for his bravery.

A truly revisionist concept of history was exemplified by the new calendar adopted by the French Revolution. The past was left behind and "Day One" of the first year began with the signing of the Constitution on September 22, 1792. At the same time, new names for the twelve months of the year were coined and adopted. They were poetic and practical for they signaled the type of weather each month was likely to bring. For instance, the second month, Brumaire (October 23-November 22) was foggy; Thermidor (June 23-July 22) was hot; Ventôse (February 23-March 22) was likely to be windy. This new calendar had a thirty-day month consisting of three ten-day weeks with a rest day at the end of each ten days that corresponded to Sunday. This meant considerably fewer Sundays and more work days in the course of a year. The revolutionary calendar was officially abandoned on January 1, 1806.

An equally revolutionary idea was the creation of a new church, the Church of the Supreme Being. After arranging a celebratory mass at Notre Dame in November 1793, Robespierre published a statement declaring that the French people "recognize the presence of a supreme being—and the immortality of the soul." Robespierre believed that people needed a religion— but he preferred that they adopt a new one. After his death, his Church of the Supreme Being dwindled and ultimately disappeared.

To defend itself against the combined forces of Austria, Spain Prussia, Holland and England, the new revolutionary French government recruited an army of volunteers. They marched to patriotic songs such as La Marseillaise by Rouget de Lisle.

Hot-air balloons, or Montgolfières, *were first used by the French army at the Battle of Fleurus (Belgium) in 1794.*

Here French Republican troops charge the Austrian Imperial army. Their victory helped Bonaparte's military advancement.

Enter Napoléon

By the end of the Revolution in 1795, the citizen soldiers of France had successfully defended their borders and even invaded the territories of the country's enemies. All of France enjoyed the sweet taste of victory. For the first time patriotism meant more than fidelity to a king or a liege lord. Under the young Corsican, Napoléon Bonaparte, foreign enemies had been vanquished and internal enemies—be they nobles or bourgeois or unruly mobs—no longer disturbed the peace.

The French began to see themselves as a united people who, under great pressure, had recreated their country. They had thrown off the monarchy and the last vestiges of feudalism and replaced them with *Liberté, Egalité et Fraternité.* Parades, plays and music all took on patriotic themes. Children played patriotic games, wearing the tricolored cockade as a symbol of liberty. One mother remarked that the children playing soldiers looked adorable "with their red-woolen caps, their carmagnoles and their big sticks."

The patriotism and military fervor that marked the period was exemplified by the inspired neo-classical painting of Jacques-Louis David. Intensely interested in the country's new social directions, David had become active in politics as a delegate to the National Convention and had voted in favor of the death penalty for Louis XVI. He then became an important arbiter of taste. Believing that the Royal Academy, with its rigid rules imposed by the *Ancien Régime* did not allow enough artistic freedom, he abolished that venerable institution and replaced it with a more liberal *Institut de France.*

During the final days of the Revolution David had been jailed, and while in his cell, painted his only landscape *View of the Luxembourg Gardens.* Shortly after his release, he met and became fascinated by the young Napoléon. Later he was named *Premier Peintre de l'Empereur.* David's huge painting of the coronation of Napoléon became one of the treasures of the Louvre. Pupils who worked at his studio in Paris included Gérard, Gros and Ingres. "To give a shape and a perfect form to one's thought," he said, "this and this only is the true meaning of being an artist."

This painting by Antoine Gros shows Bonaparte boldly touching a man's infectious tumor during a visit to a hospital in Jaffa (Syria). This kind of risk taking became part of the legend of Bonaparte; nothing bad could happen to so great a general.

177

At the Battle of Austerlitz, troopers of the Second Regiment of Hussards settle into a night bivouac. After a forced march from the English Channel to the Danube and victory over the Austrians, the **Grande Armée** prepares to face the Russians.

Wounded Russian soldiers are taken prisoner after their defeat at Austerlitz. Emperor Napoléon I won the battle using artillery barrages and infantry assaults. This scene and the one above were painted by a commandant of Hussards.

Napoléon
The Soldier

Throughout his life, Napoléon professed himself to be a true son of the Revolution. Somehow, he managed to identify his own self-interest with the ideals of the Revolution. His soldiers loved him because he always spoke to them in terms of their own self-interests. To him, glory was always secondary.

In his first proclamation to his army in Italy, he said, "I will lead you into the most fertile plains in the world; rich provinces, great cities will be in your power — you will be covered with honor, glory and riches. Soldiers of Italy, do you lack courage or fidelity?" What soldier could resist such a tempting offer?

Napoléon did not squander the lives of his men. He encouraged the factories and foundries of France to produce new, lighter and more lethal artillery. Interchangeable parts were designed for cannon and indeed for all weaponry. He organized the armies into specialized units, with different weapons and tactics for the field, the coast and the garrison.

Of all the armies in Europe, Napoléon's was the most mobile. His reputation for moving large bodies of men with surprising speed was legendary. He was seldom found where his adversaries expected him to be. To make his troops more mobile, Napoléon created a special corps of *conducteurs* or drivers, for the speedy transport of artillery. This corps also cared for the hundreds of horses needed for transport. His attention to detail, his imagination and his sense of purpose made Napoléon a formidable opponent in every battle.

He was a master tactician. He remarked that his brain was like a chest of drawers in which he had filed away great stores of knowledge. When he had need to make a decision, he would open a specific drawer of his mind, solve the problem and then close the drawer so as to be free from further thought about the matter — until the next time he faced a similar problem. Battle strategies, legal procedures, administrative crises, even personal problems, each had its separate drawer.

When hydrogen-filled balloons were invented, Napoléon was the first to use them as observation posts. This added one more advantage to his technique of surprise and mobility. One of his favorite tactics was to concentrate upon one point in his opponent's lines and then to mount a ferocious attack upon it. Massed firepower was followed immediately by bayonet charges. This tactic turned the tide of battle against the Russians at the battle of Friedland in 1807. The Russians lost upward of 25,000 men; the French less than a third of that number.

Napoléon spent most of his adult life at war. He was either planning wars, fighting wars or recovering from

Géricault excelled at painting horses. This is the original preliminary sketch for "Mounted Officer of the Imperial Guard."

wars. In all, he fought twelve major wars while most generals did not survive even twelve battles. He won his first war in Italy (1796-7); the second also in Italy (at Marengo) in 1800; the Austro-Russian war (at Austerlitz) in 1805; the Prussian War (at Iena) in 1806; a war against Russia (Friedland) in 1807 and one against Austria (at Wagram) in 1809. He suffered defeats in Egypt (naval), Spain and Russia in 1812, in Germany at Leipzig (1813), in France in 1814 and in Belgium at Waterloo in 1815. Total score for Napoléon: six wars won, six wars lost.

Out of one of his mental drawers came the inspiration for the founding of one of France's most prestigious institutions, the Legion of Honor, which Napoléon started in 1802. Awarded at first to army officers, it was the highest recognition of their service to the country. It was a popular success from its inception. In 1804, when the Constitution was adopted, a far-reaching provision was added. Though Napoléon had shown no previous interest in education for women, he now created the boarding-school of the *Maison d'Education de La Légion d'Honneur* for the daughters of the recipients of the Legion of Honor.

Napoléon
The Emperor

Few men go through life without showing some appreciation for their success, their wealth or their happiness to their mothers, fathers, wives, siblings or their friends. One of the few was Napoléon Bonaparte who said, "What I am, I owe to strength of will, character, application and daring."

He was born a Frenchman, but just barely, for Corsica had become a part of France in 1768, the year before he was born. One of twelve children born into the impoverished but noble Bonaparte family, none matched his energy, magnetism and ambition.

Young Bonaparte received his commission in the French army at the age of sixteen. Before he was twenty-one, he wrote a short history of Corsica and studied the campaigns and strategy of Alexander the Great, his role model. As a young officer, he returned to Corsica from time to time to lend his energy to the struggle for Corsican liberation which was a prelude to the Revolution in France. He gave the Revolution his full allegiance. At an early age he had expressed a revolutionary view of politics, writing: "There are very few kings who have not deserved to be dethroned."

The steps Napoléon took that led him to the leadership of France were part planning and part luck. His early military career was quite successful—he was made a brigadier general at the age of twenty-four. After a temporary setback (he was briefly put under arrest as a supporter of Robespierre), he emerged from the Bastille with a plan to protect and expand France's trade by a military campaign in Egypt. It looked to him like an easy conquest.

However, it was there Napoléon met his first defeat and made a lifelong enemy. Horatio Nelson, Vice-Admiral of the British Navy, caught Napoléon's fleet at anchor in Aboukir Bay near the mouth of the Nile and destroyed most of it.

At this point, Napoléon turned away from the sea to the conquest of continental Europe and the expansion of the French Republic. As his successes mounted, he made himself First Consul for life and still wanted more. His dream of becoming another Alexander the Great was coming true. In 1804, Napoléon literally crowned himself Emperor of the French. As in the coronation of all Holy Roman Emperors, Pope Pius VII stood ready to place the crown upon Bonaparte's head. To his astonishment, Napoléon grasped the crown, turned to face the audience and placed the crown upon his own head, thereby informing all Europe that he recognized no higher authority than himself.

His empress was the vivacious Joséphine whom he had met at a fashionable salon. Sexually predatory and with two mistresses at the time, Napoléon felt bewitched. She was a year older than he, the widow of a nobleman, Beauharnais, who had been executed during the Terror. She had two children. When an heir to the throne was not conceived, Napoléon's family, realizing Joséphine was forty years old, arranged affairs for Napoléon with two ladies of the court, Eléonore Denuelle and Marie Antoinette Duchâtel. In 1806, Denuelle gave birth to a son and Napoléon proudly admitted that he was the father. Later his Polish mistress, Marie Walewska, presented him with another son, Alexandre. Napoléon had proved he was not sterile and now the way was clear to obtain an annulment and find the ideal empress with whom he might produce an heir to the throne.

Joséphine proposed the eighteen-year-old Marie Louise, Archduchess of Austria, whose mother had given birth to thirteen children. Countess Metternich quickly relayed the idea to her husband, the Austrian Chancellor. A few days later, on January 10, 1810, the annulment of the marriage of Napoléon and Joséphine was announced. The civil marriage of Napoléon and Marie Louise took place twenty-seven days later. The religious ceremony was held the following day at the Louvre—and a year later, a son and heir was born. Napoléon called him L'Aiglon the eaglet, and crowned the infant the king of Rome. Joséphine's instinct had proved right.

As emperor, Napoléon created a satellite empire of his relatives. After making his brother Joseph King of Naples, he arranged for him to become King of Spain. His sister, Maria Annunciata, and her husband Prince Murat then became queen and king of Naples. He made his brother Jérôme king of Holland and a third brother he made king of Westphalia. Pauline, his nymphomaniac sister, became the very rich princess Borghèse. This fragile empire was held together only by the will of Napoléon, Emperor of France. With his final defeat at Waterloo, all of the satellites vanished. Only Pauline visited him in the loneliness of his exile—and she stayed for only a few days.

By carrying out the reforms of the Revolution, by creating the Napoleonic Code of Law, by making the tax system more equitable and the banking system sound, and especially by his arousal of the French spirit of nationalism, Napoléon planted a new society with its roots in an earlier France. He had made the idea of change by revolutionary methods respectable. "Equality," he wrote, "pleases the masses."

Bonaparte declared himself Emperor Napoléon I in 1804. In ▶ *this official portrait, Ingres showed him in all his glory.*

In disarray, the decimated **Grande Armée** *crosses the frozen Beresina river after its disastrous Russian campaign of 1812.*

▶▶

INGRES. P.   ANNO

This scene of an animal market near Lyon is naturalistic. A peasant relieves himself in the corner. On the left, the *two military officers on horseback may be looking for new recruits and conscripted deserters from Napoléon's armies.*

Country Life
City Life

The Revolution, the foreign wars and the Empire of Napoléon I greatly affected the peasants of France. The "new" freedoms did not concern them very much but as food became scarce and expensive, their economic conditions improved.

For generations, peasants had sent the best of their produce to market. Now they learned to hold back some until they were offered better prices for the meat, vegetables, milk and cheese that they had produced. As a result of this, some peasant families were able to accumulate enough money to purchase small parcels confiscated from the nobility and the church, and thereby move up the economic and social ladder.

These changes came slowly, for the French peasant was a very conservative individual. Change frightened him. He preferred a dependable continuity in his life. Wars might come, peace might come — there were good crop years and bad ones — so he had learned to live quietly and ploddingly, keeping close to the traditions

of his forefathers. A peasant felt safest when he was doing things just the way his father, grandfather and great-grandfather had done them. Any major change in his way of life was considered by him and by the peasants around him as strange if not disgraceful.

After the famine of 1759, the scientific academy at Besançon organized a search to find an adaptable vegetable that, in case of necessity, could replace bread. While a prisoner of war in Germany, a young pharmacist, Antoine Parmentier, had discovered the nutritive values of *kartoffel*—*pomme de terre* in French, potato in English. Parmentier won the academy's award for his suggestion. Later he presented a bouquet of potato flowers to Louis XVI and had the honor of seeing Queen Marie Antoinette wearing some of the flowers in her hair. He was also rewarded by having an important recipe named after him — *purée Parmentier*, mashed potatoes.

The peasant's life was his land, his animals and his family, often in that order. His pleasures came from the food and wine that he produced and from his traditional place in the community. As the father of the family, he had complete authority. In his marriage agreement, he promised to provide his wife only with protection.

She owed him obedience. It was part of the tradition that she prepared the food, did the house-cleaning, reared the children, helped care for the animals and worked in the fields along with her husband and her children. In most peasant households, the husband and older sons ate their meals first, the women and girls eating after the men were finished. The *veillée*, the late afternoon meeting of villagers at the end of the week, brought out all the adults and children. There, women would spin or sew and gossip while men mended tools, drank and talked. Traditional tales and ghost-stories were retold. Weddings and fairs brought dancing, mimes, tarot-readers and fortune-tellers. The peasant's life was a difficult one, but it was better than that of the poor people in the cities.

It was during this period that fantastic, almost unbelievable gossip began to filter out of Paris and the larger cities of France into the countryside. A new social class, the *Merveilleuses*, had become the pets of the nouveaux riches and the military society. It was as though this well-known word had just been rediscovered. It was used to describe fashionable women (and men) who, wearing classical Greek gowns and tunics, began attending parties and formal occasions, opera, theater, dinner-parties with one shoulder bare and one breast exposed. Another neo-classical style — the high bodice — pushed up women's breasts, often exposing their nipples. Grecian tunics of semi-transparent muslin were worn with no undergarments by the most daring of these women.

As women wore less and less, men put on more and more: elaborate bulky jackets with wide padded shoulders, and high collars with elaborate cravats worn under them. Large, almost grotesque hats derived from those of Napoléon, his admirals and his generals became popular with some men. These fashions did not last but they shocked and titillated the horrified bourgeoisie and the peasants.

In art, Ingres at age eighty-two painted an intimate grouping of some twenty nude women in his well received *Bain Turc* (the Turkish Bath). David glorified the Emperor Napoléon. Stendhal admired and vouched for the authenticity of Horace Vernet's battles, but Charles Baudelaire wrote, "I hate this man because his pictures have nothing to do with painting. They are rather a quick and frequent masturbation in paint." Delacroix posed for one of the figures in Géricault's best-known work, the *Raft of the Medusa*. During the period of the first empire, Delacroix was France's foremost romantic painter. Yet it took the French Institute thirty-two years to admit him. Baudelaire considered him "the most original painter of ancient or modern times."

▲ *The popular expression that everyone who is in need of money pulls the devil by the tail, is illustrated by this engraving.*

Madame Récamier had money, beauty and wit. Guests at her ▶ *salon were the notables of the Consulate and of the Empire.*

▲ *François Adrien Boieldieu was nationally known for his musical scores of comic operas. His chair is in the Empire style.*

Paris fashions around 1800 are depicted in an engraving on the theme of the ages of man and woman from birth to death. ▶

Baptême

Age de Discrétion

Age de M[...]

Age Viril

Age de la Jeunesse

Age de l'Adolescence

50 Ans.

40 Ans.

30 Ans.

JUGEMENT

20 Ans.

Confirmation

10 Ans.

Extrème Enfance

3 Ans. Enfance

4 Ans. Age de Puérilité.

Age Déclinant

Age de Décadence

Age de Caducité

Age de Décrépitude

Enterrement

60 Ans

70 Ans

80 Ans

90 Ans

100 Ans Age
d'Enfance et
d'Imbécillité

Communion

NIVERSEL

Napoléon I rides in the chariot of the Sun like the god Apollo. Ingres painted this sketch thirty years after the Emperor's death. The allegorical scene was to decorate the ceiling of the Emperor Room at the Hôtel de Ville of Paris.

After Napoléon, Paris reflected his desire to make it "the most beautiful city in the world and the capital of Europe." He had ordered an ornamental plan as well as one for utilitarian improvements. The *Rue de Rivoli* became a handsome central thoroughfare; fountains were designed and built in the Square of the Châtelet: *L'Egyptienne* in the *Rue de Sèvres* and the *Dieu Mars* in the *Rue Sainte Dominique*. Earlier Napoléon had expressed a desire to give Paris the look of ancient Rome. So Roman arches supported many of the new buildings. The *Madeleine* became the Temple of Glory. A Trajan column, with decorations in bronze from captured Russian and Austrian cannons, was topped by a statue of the emperor. After Napoléon's defeat in March 1814, the *Rue Napoléon* became the *Rue de La Paix*. Throughout the city, the Napoleonic and imperial symbol, the bee, was removed and the royal *fleur-de-lis* replaced it. It was Napoléon who began the huge *Arc de Triomphe* project at the *Etoile de Chaillot* dedicated to the armies of the Empire. Louis XVIII continued work on it and Louis Philippe finished it in 1836.

THE BUILDING OF MODERN FRANCE

The return of the monarchy to power is marked by the revolutions of 1830 and 1848. The Second Republic is overthrown by its elected president who declares himself Emperor Napoléon III in 1852. Defeat in the Franco-Prussian War of 1870 brings about the establishment of the Third Republic and the separation of Church and State. Railroads and canals help economic growth. Pasteur's pioneering work in chemistry has medical and industrial applications. In the flourishing fields of art, literature and theater, the Romantics give way to the Realists. The Impressionist movement brings to art a new vision of the world.

HISTORICAL CHRONOLOGY		ART CHRONOLOGY	
1820	*Assassination of royal heir.*	1822	*Asiatic Society for Oriental Studies and the Asiatic Journal reflect interest in the Orient.*
1824—25	*Charles X passes the* Law Against Sacrilege *and votes indemnity to nobles whose lands were confiscated during the Revolution.*	1824	*Delacroix paints* Massacre at Scio *in Romantic style. Ministry of Public Education established.*
1830	*Algiers captured. Revolution forces the abdication of Charles X. Louis-Philippe becomes king.*	1824—34	*Ingres paints* Apotheosis *and* Vow of Louis XIII *in Romantic and Classical styles.*
1831—34	*Anti-clerical riots. Cloth workers revolt against wage cuts in Lyon.*	1829	*Daumier issues his first satirical lithographs. He is arrested in 1832.*
1840	*Napoléon Bonaparte reburied in the Invalides. Ministry of conservative Guizot begins.*	1830	*Berlioz composes* Symphonie Fantastique.
1848	*Revolution in Paris. Abdication of Louis-Philippe and proclamation of the Second Republic. Abolition of slavery. Universal suffrage established. Louis Napoléon is elected president.*	1831—34	*Publication of* Notre Dame of Paris *by Victor Hugo,* The Red and the Black *by Stendhal and* Grandfather Goriot *by Balzac.*
		1844	*Alexandre Dumas writes* The Count of Monte Cristo.
1851—52	*Louis Napoléon overthrows the Republic and proclaims the Second Empire.*	1856—57	*Flaubert writes* Madame Bovary *which is condemned along with* The Flowers of Evil *by Baudelaire.*
1854	*France enters Crimean War against Russia.*	1863	*Manet paints* Déjeuner sur l'Herbe. *Salon des Refusés (of the Rejected) established by Impressionist painters.*
1858—66	*France brings Vietnam/Indochina under its control. Annexation of Savoie and Nice. Occupation of Peking. Expedition to Mexico.*	1864—86	*Goncourt brothers begin their novel* Renée Mauperin.
1870—71	*War with Prussia. Louis Napoléon captured. Paris rises in revolt, establishing the Commune, later crushed by Thiers. Alsace and Lorraine are lost to Prussia. Third Republic is proclaimed.*	1873	*Construction of Sacré Coeur in Paris begins.*
		1875	*Opera* Carmen *composed by Georges Bizet. Saint Saens composes* Samson and Delilah *in modern style.*
1881	*Education made compulsory for children ages 6 to 13.*	1880—1900	*Folies Bergère and attractions of the Moulin Rouge painted by Jean Béraud.*
1882	*Conservative nationalist League of Patriots founded.*	1883	*Monet (1840 - 1926) settles at Giverny. Renoir given a one-man show by Durand-Ruel.*
1884	*Le Matin first newspaper devoted to news rather than political debate or entertainment.*	1886	*Rodin's sculpture, such as* The Kiss, *revives interest in this art form.*
1885	*Louis Pasteur perfects rabies vaccine.*	1888	*Van Gogh paints* Sun Flowers *and* Van Gogh's Bedroom at Arles.
1886	*Organized labor begins with the foundation of the National Federation of Syndicates.*		
1888—89	*Possible right-wing overthrow of Republic threatens in Boulanger affair.*		

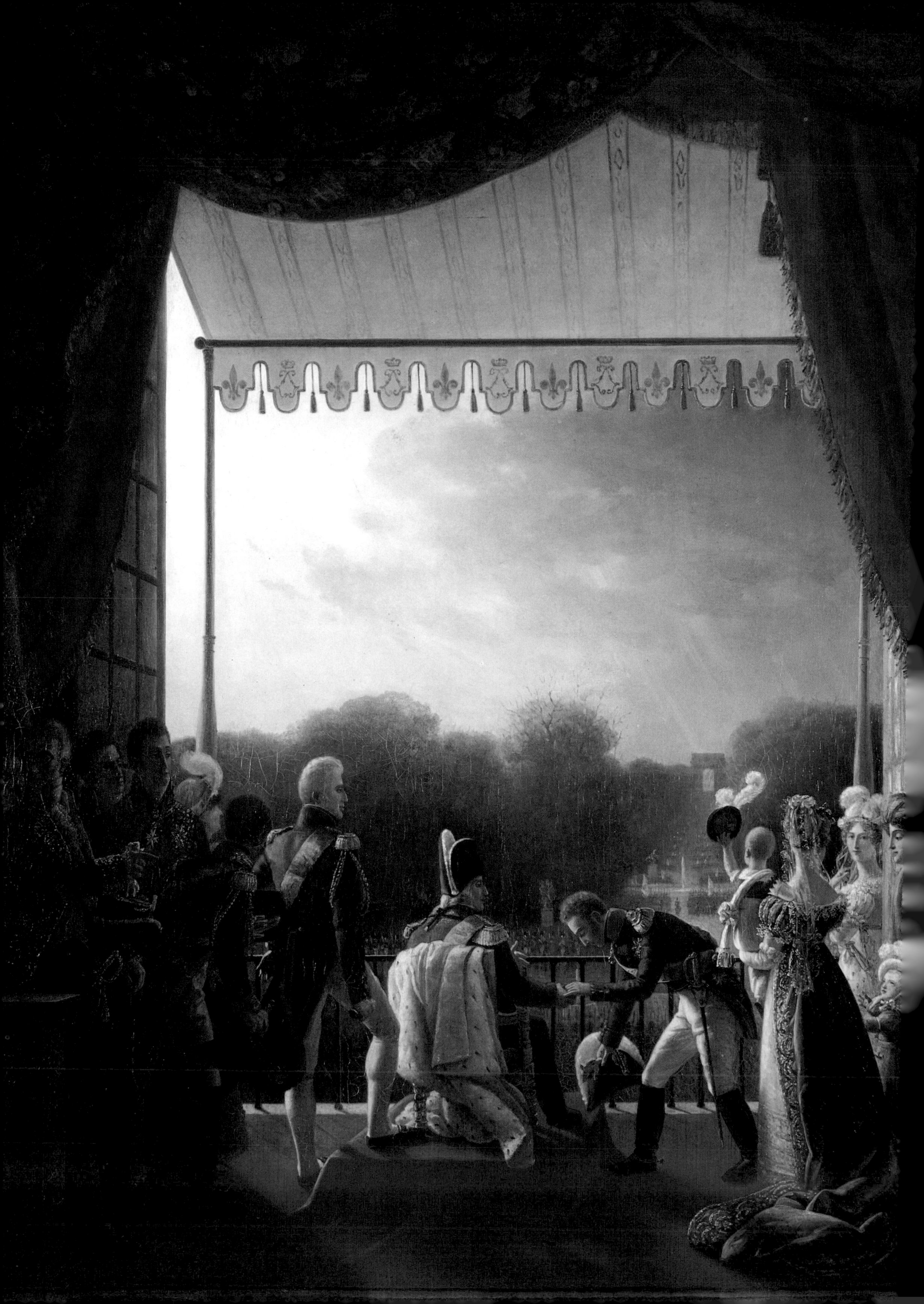

A New King
Napoléon's Final Defeat

The divine right of kings returned to France in the person of the fat, amiable, sixty-year-old elder brother of the guillotined monarch, Louis XVI. He took the title of Louis XVIII. He insisted that the years of the Revolution and of Napoléon's empire had not suspended his kingship just because he was in exile. Therefore, he called 1814 the nineteenth year of his reign as Louis XVIII. This was not an auspicious way to begin a liberal-conservative government.

Whether the king had become more democratic during his exile in England, or whether he was forced to go along with the profound changes of the past twenty years, the fact was that he did get along with the new government that was attempting to strike a balance between the Republicans and the royalists.

However, Louis had been king less than ten months when the supposedly banished Emperor Napoléon rudely disturbed him by evicting him from the Tuileries Palace on March 20, 1815.

For Napoléon, too, it would be a short stay. Greeted with cheers by thousands of Parisians and joined by most of his generals and soldiers, he moved north quickly to attack the British and Prussian armies at Waterloo. But he failed to divide the British from the Prussians and was thoroughly defeated by their combined forces. Napoléon and the remnants of his army retreated back to Paris where they were now coolly received.

This time, the European allies took no chances with the ex-emperor. When Napoléon tried to escape to the United States where sympathizers had furnished a house for him in New Orleans, the British blockaded the port of Rochefort where a ship was waiting. Napoléon wrote to the Prince Regent in England, but got no sympathy. He was permanently exiled to St. Helena.

The portly Louis XVIII shuttled back to the Tuileries, but his liberal support had entirely faded. Then a deranged veteran of Napoléon's army, who believed his mission was to exterminate the Bourbon royal family, stabbed and killed the Duke of Berry, nephew of the king.

This dramatic incident brought down Louis's two ministers, who had helped to keep the government relatively stable. They were replaced by the Count of Villèle—and the liberal influences and reforms left over from the Revolution and the Napoleonic empire were quickly abolished.

◀ From the Tuileries, Louis XVIII watches his troops celebrate victory over Spain. The Arc de Triomphe *is in the distance.*

The role in society of each of the four classes—military, church, peasant and law—is illustrated in this engraving.

A new electoral law favoring the large landowners was passed. Censorship was increased to the point where there no longer was freedom of the press. Liberal officials found their jobs eliminated. A proposal was made to indemnify aristocrats for their losses during the Revolution. And a new law was passed which was reminiscent of the intolerance of the Middle Ages. It punished sacrilegious acts in the churches with the death penalty.

Louis XVIII had the good fortune to die in bed, in 1824, after nine years of rule. His younger brother, Charles X, succeeded him. According to historians, Charles had the advantage of looking like a king—but his talent as a ruler stopped there. After six years a revolution threatened his government, so Charles gave up and went hunting. The revolt that broke out brought to the throne his cousin, the Duke d'Orléans, Louis Philippe, who became known as the citizen-king. His reign lasted until the Revolution of 1848.

The Proud Craftsmen

The custom of artisans joining organizations which they themselves controlled was known in France as *Compagnonnage*. Made up of strong-minded, independent craftsmen, these societies evolved naturally from the powerful guilds of the Middle Ages.

Secrecy was vital, for both the monarchy and the employer associations fought these organizations as strongly as they had the earlier guilds. Like the Freemasons, the societies' secret rituals and private policy-making gave them a special status. From the late eighteenth century through the entire nineteenth, these organizations of *compagnons* (companions) bore colorful names like *Enfants de Salomon*, *Enfants de Maître Jacques* and *Enfants du Père Soubise*. These names were adopted because the artisans held that they historically were the descendants of the temple builders of ancient times.

The societies were supported by dues and special assessments. Sick members were visited and cared for, funerals were provided and fêtes were given for patron saints. If an employer or contractor cut wages below the usual scales, mistreated a journeyman or tried to force an artisan to do sub-standard work, all the men would quit his workshop or jobsite until he came to terms with the association.

Because of their secrecy and the use of religious forms in their rituals, the *compagnons* were occasionally attacked by the church, particularly by one fiery Catholic order, the *Compagnie du Sacrement*. However, the greatest conflicts occurred between rival societies. In Paris, each bank of the Seine was claimed by a separate organization of *compagnons*. A worker belonging to one order often would refuse to work with a different one. It was easy for one side to recognize the other for they wore distinctive ribbons. Some orders also wore their hair in ponytails, others wore distinctive jackets and some men wore earrings with symbols identifying their trades.

The *compagnonnage* offered a special kind of on-the-job training, called the *Tour de France*. *Compagnons* who had reached minimum proficiency were sent out to travel through cities and towns to work at their trade. This not only enabled a young craftsman to learn skills not available in his own city, but also gave him a chance to learn about his country. In each town and city, the *compagnonnage* maintained a representative who arranged for jobs, supplied lodgings and made the *compagnons* feel at home with their fellow workers.

When one *compagnon* met another, they went through a ritual of greeting called *topage*, one man shouting *tope!* and the other replying with the same word. If they belonged to the same order, they drank together and exchanged information. If not, a fight often ensued with each man trying to tear off the other's insignia (considered a great insult). Sometimes they fought to the death.

After completing his Tour of France, which might take him years, the artisan—if he passed his examinations and could show an outstanding example of his work—would earn a master's certificate. A reputation for excellence in work was an important factor in a society of *compagnons*. Standards which held up for many years were set in metal working, wood working, furniture, carpentry and roofing.

The *compagnonnage* remained a conservative institution during and after the French Revolution. Its members valued their independence too much to become part of a larger class movement. Like the peasants, they did not easily change their thinking or their work patterns.

◀ Compagnons *give their ritual farewell to a carpenter leaving on his* Tour de France. *He'll work his way around the country.*

▲ *In 1825, expert fencers with the wooden rod or* bâton *were awarded this diploma allowing them to teach this martial art.*

These exquisite roofs were created by Compagnons, *master craftsmen who belonged to secret trade-union organizations.* ▶

Dancing was a social skill expected of every army officer. An officer needed a private income to be able to afford his "dress" *uniforms and pay his bills. Inspired by Emperor Napoléon III, the mustache and goatee became fashionable.*

The Military And The Marriage Contract

Young Frenchwomen in the mid-nineteenth century could not afford to marry into the military. There were plenty of soldiers — young, romantic and attractive, especially in their dress uniforms, but poor pay and army regulations kept most of them bachelors. Under only one condition could a non-commissioned officer take a wife: if the bride-to-be brought with her either an adequate dowry in cash or a guaranteed annual income.

Conditions established for officers' marriages were not much better. Careful investigations were made to be sure that the dowries were promptly paid and that other monies were wisely invested. For a time, only government and railroad bonds were considered acceptable.

The army of France was made up of men serving under universal conscription and men who had been called up but could afford to have substitutes serve in their places. One quarter of the army was thus composed of draftees; another quarter of substitutes. The other half was made up of volunteers including a high percentage of professional soldiers. By 1848, the military school at St. Cyr founded by Napoléon forty

years earlier, was turning out many officers — as were the *Ecole Polytechnique* founded by the Convention and the famous cavalry school at Saumur.

Most young soldiers had their limited sexual experiences in one of the thousands of *maisons de tolérance* (brothels), operated by the State. In them, the average young Frenchman lost his virginity by the age of sixteen. Few schoolboys would resist an initiation into sex at a brothel, and indeed such a visit was expected of him. To patronize a brothel was considered an essential rite in the mystique of becoming a man.

Priests, parents, doctors and teachers all lectured youths on the dangers of masturbation. It would drain their strength, they were told, make degenerates or homosexuals of them (one was considered as bad as the other), make their hair fall out and make their children, if they ever had any, crippled weaklings. Some church schools were said to bleed the boys they thought were indulging in this temptation of the Devil. Partly as a result of the difficulty of marrying — and the punishments promised masturbators — the number of brothels grew. Sex was sinful enough, said the clergy, but masturbation was worse. It was estimated that Paris in 1850 had 34,000 prostitutes.

Marriage was a serious business rather than the culmination of a romance in the mid-nineteenth century. Property arrangements were a vital part of the event. Most of the time, the choice of bride or groom was made by the respective parents. In bourgeois circles, the bride's contribution often was added to the husband's savings and the sum used to found a new business enterprise. Newspaper advertisements such as "intelligent man with income seeks woman with dowry, object matrimony" were customary.

Napoléon I, in his Civil Code, made marriage a contract with the provision of divorce by mutual agreement. Yet divorce was rarely resorted to by either party. Since most marriages were conducted as a business, adultery was considered preferable to the economic losses that a divorce would bring. Lovers and mistresses might come and go, but wives and husbands held on to the security of their economic alliance.

A French woman had few rights. Legally she was in the same class as a minor. A woman could not have her own bank account. It was perfectly proper for her husband to open and read her mail (who knew what she might be plotting?). He could forbid her to work and, under the Napoleonic code, the husband became the administrator of their joint estate. Any money the wife brought into the marriage was handled by her mate. A law provided that a wife had no voice in deciding where the couple lived—she had to follow her husband wherever he chose to go.

It was repeated as gospel that women could not be given the right to vote because they would be too influenced by the Church. Men believed that, except for a few outstanding women (George Sand might be one), just about the entire sex did not have enough intelligence to vote wisely and independently. This, in spite of the fact that throughout the history of France women had influenced the decisions of kings, politicians, businessmen, shopkeepers, laborers and farmers. Their ideas had been transmitted and used—even when they originated in pillow politics.

In the difficult days of the Revolution of 1848 and during the trying years afterwards—specifically the Franco-Prussian War and the days of the *Commune* that followed—many women became politically active. They formed literary and social clubs, and raised money for the budding feminist cause. Hope for women's progress was seen in the growth of humanitarian and socialist ideas. In 1830, Delacroix had painted *Liberty Guiding the People* showing a patriotic woman leading a crowd, and he received the Legion of Honor for it. After 1870, Marianne, the Phrygian-capped figure named for contemporary secret societies, became the feminine symbol of French leadership.

"The great family quarrel" is the title of this caricature of the dissension in a French family. An alternative title *was "Who wears the pants?" These hand-colored woodcuts from Epinal (in eastern France) were cheap and sold in quantity.*

Exotic costumes prevail in this gay carnival scene on the Place de La Concorde in Paris c. 1845. Honoré de Balzac wrote about carnivals like this: "Since 1830, the carnival in Paris has developed tremendously, making it European

Romantics And Realists

The Romantic period in French history was a time for opening up one's vistas and becoming part of a more sensitive and humane world. Classicism and the icy coldness of the intellect were buried under a more compassionate outlook. Among the Romantic painters of the period, Corot reflected a world of nymphs and shepherdesses in dream-like fields; Millet glorified the peasant and his wife, with their hands and feet planted in the fecund earth. These artists left Paris for the village of Barbizon where they could paint the meadows, forests and hills of the Fontainebleau region. Among those who joined them there were Théodore Rousseau, Daubigny and Harpignies. But one of the most gifted of all French painters stayed behind. He was Eugène Delacroix and he belonged to no specific school. He was a neo-classicist, a realist and a Romantic. Like the others, he was a rebel who had finally broken with the neo-classicism of the Academicians.

The writers of this nebulous Romantic School were, like the artists, experimenting with new-found sensitivity, searching for a way to live and work in the discouraged France left to them by the monarchy. Romanticism was a means of avoiding the rational acceptance of their fate. There was new, or revised, thinking about literature, music and poetry. Hector Berlioz composed the "Roman Carnival Overture" and his famous opera "The Damnation of Faust." Chateaubriand wrote *Le Génie du Christianisme*. The wit and wisdom of Shakespeare, and the symbolism of Dante and Goethe were appreciated for the first time in France.

One man encompassed both the Romantic and mystical schools in art and also wrote romantic-lyrical poetry. At first Victor Hugo was an artist—a painter whose fantastic paintings and drawings showed not only his great imagination but also his ability to look beyond the realities of France in the mid-nineteenth century. Later he turned to writing, publicizing the pain, misery and unfairness visited upon the mass of workers. Only through education for everyone, he wrote, could France progress. "Everywhere," he said, "there is a mind, everywhere there should be a book. No commune must be without a school and no town without a college." Ordered into exile for his criticism of the empire of Napoléon III, he wrote the ten volumes of *Les Misérables*

and rather a burlesque, better animated than the Venice carnival." Carnival was every year's most uninhibited popular festival.

With circular brush strokes, Daumier conveys the haste of the laundress carrying a heavy load and her concern for her child.

Lawyers and the courts of justice were targets of Daumier's social satire. He was jailed for a caricature of the king.

to expose the lack of justice in France for the poor and the weak. He diagnosed and suggested cures for the chronic disease of poverty. His influence was widespread and he lived a long and useful life. Hugo died in 1885 and was buried in the *Panthéon.*

Charles Baudelaire, nineteen years younger than Hugo, also opposed the smugness and opportunism of the era and managed in his short life (he died at forty-six of alcohol and drugs) to make a lasting impression on his times. Like Hugo, he was a liberal thinker (he fought on the barricades in 1848) and led an incredibly active literary career. Speaking of his translations of the macabre stories of Edgar Allan Poe, he said that they had dreamed the same dreams and thought the same thoughts. These translations were successful but even more so was Baudelaire's poetry which reached deep into the decadence of the soul, revealing the beauty to be found in the corrupt and disintegrating society. To Baudelaire, the goal of poetry was to show the similarity

◀ *The dark shadows and deep colors in this painting by Daumier create a mood of peacefulness in the familiar heart of Paris.*

and the dissimilarity in both good and evil. His widely known masterpiece, *Les Fleurs du Mal*, was banned until he removed six poems considered obscene — but then he added thirty-five more. To the Secretary of State he wrote: "I cannot feel guilty — I am proud of having written a book that inspired nothing but fear and horror of evil."

Two young men who had been friends and admirers of each other since childhood were among the seminal contributors to the Romantic period. They made a strange-looking pair: Emile Zola, short, dark and bespectacled, and Paul Cézanne, tall, ungainly and thin. As youths, they had hunted together in the countryside near Aix-en-Provence and spent many hours reading Victor Hugo and the works of Alphonse de Lamartine. Together they went to Paris. There Cézanne tried desperately to learn to paint by attending the Suisse Academy where he met young Pissarro who would, like himself, become an important part of the Impressionist movement. Zola got a job in the advertising department of the publishing firm of Hachette. Zola later wrote to Cézanne: "Let us eat, think and satisfy our appetites but let us keep our souls sacred and apart."

203

The Second Republic, The Second Empire

When Nicolas Tassaert, one of the leading painters in the mid-nineteenth century, painted the misery of the poor in Paris, he was severely criticized. The critics held that an artist could not create high art out of such low subjects. Tassaert's people were on the sordid side of extreme poverty—as were many workers' families in Paris.

At the time, the laborers, artisans and street people of Paris were restive. They had learned that work stoppages, riots and strikes brought reform. Disturbances in Paris and Lyon had brought about a higher scale of wages in 1843. Two years earlier, a law had been passed controlling the hours and ages of working children. For the first time the government came to their aid by law fixing the minimum age at eight years. The work day was reduced from thirteen hours to eight except for children over twelve who were permitted to work a twelve hour day. This law was considered too liberal by some of the *députés* who felt that with shorter hours, children would not have enough opportunity to learn to be good workers and would not have sufficient time to learn obedience.

Once again liberals suggested that all Frenchmen be given the right to vote, but this new proposal for universal suffrage was rejected. But the specific activity that led to the Revolution of 1848 was nothing more radical than a series of banquets organized by workers to raise funds and public consciences. After one such banquet was sold out, the government decided to ban it and the angry workers rioted. The government ordered out the National Guard, but the troops joined the workers. Then the army was called in, shots were fired and the Revolution of 1848 erupted.

It was a Parisian revolution, not a national one for the remainder of France stayed calm. The widely respected poet and patriot Lamartine was elected to head the provisional government. For the first time, a Constitutional Assembly was voted in by the people. The Second Republic was proclaimed, and in December an open election voted on nominees for the office of president. The winner, to no one's surprise, was Louis Napoléon Bonaparte, nephew of the former emperor. He was elected for four years by a huge majority, but when the assembly refused to ratify a law permitting

his reelection, Bonaparte did not wait for his term to expire. In a *coup d'état* on December 2, 1851—the anniversary of the battle of Austerlitz, forty-six years earlier—he successfully used the army and his personal popularity to take over the government. In a matter of weeks, he held the power once held by his famous uncle. Napoléon's son, the Prince of Rome who had died at the age of twenty-one, had been Napoléon II, so Louis now took the title of Napoléon III.

Napoléon III professed to be a socialist. Without question, he was far more liberal than his predecessors. He had written a book entitled *An End to Pauperism*. He funneled money into educational channels; press censorship was minimal; workers' associations were recognized. Free trade was encouraged, and the French found that their products could compete in the international market. In 1864, when French workers won the right to strike, Louis Napoléon stood at the height of his popularity. He engaged in and was victorious in the Crimean War and the Italian campaign. In 1870, he supported a new liberal constitution. His aim was to build a parliamentary empire.

But a foreign intrigue diverted him. Influential Mexican conservatives led him to believe that Mexico would welcome a French alliance. Expecting an easy victory, his well-equipped expeditionary force, led by Archduke Maximilian of Austria, marched into Puebla where it was defeated by a Mexican army two-thirds its size. The date of this battle, May 5th, 1862 became a national holiday in Mexico, Cinco de Mayo (Mexican Independence Day).

Napoléon was furious. In retaliation, he dispatched 28,000 soldiers to capture Puebla and Mexico City. However, Juarez, the Mexican popular leader, fought a guerilla war and kept the French off balance. Their troops were defeated and ridiculed. Maximilian, a well-meaning Austrian aristocrat, found himself and his wife Carlota unpopular and unsupported. The emperor decided to abandon Maximilian and ordered General Bazaine to evacuate his troops. On June 19, France's Mexican adventure ended when Maximilian with his two generals, Miramón and Mejía, faced Juarez's firing squad.

After a fancied insult to France which had been carefully orchestrated by Bismarck, the French government declared war on Prussia. It was the most disastrous decision Napoléon III made—more disastrous than his Mexican expedition. The efficient and modern Prussian army was fully prepared when the ill-equipped French attacked. Napoléon III, who personally led the French into defeat, was ignominiously captured. By beginning this unnecessary war and losing it, he made it possible for Bismarck to unite Germany with far-reaching consequences for France. After the capture of Napoléon, the Prussians invaded France which was fiercely defended by a provisional government led by Léon Gambetta. The war could have ended had France

In the War of 1870, a French infantry unit charges through a village in the east of France occupied by the Prussians.

Defeated, Napoléon III capitulated. The Third Republic was proclaimed and had to relinquish Alsace-Lorraine to Germany.

been willing to cede Alsace to Prussia — but Jules Favre vowed that France would fight on and never yield an inch of her soil. After a four-month siege, artillery shelling and starvation, Paris was forced to surrender.

France had to pay the huge amount of 5,000 billion gold francs in reparations — and lost Alsace anyway and most of Lorraine, that priceless region which contained the rich coal mines.

The Place de la Concorde *became a battlefield when Minister Thiers sent troops from Versailles to Paris to suppress the* Commune *uprisings resulting from the Prussian siege of the capital. The rebellion against the government installed in*

Versailles lasted just over two months. Before giving up, the Communards set fire to many buildings. The Franco-Prussian War cost over 50,000 French lives. During the Paris Commune 25,000 Frenchmen and women were killed by their compatriots.

A sketch by Delacroix for the painting The Sultan of Morocco Receiving the French Ambassador *demonstrates his fluid line* *and masterful use of color that influenced many of the early French Impressionists. Delacroix visited Morocco in 1832.*

The Impressionists

A chain of friendships forged among talented young artists who met by chance, and helped each other to increase their knowledge and develop their skills, resulted in a new vision of the world. They would be known as the Impressionists. All were rebelling against the neo-classic art forms which had squeezed the life out of art. In the dark, artificial atmosphere of studios, beautiful flesh and blood models had been transformed into cold Greek and Roman figures. Art had moved indoors, out of sun and shadow, losing touch with the invigorating effects of natural light and natural motion. The young rebels of the 1860s-1880s were inspired by earlier examples—the older artists who had gone to Barbizon and two other pioneers, Courbet and Delacroix.

A physical giant, Gustave Courbet had opened his own salon so that he could paint as he pleased. He shocked viewers with the reality of a painting of two nude women asleep, with their legs and arms amorously intertwined. Called sometimes *The Friends*, other times *The Sleep*, it is now in the Petit Palais in Paris. His was an instinctive approach to painting as opposed to intellectual. He forced his viewers to see the realities of human beings in genuine environments. The other rule-breaker was Eugène Delacroix of whom Degas said, "He paints like a man who enjoys everything." Both Delacroix and Courbet had been through the neo-classic era and then had moved out of it, demonstrating that neither art nor they were anchored in the past. Zola could have been speaking of Courbet and Delacroix when he wrote, "A work of art is an aspect of creation seen through the sensitivity of a temperament."

The life of Claude Monet runs like a multicolored thread through the intricate pattern of the Impressionist school. A fifteen-year-old with a talent for caricature and for winning friends, he met Eugène Boudin, a pre-Impressionist artist whom Baudelaire had called "king of the skies." Young Monet became fascinated with the possibility of becoming an artist like Boudin and later was to write, "It was as if a veil had been removed from my eyes—in a flash I could suddenly see what painting really meant."

Le Déjeuner sur l'Herbe *by Edouard Manet was rejected by the Academy but hung in the* Salon des Refusés *where it caused a scandal. Critics found erotic symbols, but Zola saw it as a "fragment of nature rendered with just the right simplicity."*

Monet moved to Paris as did most young artists at the time. Because he had very little money, he attended the *Atelier Suisse* operated by Monsieur Suisse who was not Swiss. There wasn't much instruction, but by paying a small fee for the use of the model and the space for an easel, a beginner could learn by doing—and by observing other painters. There Monet met Pissarro, a painter with original ideas, and set up an easel next to his. Monet's stay at the *Atelier* was a short one for he was called up by the army and sent to Algiers. When he returned, he enrolled at Gleyre's studio, which was actually run by a Swiss with academic credentials. There Monet met four young artists who were destined to rank among the great painters of France. They were Sisley, Bazille, Manet and Renoir. When Renoir was sarcastically asked by the stodgy Swiss instructor whether he painted "only to amuse himself," Renoir replied that he had never thought of painting for any other reason.

The congenial Monet suggested to his friends that they all move out of Paris to paint outdoors in the forest of Fontainebleau. There Manet painted his *Luncheon on the Grass (Déjeuner sur l'Herbe)*. His friend Bazille obliged him by modeling for one of the two men in the picture.

Meanwhile in Paris, because the works of many unknown artists were being regularly refused by the Academy, Napoléon III agreed to the opening of an exhibition hall where the rejected pictures could be shown, *Le Salon des Refusés*. Its first showing of Manet's *Luncheon on the Grass* caused onlookers to riot and threaten to wreck the building. The painting was condemned by all the critics. One wrote: "The nude does not have a good figure and one cannot imagine anything uglier than the man stretched out beside her." Another: "I see garments without a human frame beneath, I see fingers without bones and heads without skulls." None of those who objected criticized the quality of the painting or the coloring. None mentioned the real reason that they were so disturbed, which was simply that the painting reflected the artist's unconventional ideas. Women were represented neither as servants nor models but as equals—it was a shock after the way women had been portrayed in classical and neo-classical paintings.

The Impressionists became a tight circle of talented artists. Most of them were friends who convened regularly at the *Café Guerbois*. Every Friday evening, Manet, Degas, Bazille, Guys, Duranty and Renoir met there and, when they were in Paris, Monet, Pissarro

209

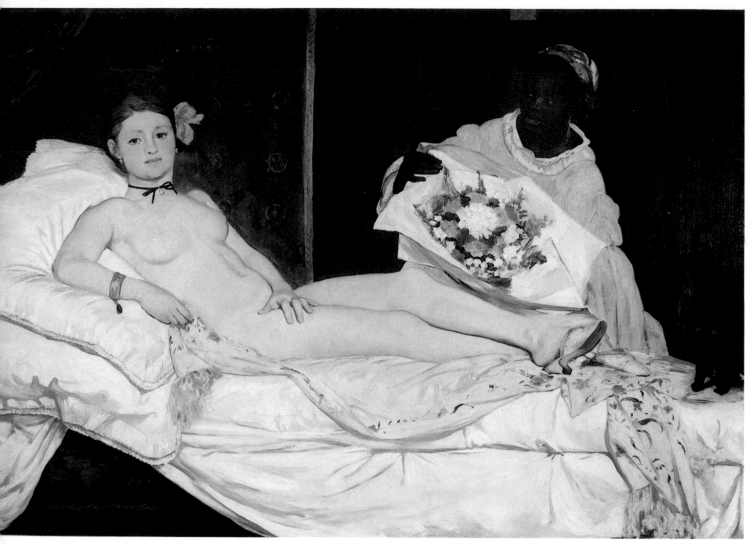

Most critics received Edouard Manet's Olympia *with derision. One of them wrote, "Nothing so cynical has ever been seen as* *this Olympia, a sort of female gorilla." But Cézanne wrote, "It is a new stage of painting, our Renaissance dates from it."*

and Sisley joined them. Zola was a regular at these meetings, where exhibitions were planned, esthetics discussed, philosophies examined and techniques of art around the world discussed until the late hours. Japanese art particularly interested them. When the 1867 World's Fair opened in Paris, most of the Impressionists went to see the prints of such Japanese masters as Hokusai and Utamaro, and the screens of Taiga. The Ukiyó-e drawings and woodblock prints were admired and purchased whenever possible. Manet later inserted Japanese prints into the background of his *Portrait of Zola*. In *Portrait of the Artist James Tissot*, Degas painted a scene of Japanese women, possibly dancers, in a garden setting. The Japanese influence on Degas's work, especially in his later compositions, became marked.

Although he occasionally set himself apart from it, Degas belonged to the Impressionist movement. In 1877, when the Impressionists were the talk of Paris, he deeply involved himself in the design of an hilarious,

satirical theatrical production. This was called *The Grasshopper (La Sauterelle)*, and the Impressionist movement furnished the comedy. The protagonist, a composite of a number of prominent artists, declared: "We no longer are Impressionists — we are Intentionalists, we do it on purpose!" In one satiric skit, an artist keeps trying to paint a laundress while her tub of laundry splashes all over him. Another complains that he has worked on a painting for ten whole minutes and that it is still unfinished. In a major scene, a large canvas is brought in, the top half red, the bottom half blue. At first it is titled *Sunset Over the Ocean*; when it is turned upside down, it becomes *Blue Sky Over the Desert*. Monet, it should be known, in an early exhibition had shown a painting that he called *Sunset, an Impression*.

Working in pastel, Degas captures the raucous atmosphere of ▶ *of an evening at the* Café-Concert aux Ambassadeurs.

Pierre Auguste Renoir lived seventy-eight years and worked at painting for sixty-five of them. At the age of thirteen, he got a job as a decorator in a Paris porcelain factory. He was twenty-one when he finally could afford to go to art school. Those years, while Renoir progressed from painting shepherdesses and Marie Antoinette on porcelain to studying at the Atelier Gleyre were among the most progressive and productive in the history of France. The entire country was surpassing itself in architecture, art, literature, science and industrial production.

In the early 1850s, Baron Haussmann began to redesign Paris, keeping much that was beautiful, yet making the whole city accessible and efficient. Thousands of old houses were demolished but for every one destroyed, two new buildings were erected. The boulevards were straightened; the Champs Elysées and other avenues were planted with trees. It took Haussmann seventeen years to make Paris into a magnificent, modern city.

In 1861 the design competition for a new opera house had been won by Charles Garnier, the winner over 171 contestants. When the Paris Opera finally opened, Parisians gasped with delight and awe at the sight of what was then the largest theater in the world. Its stage could accommodate 450 performers at once. Patrons drove up a ramp in their carriages and then strolled up a marble staircase to their boxes.

The new age of applied science was marked by the discoveries of Louis Pasteur who, by proving that living organisms were responsible for fermentation, contributed to the health not only of the nation but of the world. Pasteurization was widely used to purify milk and retard its souring and was also used in the preservation of wine. When the French silk industry was threatened by silkworm disease, it was Pasteur who found a cure. He also developed the rabies vaccine.

Three years before Renoir was born, the first French railroad was begun, and during his youth, the network of steel rails grew to crisscross all of France. With facile transport available, the market for food expanded, adding considerably to the prosperity of the farmers and the city people involved in food distribution. Of course, there were the usual skeptics who worried about

Renoir was the first Impressionist to settle in Montmartre, then a rural suburb of Paris. He shows Parisians dancing at the Moulin de la Galette *where the sun and trees create a dappled effect on the women's gowns and the men's straw hats.*

The clinging beauty is Suzanne Valadon, a frequent model for Renoir and Toulouse-Lautrec and a painting student of Degas.

For The Country Dance *Renoir used his wife as model. He started his long career at thirteen as a porcelain painter.*

the railroads. Victor Hugo sent word from exile castigating the "demon of speed." Lesser critics predicted that the tunnels would collapse, that the motion of the trains would cause pregnant women to miscarry and that the moving landscape would result in an epidemic of eye infections. But none of these warnings dampened the enthusiasm of the Parisian bankers who eagerly bought railroad bonds, or of the prospering shippers of wine and produce. Artists also found the trains fascinating as something new to paint. Claude Monet did seven views of the Saint Lazare railroad station, while Pissarro, Sisley and Manet also completed affectionate studies of trains.

The literary world, meanwhile, was replete with talent. There was Amandine Aurore Lucie Dupin who,

writing under the *nom de plume* of George Sand, turned out ninety novels in a lifetime full of romance and disasters. Gustave Flaubert became one of the best-selling authors of the time when his *Madame Bovary* was banned for immorality. When curious readers asked him the true identity of his heroine, Flaubert replied: "I, I am Madame Bovary." Flaubert served as an inspiration to Emile Zola who, in 1867, became the most discussed author in France with the publication of his novel of adultery and murder, *Thérèse Raquin.* It too became a best-seller when the authorities banned it as pornographic.

All of France seemed to be in a creative ferment while Renoir was launching his long career in art. In the next half century, he would paint hundreds of unforgettable, evocative impressions of his times.

The Bathers *was painted by a mature Cézanne in his native Provence. He entered the first Impressionist Exhibition at age thirty-five. While many Impressionists tried to capture the moment, Cézanne also analyzed colors with great subtlety.*

Cézanne

With the outbreak of the Franco-Prussian War, the Impressionists were torn apart. Renoir joined the 10th Regiment in Bordeaux; Bazille was killed; and Manet became an officer in the National Guard. Three of the artists — Monet, Pissarro and Sisley — went to London where they discovered the art of Turner and were permanently influenced by his use of light. To avoid the armies, both French and Prussian, Paul Cézanne escaped to the small village of L'Estaque.

Cézanne's paintings were admired by his colleagues, but no matter how much one appreciated his work, Cézanne was a difficult man to like. To him, painting was everything — friendship, nothing. He painted himself as a fierce-looking cynic with downturned mouth, thin nose, dark smoldering eyes and a battered slouch hat. The portrait was of a man who disliked the world. His conservative father had considered him worthless and never stopped reminding him of his failures. The press held him and his work up to ridicule; one critic warned pregnant women not to look at his paintings lest their children be born yellow and green.

If Cézanne was discouraged, he never showed it and never stopped painting. Until he was fifty-six, his work had been exhibited only four times in group showings. Finally, the astute critic and art-dealer Ambroise Vollard gave him his first one-man show in Paris (as he would do with Picasso six years later).

As a result of this exhibition, Gertrude Stein and her brother Leo bought a portrait of Cézanne's wife Hortense called *The Woman With the Fan*. They also bought a yellow-green landscape, *The Bathers*. Vollard was pleased to find two Americans with such excellent taste. He firmly believed that Cézanne was the greatest artist in France. Later, the Steins would buy Renoirs, Monets, Manets, Daumiers, Matisses, Massons, Picassos — and more Cézannes. As art collectors, they could tell one rose from another.

Seurat

Some of the Impressionists felt that Georges Seurat was a conservative member of the "artistic establishment." After all, he had studied at the *Ecole des Beaux-Arts* and took a scientific attitude toward his painting.

In 1884, they were surprised when he exhibited the first work using his new technique: painting created by dots. It was called Divisionism, neo-Impressionism and especially — Pointillism. One anonymous critic wrote: "The city has ordered that the exhibition be closed as three visitors have succumbed to smallpox caught in front of a painting created by dots; others have been taken ill." However, the poet and critic Guillaume Apollinaire liked what he saw: "A canvas like *Le Cirque* or *Le Chahut* are (like) ballets full of grace, lyricism and good sense." Félix Fénéon, the most important art reviewer of his time, wrote of Seurat's *A Sunday Afternoon on the Island of La Grande Jatte*: "The atmosphere is transparent and singularly vibrant; the surface seems to quiver."

At the final exhibition of the Impressionists, Edouard Manet opposed the inclusion of a number of young artists including Seurat, Henri de Toulouse-Lautrec, Paul Gauguin and Odilon Redon. However, Manet died before the exhibit opened. Degas agreed to let the new artists into the show on condition that the word "Impressionist" be omitted from the advertising poster. When the newcomers were accepted, Renoir and Sisley withdrew. The Impressionists, it seemed, had become the conservatives. Now the neo-Impressionists had succeeded them as the *avante-garde*.

Seurat's models undress in Les Poseuses *which he painted between 1886 and 1888. The term Neo-Impressionism was coined for his new style. Using his brush to create myriads of dots, Seurat deftly achieved an optical effect known as pointillism.*

A Sunday painter with an admiration for the Impressionists, Gauguin left Paris for Tahiti in 1891. Breaking naturalistic conventions, he captured the daily life of the then unspoiled Polynesians. He grew to love the South Seas and died there.

A visionary, van Gogh made more than 200 paintings before killing himself. The Church at Auvers is among his last ones.

They met in Paris in the Fall of 1888. Both were artists with only one ambition—to paint. Both were symbolists and believed that the secret of great painting lay in the heart rather than in the eye or in the mind.

At their meeting they responded immediately to one another, and each tried to convince the other to join him. Paul Gauguin wanted Vincent van Gogh to work with him in Brittany, but he finally agreed to van Gogh's insistence that he come to Arles. The insecure van Gogh hoped that he and the confident, ebullient Gauguin would become close friends and then there would be no limits to what the two artists might accomplish. After only two months, however, they argued constantly. Van Gogh could no longer stand Gauguin's sarcastic wit. At a café, van Gogh threw a glass of absinthe at his former friend, and a few days later lunged at him with a razor. Gauguin left.

A few days after Gauguin's departure, van Gogh was found in bed with his head bandaged. It was Christmas; he had cut off his ear and sent it to a prostitute he had recently visited as a Christmas gift to remind her of how she had teased him about his large ears. A few months later, van Gogh shot himself. Gauguin, meanwhile, had gone off to Tahiti.

This facade of the cathedral of Rouen in 1894 is one of four versions Monet painted in the different light qualities of the changing seasons. In 1874, critics used the title of his canvas An Impression to name the new trend in painting.

Photography was both a business and an art in 1878 when a Lyonese painter immortalized this bourgeois wedding party at the photographer's studio. Film plates were slow and the only illumination came from the adjustable skylight. Thirty-

five years earlier, the French Academy had honored Daguerre and Niepce for their invention of the photographic process.

Photography, A New Art

With the introduction of the daguerreotype in France in 1840, photography became immensely popular. It was the invention of Louis Daguerre, a painter whose wife described him in a letter: "He has for some time been possessed by the idea that he can fix the images of the camera. He is always at the thought, he cannot sleep at night for it. I am afraid he is out of his mind."

Fortunately, Daguerre was not mad, simply persevering. With the help of Nicéphore Niepce, who had invented heliography in 1826, he succeeded. In 1839 the French Academy and the French government accepted and financed his camera and process. Photographers — or rather camera operators — opened shops first in Paris, then in London (where Fox Talbot had his own process) and ultimately the daguerreotype craze spread all over the world. Everyone wanted to be photographed; millions of daguerreotypes were sold. By the 1850s, a new process which permitted several prints to be made from the same negative (the daguerreotype made only one) was introduced in Paris by a caricaturist-lithographer named Gaspard Félix Tournachon, who called himself Nadar. Through his newspaper connections and his charm, Nadar was able to convince celebrities to pose for his camera. Nadar photographed Charles Baudelaire on at least two occasions. They became close enough friends for Baudelaire to borrow money from Nadar. Among Nadar's other subjects were Victor Hugo, Franz Liszt, Alphonse Daudet and Charles Garnier, the designer of the Paris Opera.

Nadar was most successful with his portraits of women. He photographed George Sand at least twice, and did a sensuous portrait of Sarah Bernhardt. Critics complained that his photographs were too realistic; by showing every wrinkle, squint and mole, they destroyed people's illusions. But these reservations did not affect the popularity of photography.

Nadar, a friend of many artists, loaned the Impressionists his studio on the *Boulevard des Capucines* for their first group exhibition in 1874. One of his artist friends, the painter-sculptor Edgar Degas, became fascinated by this new art form and took many excellent photographs.

One morning in 1886, Nadar was asked to come with his camera to Victor Hugo's house. Arriving, he was told that Hugo had just died. Nadar set up his camera in Hugo's bedroom and, as the sunlight streamed through the window and onto the bed, he made the final photograph of this great man — preserving that event for posterity in the new medium. It would not be long before photography was accepted in France as art.

219

The Theatre

In the 1850s, Eugène Scribe was Paris's favorite playwright with his entertaining comedies that featured heiresses pursued for their dowries and bankers involved in adultery. However, his plays were not applauded by a new naturalist group which wanted a different kind of theater.

Its hero was André Antoine, the director-manager of the *Théâtre Libre* (Free Theater). Well known in Paris theatrical circles, originally the leader of a claque, his first production was a new play by Emile Zola. It established his "little" theater, in which he presented plays on realistic themes done by actors who performed them that way. His actors behaved naturally, even turning their backs to the audience while talking.

A leading playwright of the time was Edmond Rostand, originally from Marseille, whose *Cyrano de Bergerac* contained all the qualities of a great melodrama: it was sentimental and romantic, and yet it included "serious" bits of history.

In the last quarter of the nineteenth century, Paris offered a great variety of theater. In 1875 and 1876, Bizet's *Carmen* was produced, Léo Delibes wrote the ballet *Sylvia* and Saint Saens composed *Samson and Delilah*. At the Comédie Française, one could see the operettas of Jacques Offenbach, who wrote *La Vie Parisienne*, *La Belle Hélène* and was working on *Les Contes d'Hoffmann* (The Tales of Hoffmann) when he died. In 1881, Paris's first cabaret *Le Chat Noir* began its musical evenings which became the rage of Paris.

The brightest star of the theater stage, not only in France but in England and the United States as well, was Sarah Bernhardt. Born Rosine Bernard in 1844, she became "the Divine Sarah" and, at the height of her fame in 1893, bought her own Paris theater. There, among other great portrayals, she daringly played a man's role — Hamlet. She went on acting even after her leg was amputated in 1914. Only her death, in 1923, took her offstage.

◀ *Portrayed at age thirty-five as the leading actress in a drama by Victor Hugo, Sarah Bernhardt was the darling of the* Comédie Française. *Her international career lasted almost sixty years. Critics and fans called her the "Divine Sarah."*

During an entr'acte at the Comédie Française, *Victor Hugo, Alexandre Dumas and Emile Zola are shown. This imaginary scene allowed the artist to portray the most important men of the 1880s. Orchestra seats were reserved for men only.*

The mother and child theme was a favorite of the American-born artist Mary Cassatt who, living in Paris, exhibited with the Impressionists.

Education, The Separation Of Church And State

A new kind of missionary appeared in France toward the end of the nineteenth century. Unlike the usual missionary who preached Christianity, he was a secular teacher employed by the State to teach reading, writing, mathematics and the sciences to children in the elementary schools throughout France.

The Third Republic had inherited a system of state elementary schools dominated by the Catholic clergy. Jules Simon had attempted to secularize the school system but was opposed by Church and monarchist sympathizers who combined to defeat him.

Then, the proponents of change found new arguments in France's disastrous defeat by the Prussians. In 1871, the distinguished philosopher, historian (and former priest) Joseph Ernest Renan wrote: "In the conflict which is just ended, the inferiority of France was mainly intellectual; what we lacked was not heart, but head. Public education is of paramount importance; French intelligence is enfeebled and must be strenghtened. Our greatest error is to believe that Frenchmen are born already educated . . . Lack of faith in science is a grave failing . . . Catholicism permits transcendant mysticism to flourish side by side with ignorance . . . It has a fatal influence on the development of the brain. A pupil of the Jesuits will never be an officer capable of opposing a Prussian officer; a pupil from a Catholic elementary school will never be able to engage in a scientific war with improved weapons."

Renan's message had considerable effect but it was not until the minister of education of the Third Republic, Jules Ferry, actually implemented Renan's ideas that the battle against clerical education began. His first step was to expel the bishops from the Superior Council of Public Instruction. He then decreed that only the State could grant degrees and other qualifications. Education in the public primary schools was made free and—shortly afterward—compulsory. New schools for girls were opened to train women teachers. Religious instruction was excluded from state schools.

Some of these new laws were ignored and fell into disuse, but in July 1904 they were revived by a new decree that prohibited members of religious orders from teaching in the public schools. That did it. The separation of Church and State in the area of public education had been accomplished.

The first bath of his newborn daughter Bernadette, given her by two midwives, was painted by the Nabis artist Maurice Denis. ▶

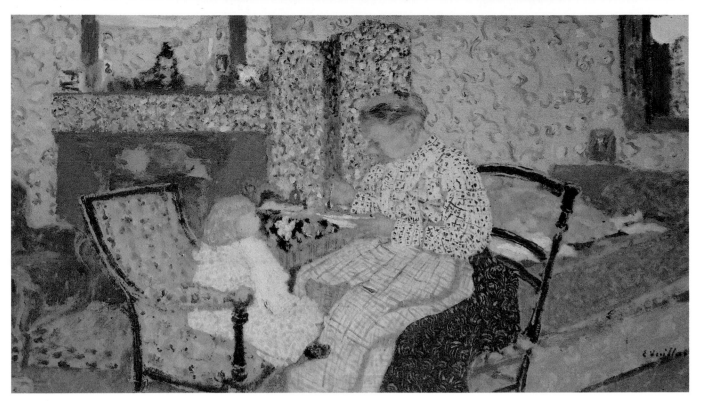

Annette, the daughter of Edouard Vuillard is having her first soup. A soft blend of light tones suggests the intimacy and the joy of the occasion. Vuillard and his closely knit Nabis ("prophet" in Hebrew) group painted at their best c. 1900.

In this naive scene, airborne Liberty directs the artists of all nations to come exhibit their works with the Society of the Indépendants. Henri Rousseau, a Paris douanier, painted it about 1905. He had begun exhibiting there in 1886.

1889 - 1940
SURVIVAL AND PROGRESS

Prosperous and at peace, France enjoys *La Belle Epoque*, dedicating Eiffel Tower and opening Paris Exposition to display its industrial progress. Dreyfus trial divides country. World War I begins. German troops almost reach Paris; battle of Verdun turns the tide. Victory is won in 1918. Paris becomes fashion capital of the world. In art, Picasso and Matisse become prominent. The Fauves are followed by Dadaists, Cubists and Surrealists. World War II begins. France is defeated and occupied. De Gaulle forms a government-in-exile.

HISTORICAL CHRONOLOGY	
1894—99	Dreyfus Affair. Ultra-conservative nationalist group Action Française founded, condemned by Pope in 1928.
1898—99	Pierre and Marie Curie discover radium and polonium. Construction begins on Le Métro, underground railway in Paris.
1890—1904	France leads world in the production of motor cars.
1904	Adoption of the Ten Hour Day Law and introduction of law for the separation of Church and State.
1909	Blériot makes first flight across the English Channel. Beatification of Jeanne d'Arc.
1912	French protectorate over Morocco established.
1914	World War I begins. President Poincaré calls upon the French to lay aside differences and form a "sacred union."
1916—17	Battle of Verdun; "they shall not pass." The United States enters the war on the side of France and Britain.
1918—19	End of World War I. Alsace-Lorraine is returned to France at Treaty of Versailles.
1923—24	France occupies the German Ruhr to collect unpaid reparations.
1926—28	Proto-fascist organization, Action Française, is condemned by the Pope.
1928—9	Construction of the fortified Maginot line along French-German border begins. Worldwide depression follows Wall Street crash in the United States. French economy slumps.
1936	Left-wing coalition, the Popular Front, wins the elections.
1939	World War II begins.
1940	German occupation of France. Collaborationist regime established in Vichy by Marshal Pétain. De Gaulle forms a government-in-exile in London.

ART CHRONOLOGY	
1891—93	Paul Gauguin paints his Tahitian pictures.
1894	Debussy composes **Afternoon of a Faun**. inspired by Mallarmé's 1876 poem.
1895	Moving pictures first shown by Lumière brothers who invented the projector.
1900	Paris becomes the fashion capital of the world. Fashion houses of Worth and Paquin are established.
1904	Mistral wins Nobel prize for literature.
1905	First Fauve exhibit in Paris introduces works by Matisse, Derain, Vlaminck and Dufy.
1907—08	Braque and Picasso experiment with Cubism. Picasso paints Demoiselles d' Avignon. Matisse founds his academy and publishes **Notes d'un Peintre**.
1912	Ravel composes **Daphnis and Chloé** for the Diaghilev ballet. Mystical, conservative Catholicism reflected in **The Announcement Made to Mary** by Paul Claudel.
1913—9	Marcel Proust writes **Remembrance of Things Past**. Nude Descending a Staircase by Marcel Duchamp creates a sensation.
1915	Romain Rolland wins Nobel prize for literature for his **Jean-Christophe**.
1918	First jazz band appears in France at Casino de Paris.
1920	**Chéri** written by Colette.
1923	Fashion designer Coco Chanel creates her Chanel No. 5 perfume.
1924	**Manifesto of Surrealism** issued by André Breton.
1926—27	André Gide writes **The Counterfeitor** which brings him a Nobel prize in 1947.
1931	Vision of freedom from industrialism portrayed in René Clair's film **A Nous la Liberté**.
1934—38	André Malraux writes about social justice and personal integrity. Roger Martin Du Gard wins Nobel prize in literature. Publication of **Nausea** by existentialist Jean-Paul Sartre.

Young ladies prepare for the ball by practicing the waltz. The dance had been introduced more than fifty years earlier, *but conservative society still considered it dangerously intimate. Marius Avy painted* **The White Ball** *in 1903.*

1889

La Belle Epoque, which can be translated as the Happy Years, the Glorious Period or the Beautiful Age, was a time when France was at peace with the world and with itself. The year 1889 opened with the dedication of the tallest structure in the world, the blue-steel Eiffel Tower, approximately 1,000 feet high. It had been designed by Alexandre Gustave Eiffel, an engineer who five years earlier had created the metal framework for Bartholdi's *Statue of Liberty.*

Since 1889 was also the hundredth anniversary of the fall of the Bastille, all of France and especially Paris celebrated the event on July 14 with fireworks and festivals. It was the year of the International Exposition where, on the Champs de Mars, an elaborate structure housed an exhibit of new machinery, a symbol of the rapid progress of French industry. It *was* a happy time.

True, there had been some problems. The government of the Third Republic had changed six times in the ten years between 1879 and 1889. And Jules Ferry, the statesman who had served twice as premier during those years, had been assassinated by a man who felt that the government was not doing enough to relieve poverty. Yet almost everywhere people looked there was reason for optimism. France had recovered from the defeat of 1870 and the indemnities it had been forced to pay Germany. New investments had poured into industry, banking and transportation. The French empire was flourishing. It still held the colonies of Martinique and Guadeloupe in the West Indies and benefited from the growth of the sugar and coffee industries. The government had established protectorates over Tunisia, Madagascar and Sénégal in Africa and deepened its control of Vietnam, Cambodia and Laos through the Indochinese Union. Now with the International Exposition, France was ready to invite every nation to the city it considered the capital of the world.

Entertainment to match every taste was to be found in Paris and one could travel around the city easily on the new *Métro.* The greatest diversions were offered in Montmartre, on the hill called *La Butte.* Since the late nineteenth century this picturesque quarter, three miles from the center of the city, had been the home of hundreds of composers, writers and artists. It was an area where prices were low, where many members of the working class lived and where all classes mixed. Seamstresses and laundresses became the models and sometimes the mistresses of artists and writers. Poets recited their poems, and composers sang their new songs as they met in the inexpensive cafés. In Montmartre, a

An elegant crowd strolls along the Champs Elysées near the Arc de Triomphe in this Impressionist painting by Raffaelli

c. 1900. No automobiles are in sight, although the Paris police department began issuing driver's licenses in 1893.

philosophy of live-and-let-live prevailed. The rest of Paris was dominated by a highly conservative society, which expected its members to live by the traditional rules. In Montmartre, there were no rules.

In October 1889, a *boîte* (night club) named *Le Moulin Rouge* (the Red Mill) opened in Montmartre. From the beginning, it was a phenomenal success. Opening each evening at ten, it offered two and one-half hours of divertissement. Its singers included Aristide Bruant, Jane Avril and May Belfort. One of the dancers was the blonde and supple *La Goulue* (the Glutton), who ate and drank at every opportunity. Her partner was a tall, rubber-legged dancer called Valentin-le-Désossé (the boneless). One of the early stars of the Moulin Rouge was billed as The Incomparable Pétomane (Fartingman). He had such control of his abdominal gases that he played operatic arias, with a tuba-like resonance, by breaking wind.

Two bands played for dancing, one of them in the shadowy light of the outdoor garden. In addition, there were fortunetellers, a shooting-gallery and, late in the evening, a chorus of belly-dancers. Certainly one of the most popular attractions was a large room next to the entrance with candlelit tables for two. At each one sat an attractive young woman waiting for a customer to join her and then negotiate for drinks, dancing and possibly a more intimate relationship.

The Tabarin night club in Montmartre offered popular shows with provocative dancers like this one painted by Rouault.

227

It was in the steamy atmosphere of Montmartre that a young artist from an aristocratic family found a home. Crippled as a child by two accidents that broke both his legs at the thighs, Henri de Toulouse-Lautrec grew up to be only five-feet one-inch tall. After two unsuccessful operations, the lonely, unattractive youth turned to painting. Against his parent's wishes, he moved to Paris where he studied at the Ecole des Beaux-Arts. Then he found the kind of life that suited him in Montmartre.

At the Moulin Rouge, young Toulouse-Lautrec first made sketches to please himself, but soon found people that wanted to buy them. That brought him money and, even more important, lots of friends. Well liked for his wit, his good humor and his talent for reproducing the life at the Moulin Rouge, he became friendly with the performers and with customers as well. Dressed in checked trousers, black jacket, cane and scarf, he regularly visited the cafés and houses of prostitution, always ending his tour at the Moulin Rouge. He became famous outside Montmartre. While still in his twenties, he contributed to important exhibitions in both Paris and Belgium.

In the posters Toulouse-Lautrec created for the Moulin Rouge, he used the entertainers as models. An expert craftsman, he made lithographs and personally supervised their printing. The French magazines, *Le Mirliton, Paris Illustré* and the satirical magazine *Le Courrier Français* used his work.

Toulouse-Lautrec became the lover of Suzanne Valadon, whose illegitimate son grew up to become an important artist—Maurice Utrillo. Their liaison continued for three years until, tired of her suicide threats, he walked out.

He found a way of life that seemed perfectly suitable—spending most of his time in one of the largest brothels in Paris. The madame liked him, and he had models who would pose for him night and day. He loved to observe and paint nudes and semi-nudes. He played cards with the girls, told them jokes (he had such a large penis compared to his dwarfed body that he referred to himself as a "coffee pot with a large spout"), gave them advice and remembered their birthdays.

Toulouse-Lautrec regularly broke away from life in the brothel to go to the races, to the seashore and to the circus. He loved the sporting life and backed a bicycling team. All of these activities showed up in his paintings and posters. Toulouse-Lautrec was in pain a great deal of the time and turned to alcohol. When he developed delirium tremens, his father briefly committed him to an asylum, then hired a male companion to keep him away from alcohol. But Toulouse-Lautrec became chummy with his guardian and still drank. He died in 1901.

Toulouse-Lautrec, sketching in Montmartre cabarets, captured the earthiness of La Goulue *and* Valentin-le-Désossé.

CINÉMATOGRAPHE

In 1895, when Parisians queued up to see the first motion pictures, they were enthralled. The new entertainment was called **Cinématographe Lumière**, *after the two brothers who had invented the equipment. Audiences were astonished*

The Motion Picture

The French aptitude for combining business with pleasure reached a new peak with the invention of the motion picture by the Lumière brothers in 1895. At the first showings, audiences chuckled when they saw a horse pulling a cart along the Place Bellecourt in Lyon — on the screen. They were even more astonished when a train puffing smoke moved across the screen as it left the railroad station. But their greatest applause went to a baby girl drinking soup.

Everyone in Paris wanted to see the pictures that moved. Soon the Lumière brothers were taking in 2,000 francs a day and lines of people formed outside the Grand Café to see the ten-minute motion picture. Camera operators bustled throughout France photographing everything that moved. Audiences saw King Edward VII visiting Paris, men and women dancing the questionable new dance called the *Valse* and the first motor-driven bicycles and early motorcars tootling along Paris streets. Elephants walked, ducks swam and birds flew. A new form called the "newsreel" became a weekly feature at the movies and a French company headed by Charles Pathé monopolized this field for ten years.

The first motion pictures that used actors to tell a story were the work of Georges Méliès, who in 1897 began employing his knowledge of magic and illusion to create a series of fanciful films. One of his first was *A Journey to the Moon*. Using ropes and pulleys outside camera range, he moved actors and props around while he photographed them. The audience saw the moon rise and his actors, propelled from a sort of cannon, land on it. He even added a *soupçon* of sex to his films. In *A Journey to the Moon*, he showed ten shapely models, wearing very short shorts and low-cut nautical blouses. Other Méliès films released at the turn of the century were equally imaginative: *The Doctor's Secret* and *Disappearing Woman*.

Eight years later, out of the fertile imagination of French artist-director Emile Cohl came the first animated cartoon. It was shown in 1908 (Walt Disney was then seven years old) and required hundreds of drawings — each one slightly different. The film was called *Drame chez les Fantoches* (Drama at the Home of the Puppets).

In 1911, Sarah Bernhardt appeared on the screen as Queen Elizabeth. In 1924, the innovative Abel Gance produced and directed the epic film *Napoléon*. In that same year Jean Renoir, the talented son of the Impressionist-painter Pierre Auguste Renoir, directed Emile Zola's *Nana* which included a lusty version of the Can-Can.

The first movies were shot outdoors in bright sunlight with simple sets. French movies were one of the excitements of the 1900 Paris Exposition. Méliès, an amateur magician, was the first to use plot lines and special effects in his films.

In 1930, a new kind of film was released when Jean Cocteau, poet, artist and playwright, did for the motion picture what the Surrealists a few years earlier had done for art. His imaginative and important avant-garde film, *The Blood of a Poet,* had a lasting effect on film makers throughout the world. *The Blood of a Poet* ran for over a year in motion-picture theaters in New York, Paris and London. Luis Buñuel and Salvador Dali then collaborated on a film which rivaled Cocteau's in avant-garde appeal, *Le Chien Andalou.* Buñuel, who had been a poet, directed and the artist Dali designed the sets and costumes. Their film, they predicted, "would plunge right into the heart of witty, elegant and intellectualized Paris..." *Le Chien Andalou* used outrageous symbolism like a young woman sucking the toe (of a statue) of the Pope. People's nerves tingled as they saw ants crawling over an actor's hands. Dream images of two dead donkeys, each lying inside a grand piano, made viewers gasp—and wonder what was going on.

These films did lead to the rise of a new and special kind of small, yet profitable movie theater. Such specialized "art houses," in contrast to the ever larger, ever more grandiose movie palaces of the 30s and 40s, spread to cities everywhere.

Even after the advent of sound, the French films of the 30s and 40s reached out to audiences in Europe and the United States. Despite the use of subtitles, French movies in the fields of social criticism, comedy and romance were successful abroad. French actors like Raimu, Arletty, Michèle Morgan, Louis Jouvet, Pierre Fresney and Jean Gabin became familiar names to the world's movie-goers. So did French directors like René Clair, Luis Buñuel, Marcel Carné, Jean Renoir, Jacques Feyder, Jean Duvivier and some of their films like *Sous les Toits de Paris, A Nous La Liberté, Marius, Fanny and César, The Baker's Wife, L'Enfant du Paradis* and *La Grande Illusion.* One hungry critic, Parker Tyler, called the French movies of this period the "caviar" of films.

232

When Rouault painted The Accused *in 1907, Captain Dreyfus had finally been freed. A Jewish army officer, Dreyfus had* *been convicted on forged evidence of being a German spy. The unfair trial was publicized by Zola in his famous "J'Accuse."*

Zola: J'accuse!

In 1894, an undated and unsigned letter indicating that a French army officer had passed along information to the Germans was discovered. Captain Alfred Dreyfus of Alsatian-Jewish descent was accused of treason and ordered to stand trial. An anti-Semitic journalist, Edmond Drumont, published a series of articles entitled "Les Juifs dans l'Armée" and shortly afterwards founded the Anti-Semitic League. A secret court-martial quickly found Dreyfus guilty and sentenced him to life imprisonment in solitary confinement on Devil's Island. The case was closed—or seemed to be. Then a new officer in the intelligence office, Captain Georges Picquart, found a letter addressed to a Major Marie Charles Esterhazy, whose handwriting matched that of the original incriminating document. The War Office immediately transferred Captain Picquart to a combat unit in Tunisia.

From Tunisia, Picquart wrote an important Alsatian senator, who approached the War Ministry and requested a new trial. Emile Zola, who had investigated the case, now wrote his famous letter *"J'accuse"* in which he accused the army of covering up the facts and falsifying the evidence. The army countersued. Zola was found guilty of libel and of insulting the army. His fine and sentence were annulled on appeal but the anti-Semitic press made life so difficult for him that he moved to England for a year. The country became divided into Dreyfusards and anti-Dreyfusards. In Alsace, Jews were attacked and their property looted.

When the army cover-up was disclosed, Lt. Col. Hubert Henry, the officer who had originally manufactured the evidence, committed suicide. Esterhazy, certainly the guilty party, escaped to England. Still, a new trial was held. Dreyfus was again convicted and sentenced to ten years of detention. Everyone realized that he had been unjustly imprisoned. President Emile Loubet gave him a full pardon and awarded him the Legion of Honor. Dreyfus, a good soldier, took up his career again as a captain of the army of France.

The first Congress against pornography was held at the time this colorful caricature appeared. It shows a busy boutique, *where love is for sale. Teenage boys often had their sexual initiations in the legalized* maisons de rendez-vous.

Destination Paris

People came to Paris from everywhere: from the provinces of France, from other countries on the European continent, from Britain, the Americas, Asia and Africa. They came for its *joie de vivre,* for its art and artists and for its incomparable cuisine. Many were students; young people from exotic places like Indochina, Morocco and Equatorial Africa met, studied and exchanged ideas in the classrooms, hotels, restaurants and cafés of the Latin Quarter, the site of the University of Paris otherwise known as the Sorbonne.

It had begun in 1252 when Robert de Sorbon founded a theological school there for sixteen poor students. By 1900, over a dozen colleges occupied the quarter on the left bank of the Seine, and there were so many students that they — and the artists and writers who lived among them — had spilled out of the Latin Quarter into neighboring Montparnasse. They shared the camaraderie of the Montparnasse cafés with artists like Pascin, Moreau, Steinlen, Foujita and Vlaminck, frequenting the *Dôme,* the *Coupole* and the *Rotonde.* Aristide Bruant, an attraction in Montmartre for his songs and poetry, also sang and recited in

Montparnasse. The *Douanier* Rousseau had his studio in Montparnasse's *Rue Perrel.* Crowds often gathered to watch the artists as they sketched, and every morning in the *Rue de la Grande Chaumière* there was a models' "market."

When Pablo Picasso first arrived in Paris in 1900, he came not as a student, but as a professional artist. He had studied art in Spain, notably in Barcelona. It took him three trips before he decided to make France his home instead of Spain.

One of the great attractions of Paris was its restaurants. By 1910, the *haute cuisine* was standard fare in the good restaurants, while the great ones served the *grande cuisine* — cooking fit for royalty. Struggling artists paid for their meals with canvases, so some restaurants amassed first-rate collections. Both Toulouse-Lautrec and Renoir illustrated menus and one of Renoir's sketches shows a chef at work, each dish drawn in detail and labeled.

Some of the great restaurants like Fouquet, La Grande Véfour, La Tour d'Argent, La Pérouse and Maxim's already were famous before World War I. Maxim's had opened in 1890 and had been a social and financial success from the start. There were restaurants for every taste in Paris before 1900; a restaurant guide of the time listed nearly 1,000 places to eat. In 1900, the President of France gave a banquet for all of the country's mayors. The caterer served 22,695 men. The hall was so large the maîtres d' rode around on bicycles.

Pablo Picasso was twenty-five years old when he painted this self-portrait. He was living in Paris at the time, having left Barcelona a few years previously. He had moved there to participate in the excitement of the avant-garde art world.

235

Soldiers, during World War I, are portrayed as machine-tooled weapons in this comment on war's inhumanity by Marcel Gromaire.

World War I

In 1904, a German staff officer — his head swathed in bandages to hide his identity — sold to a French Intelligence agent several documents which described the Schlieffen Plan, the German General Staff's top-secret scheme to attack France in the next war by sending an army through Belgium, whose neutrality all the major European powers had guaranteed. The chief of the French General Staff believed the information was authentic, but his colleagues were skeptical. They suspected it was a trick, to draw French attention away from the real German intention — a drive into central France from Alsace. They pointed out that the Germans would not be so foolish as to violate Belgian neutrality since that would ensure England's entry into the war on the French side. No, said the doubting French generals, the Germans would attack Russia first, then turn on France and definitely leave Belgium alone. There would be time to mobilize, they insisted, while France's Russian

allies bore the brunt, and then would come *revanche* (revenge for the 1870 defeat): The French army would beat the Germans, liberate Alsace and Lorraine, and march triumphantly to Berlin. However, the documents were genuine and the skeptics on the French General Staff were wrong. When the war began in 1914, the Germans did follow the Schlieffen Plan and swept across Belgium in an enveloping maneuver so wide that the prediction of Count Alfred von Schlieffen almost came true: "When you march into France, let the last man on the right brush the Channel with his sleeve."

This was not France's only mistake as it faced the inevitability of another war with an aggressive Germany that intended to dominate Europe. The Germans put their hopes in new military technology. The French, for their part, hoped for the restoration of French self-confidence, a return to Napoleonic *gloire* (glory). General Ferdinand Foch, director of the *Ecole Supérieure de la Guerre* (War College), said what France needed was to believe in a mystique of will which he expressed in aphorisms, "The will to conquer is the first condition of victory," and "A battle won is a battle in which one will not confess oneself beaten." His philosophy was translated into new field regulations by the General Staff which proclaimed: "The French army admits no law but the offensive."

The French *poilu* (infantryman) was lectured on *volonté* (will) and *cran* (guts) but not much was done about his equipment and his firepower. Proposals that his uniform be changed so as to make him less conspicuous in combat were shelved. The British had changed to khaki and the Germans had switched from blue to field-gray, but French troops still went on wearing blue coats, red kepi and red trousers that made them easy to spot in this new era of long-range artillery. Nor did the French General Staff press for the kind and numbers of heavy artillery with which the Germans were equipping their forces, along with other new weapons: tanks, detachments of light and heavy machine-guns, regiments of balloons (for artillery spotting) and poison gas. Krupp had manufactured a giant cannon, nicknamed "Big Bertha," which could fire a shell sixty miles. The Germans were developing airplanes for observation and primitive bombing. And the German navy was sending to sea hundreds of submarines as well as giant dreadnoughts.

On June 28, 1914, a Serbian patriot assassinated the heir to the Austrian throne, Archduke Ferdinand, and his Duchess in Sarajevo and the Germans insisted that their ally, Austria, attack Serbia in retaliation. When Russia went to the defense of the Serbs, Berlin declared war on the Tsar's empire. France immediately moved to the aid of Russia, her ally. The day after the Kaiser

The violent German offensive in the north of France destroyed ▶
the cathedral of Soissons along with many industrial plants.

François Flameng. Soissons. 18 mai 1915.

The Germans first used poison gas in 1915 in an attempt to end the deadly impasse of trench warfare. It did not work.

for peace with Germany.

In the West, the war in the trenches went on—a terrible orgy of mud and blood—with neither side able to win decisive battles. The Royal Navy blockade of German ports was effective. In February 1915, Kaiser Wilhelm retaliated by declaring all the sea approaches to the British Isles and France war zones and ordering his U-boats to attack all ships carrying goods to England or France without warning. Two ships, the American tanker *Gulflight* and the British Cunard liner *Lusitania*, the latter with 1,100 passengers including 128 Americans, were sunk without warning. Most Americans were determined to stay neutral. President Wilson said: "There is such a thing as a man being too proud to fight."

In February of 1916, the Germans attacked in force at Verdun. They had planned this offensive carefully, knowing that the great fortress of Verdun stood exposed and that its fate would affect every Frenchman. If Verdun fell, the Germans believed, France would give up. The Allied high command knew that the fall of Verdun would seriously affect the French morale and gave orders to defend it at all costs. General Philippe Pétain told his troops, "They shall not pass," and they did not, although the number of French and British killed was incredibly high. By the time the German assault had been turned back, each side had lost a quarter of a million men. In another bloodletting—the battle of the Somme—the French and British lost over 200,000 men in exchange for limited advances. The stalemate in the trenches went on.

German diplomatic blunders were moving the United States closer to war. The British intercepted and decoded a message to Mexico City proposing an alliance whereby Mexico would attack the United States from the south and in return would get back Texas, New Mexico and Arizona. At the same time, Germany tried to entice Japan to attack Hawaii, promising it those islands as booty. On April 6, 1918, President Wilson declared war on Germany. Conscription began immediately and over a period of a year, two-million American doughboys were dispatched to France. The American expeditionary force and its commander, General John Pershing, served under General Foch who had become supreme commander of the allied forces. With American reinforcements and aid, the war of attrition in the trenches began to end. On May 28, 1918, the British, French and Americans took the offensive against the Germans.

In July came the second battle of the Marne. The Germans attacked simultaneously on both sides of Reims, but after three days of fighting, they were exhausted and their advance halted. The Allies counterattacked at Soissons and their victory turned the tide of the war. On that day, the 18th of July, the German chancellor would later write, "even the most optimistic among us knew that all was lost." When the British crashed through the "Hindenburg Line," Germany's last line of defense,

declared war on Russia, a million German troops swept into Belgium. As expected, the British entered the war—allying themselves with France, Russia and Italy. By the time the French had mobilized and begun their attack on Germany through Alsace and Lorraine, the Germans had crushed Belgium (with more resistance than they had expected) and were rapidly advancing on Paris. When the Kaiser's troops reached the Marne, twenty-five miles from Paris, and prepared to attack, the French brought them to a halt with a dramatic last-moment rally.

Out of the city rushed private cars, produce trucks and taxicabs carrying every soldier they could muster directly into battle. The defense at the Marne signaled to the Germans that France would not be a pushover this time. Both armies dug in, and began fighting a static war from trenches that eventually ran across France in a jagged line from the Swiss border to the English Channel. Trapped in a deadly standstill on the Western front, the Germans turned their attention to the East and the ill-equipped Russians. Outnumbered and outgunned, the Russians fought on, suffering the loss of nearly one million men. Their defeats and the consequent demoralization behind the lines contributed to the political and social unrest inside the country and, in November 1917, the Bolsheviks seized power and sued

During the six months of the Battle of Verdun in 1916, the French lost 315,000 men while the Germans who had superior firepower lost 281,000 men. The young officer, Charles de Gaulle, commanding an infantry regiment, was taken prisoner.

in the North, the Fatherland lay exposed to invasion. Realizing the war was over, the Kaiser abdicated and Germany quickly established a parliamentary form of government, which sued for peace. Marshal Foch negotiated an armistice which was signed in his railroad dining car in the forest of Compiègne at 11 a.m. on November 11, 1918. The costliest war to date in terms of human lives and property had come to an end.

The total number of men killed, not including the wounded who died later, came to at least seven and one-half million. The Germans lost the most: 1,800,000. The Russians lost 1,700,000, the French 1,400,000, the Austrians 1,200,000, the British 900,000, the Italians 200,000 and the Americans 100,000. Germany's attempt to dominate Europe had been stopped, but at a frightful price.

President Wilson, who came to the Versailles peace conference, insisted that his Fourteen Points be the basis of the peace. French Premier Georges Clémenceau did not entirely approve, saying: "President Wilson and his fourteen points bore me. Even God Almighty only had ten." Defeated Germany was occupied, demilitarized and ordered to pay reparations. Alsace-Lorraine became French. When the German government failed to pay reparations, French troops occupied the Ruhr. The future of the iron-rich Saar was to be decided by a plebiscite.

The French, like other Europeans, hoped that the new League of Nations, established in Geneva, would bring an era of international cooperation. However, the United States, which had become the world's greatest industrial power, chose to retreat into isolationism and refused to join the League.

Paris In The 1920s

The postwar expatriates in Paris were British, Italian, Russian and American. Most were young; many were talented painters or writers. A few were rich dilettantes. Ernest Hemingway was creating memorable characters, including himself. He modeled the beautiful and sensuous Lady Brett Ashley in *The Sun Also Rises* after the very real Lady Twysden. James Joyce, writing his masterpiece *Ulysses*, was being supported by Sylvia Beach whose bookstore, Shakespeare and Company, was a home away from home for writers. Isadora Duncan, the American dancer, was writing her autobiography and occasionally gave recitals. Among the American writers were Ezra Pound, F. Scott Fitzgerald, Sinclair Lewis and Elliot Paul who lived on and wrote about the *Rue du Chat Qui Pêche* (Street of the Fishing Cat).

At Bricktop's, black musicians, mostly from the United States, played jazz until dawn while Bricktop herself sang old favorites like "Bill Bailey" and new hits like Cole Porter's "Love For Sale." At the Jockey Club, the wealthier expatriates convened: people like publisher Robert McAlmon and his heiress wife Bryher; Nancy Cunard (of the shipping fortune); and Caresse and Harry Crosby, the American couple who later would help support the American writer Henry Miller. Also to the Jockey Club came Frenchmen like Louis Aragon, the author; Marcel Duchamp, the painter; René Cervel and Jean Cocteau, the artist, designer, composer and author.

At the Boeuf-sur-le-Toit, Erik Satie gathered around him a younger generation of Parisian composers: Georges Auric, Arthur Honegger, Louis Durey, Germaine Taillefere, Francis Poulenc and—the youngest of the six—Darius Milhaud. All were beginning their careers, all would become famous. The music world of Paris knew them as "The Six," a title given them by music critic Henri Collet. Cocteau acted as an unpaid publicity agent for the young musicians and on occasion played the cymbals with them. Satie already had earned his reputation for his *Gymnopedies*. Now he wrote songs for Montmartre music-hall singers and studied counterpoint, a technique opposed to the current harmonics. It would not be long before the young composers with whom he associated would reject

Clémenceau's political career spanned more than forty years. Quick to pounce on an opponent, his nickname was "The Tiger.

◄*Cocteau (right rear) with* The Six; *the composers shown are Honegger, Auric, Durey, Milhaud, Poulenc and Taillefere.*

Auguste Rodin's sculptures of lovers were censored. He was criticized for the stark realism of The Thinker *and* Balzac.

241

musical impressionism and strive for polytonal construction, clarity and humor, all basic in Satie's compositions.

At these cabarets and clubs, much of the talk revolved around four art movements that had followed Impressionism. First had come the Fauve movement. At the Salon d'Automne a group of artists had shown their new works: Henri Matisse, Georges Rouault, André Derain, Maurice de Vlaminck, Raoul Dufy and Kees van Dongen. All painted in brilliant colors and most of them seemed to have been influenced by van Gogh. Their painting was charged with energy and excitement. Landscapes, figures and street scenes were painted in colors as brilliant as a tropical jungle. A critic writing of the event described the room as "a cage of wild beasts" *(une cage à fauves)*, and the name "Fauve" was adopted to describe this new art form. While colorful and representational enough to be considered

a new Romantic movement, it was more than that for it contributed to the recognition of pure color as a separate factor in itself. As such it contributed to the Cubist movement, still another new form.

There was much conversation about Cubism. The Cubists, at least for a time, absorbed the techniques of color laid down by the Fauves and developed them in depth. Its major inspirations were Cézanne and Seurat whose reflections could be seen in many Cubist works.

In the year 1910, a number of talented painters were working toward a feeling of solidity and depth by using three-dimensional forms. Among the most effective in this new departure were three Spanish painters, and one Frenchman. They were Pablo Picasso, Amédée Ozenfant, Juan Gris and Georges Braque. Each of the four advanced the Cubist movement but, because each was going in his own direction, Cubist art became highly individualistic. Picasso and Gris moved toward a solidly

In 1914, at the age of forty-five, Henri Matisse went to spend the winter in Nice on the Riviera and stayed on for most of
the rest of his life. In this storm scene in Nice, Matisse does not use the brilliant colors typical of the Fauves.

based lyrical quality. Braque went in the same general direction but with more decorative feeling. Picasso should be considered the seminal influence. His *Demoiselles d'Avignon* painted in 1907, and his *Three Women* done the following year had strong Cubist elements. Later, Marcel Duchamp and Fernand Léger made important contributions to this controversial movement.

Next came Dada, which took a humorous view of art, ridiculing the seriousness with which too many painters looked at themselves. It was born (some said aborted) in 1920. The aim of Dadaism was to create art spontaneously, including its satiric commentaries on serious work. Dadaists painted a mustache on the serene visage of the *Mona Lisa* (Salvador Dali), made an art object of a porcelain urinal (Marcel Duchamp), created a fur-lined bathtub and published the satirical magazine *391*, a continuation of the earlier *291* published by Stieglitz in New York. Prime movers among the Dadaists were Francis Picabia, André Breton, Joan Miró, Louis Aragon and Marcel Duchamp.

In 1924, Breton issued the *Surrealist Manifesto* which proclaimed, "a dictate of the mind, without any control by the reason," and said that a work "will thus refer to a purely interior model or it will not exist." The roots of Surrealism, he wrote, lay in symbols that arose from unconscious mental processes. The movement was doubtless influenced by the metaphysical works of France's non-realistic artists de Chirico, Moreau and Redon. It admittedly owed a great deal to Goya, Blake and Sigmund Freud. Surrealism's most notable artists were Picasso, Dali, René Magritte, Joan Miró and Max Ernst. André Masson's contribution was automatic painting; he said his brush was controlled by his subconscious mind. The Surrealist movement in art has gone through many incarnations since 1924, but its influence is still apparent.

Raoul Dufy, influenced by the Fauve movement, used simplified forms and bright colors in a gay, light-hearted and decorative style. Like Toulouse-Lautrec, he enjoyed the social life at the racetracks and painted the fast horses and elegant women.

Gromaire 1927

On The Riviera

In 1871, an English travel writer predicted: "The time is fast approaching when tens of thousands from the north of Europe will adopt the habits of the swallow and transform all the towns and villages of the Riviera into sunny winter resorts." English, Belgian, German and Russian noblemen showed French aristocrats and industrialists how enjoyable it was to pass winters along France's Mediterranean littoral.

From the 1920s onward, the burgeoning automobile industry, improved roads and deluxe railroad trains made it easy for Frenchmen to travel south to St. Tropez, Cannes, Nice and Menton where flowers bloomed even in winter. The residents who had been fishermen and flower-growers adapted their skills to the tourist trade. Some became entrepreneurs, running country inns, small seaside hotels and restaurants specializing in the Provençal cuisine of the region. Others worked as waiters and croupiers.

Winter vacationers avoided the beaches, preferring to promenade along the seafront, inhaling the sea air which they believed might prevent tuberculosis (a scourge in those days). Swimming in the Mediterranean was considered foolhardy: cold water, sea-urchins and jellyfish. A few pioneering resorts stayed open for the summer. The American Frank Jay Gould, who lived in Cannes, built a resort for summer visitors at Juan-les-Pins. In 1922 the Tennis Club of Nice decided to stay open year-round. More people swam and sailed when the water was warm. The first businesses offering yachts for charter opened.

By 1925, men and women on the Riviera began to wear what was then considered the skimpiest of beachwear so as to move freely when swimming and get the maximum tan on their bodies. Women wore bathing suits that displayed their contours; men wore only shorts, baring their chests.

During the 1930-39 Depression and World War II, the Riviera was a sad place. In 1944, Allied forces landed on its beaches to end the Axis occupation of southern France. After the war, it came back to life. The first Cannes film festival, in 1947, received worldwide attention. In addition to making films and film makers famous, it publicized the Riviera as the land of the bikini — the tiny swimsuit that revealed everything but three strategic areas of the female body. Twenty years later, only one strategic area was still covered on public beaches. In private coves and on yachts, nothing was hidden.

Along the French Riviera, bathing suits became brief while some women went topless on the beach as early as the 1920s.

245

The Queen
Of Haute Couture

The French created a high standard of excellence with their cuisine, their wines and their genius for dressing women. In the last quarter of the nineteenth century, *Maison Worth* established by the Englishman Charles Frederick Worth made gowns and dresses for the royalty of Europe, actresses and society leaders. Worth's ingenuity, taste and expert seamstresses paved the way for Paris to become the world's fashion capital.

Shortly after Worth's success, Madame Paquin opened a dressmaking establishment only two doors away from his. Like Worth, she made one-of-a-kind dresses, capes and coats for the elite. But she was interested in functional clothing and mass production as well. In 1910, with the backing of the French government, Paquin toured the United States with a group of mannequins. Her fashion shows were so popular that admission prices were raised from three to five dollars to discourage the crowds. In 1913, the French government awarded Madame Paquin the Legion of Honor.

Fashion in France had always been a perquisite of the aristocracy. From the time of Louis XIV and Colbert, members of the guild of couturiers had played an important role in dressing royalty. It was, in fact, the Empress Eugénie who had first patronized Worth.

But in the 1920s, Gabrielle Bonheur Chanel to use her full name, which few people did — they knew her as Coco Chanel — proclaimed: "Fashion is no longer dictated by aristocracy." She ridiculed the heavy and elaborate clothing of Worth and Paquin. She also said: "Princesses and duchesses rarely pay their bills."

Chanel's clothing was elegantly simple. "Throw away your corsets," she said. "You can't drive a car in a crinoline skirt." Her graceful, knee-length skirts and cardigans, and her jersey dresses became classic couture.

Chanel had a tactile sense about clothing. She needed to feel the fabric, to shape it in her hands, to pin it together again and again until it looked and felt exactly right. She did not sketch her designs but, like a sculptor, molded her dresses, skirts and blouses directly on her models. She admitted learning a great deal about men's clothing from her lovers.

Her mother's early death and her father's desertion when she was six (it was he who called her Coco), left her to be raised by aunts. When she was fifteen, she ran away with a young cavalry officer, Etienne Balsan. After living together for ten years, they drifted apart. For a short time, she ran a small millinery shop in Paris,

then spent a summer in Deauville where she opened an exclusive hat boutique. The next year she was back in Paris and opened a fashion establishment at 31 *Rue Cambon*. In Paris she met Arthur Capel, called "Boy." Like her first lover, he was rich and socially prominent.

Now Chanel began her career as designer and dressmaker. Within five years, with her emphasis on simple and graceful lines, she had become a recognized figure in the fashion world, and within ten years, she had a rich international clientele wearing her "poor girl" look. At the peak of her success, she employed 3,500 people in fashion, textiles, perfume and costume jewelry. She became a famous Parisian figure, slim, dark, graceful, noted for the sharp edge of her wit.

After the death of "Boy" in an auto accident, she and Cocteau were constant companions. For the next few years, she was seen regularly with Cocteau and his young lover Raymond Radiguet. When Radiguet died, it was Chanel who paid for his funeral. During the Occupation, she put Cocteau up at the Ritz. He said that she had the head of "a little black swan" to which she added, "and the heart of a little black bull." She was generous to her artist friends and often seemed able to make things work out for the best. One evening, as she was dressing to go to the Opera, the hot water heater in her Ritz Hotel bathroom exploded, and smoke and soot covered her long hair. She reached for her scissors and cut most of it off. Her appearance that night in a simple white gown with short jet-black hair caused a new vogue for bobbed hair that swept the world. When she began her affair with the second Duke of Westminster, Hugh Grosvenor, he presented her with a collection of large and valuable gems. Practical Chanel put them away in the safe-deposit box after having copies made for herself — and then made more copies to sell to her customers. When after a sojourn on the Duke's yacht Coco returned from Cannes with a deep suntan, she was credited with creating the new healthy tanned look.

Her biggest moneymaker was the perfume she promoted, Chanel No. 5 (her lucky number) which had a light elusive odor. When someone asked why she did not make perfumes with the odor of flowers, she replied: "Women are not flowers — why should they smell like them?" Other Chanel wisdom: "The problem is to rejuvenate the woman, to make women look young. Then their attitude towards life changes, they feel more joyous."

During the German Occupation of World War II, Paris fashion became a ragbag of old clothes madeover, skirts short enough for bicycling and wooden shoes. In 1947, the city reclaimed its fashion title when Christian Dior introduced the "New Look," a lavish farewell to wartime austerity. After Dior, the trendsetters included Yves St. Laurent, Marc Bohan, Courrèges and Paco Rabanne.

When Marie Laurencin painted Coco Chanel in 1923 at the age of forty-one, Chanel dominated the high fashion scene and had just launched her "Chanel No. 5" perfume. Both Laurencin and Chanel were then designing for the **Ballets Russes** of Diaghilev.

Raised in Montmartre, Maurice Utrillo was encouraged by his artist mother, Suzanne Valadon to take up painting to overcome his alcohol and drug addictions. He became celebrated as a painter of the hilly streets and old buildings of Montmartre.

Communists And Catholics

Two new political movements emerged in France in the 1920s, Communism and Christian democracy. Radically opposed to one another, both became important mass movements which strongly affected the direction of the government and the nation's social climate. Both ideologies directed their recruiting to the youth and the working class.

The Russian Revolution had had a profound effect on the younger generation of France. The idealistic aims expressed by the early Bolshevik leaders convinced many people in other countries that Communism had the same goals as Socialism, that Bolshevism was only "socialism with tartar sauce" and that "the dictatorship of the proletariat" was a temporary expedient before a free workers' state would come into being. In the 1920s, when the French Socialists voted overwhelmingly to join the Third International, the opponents of the move, suspicious of what Moscow had in mind, seceded and formed their own party.

The majority became the Communist Party of France denouncing the Socialists in violent language that would become familiar and abandoning the unity of the Left. Now there were two parties on the Left: the Socialists, democratic and idealistic, and the Communists, a tight, highly disciplined branch of the Third International divided into cells which operated under strict party discipline and had no influence of their own on policy.

Peasant women with their children out for a Sunday stroll wore their Sunday clothes. After their victory in 1936, *the Socialists and Communists in parliament legislated paid vacations and increased allowances for large families.*

Every move the party made was controlled or edited by instructions from Moscow.

In 1934, worried about the rise of fascism (Hitler had come to power in Germany), the French Communists switched from internationalism to patriotism in one swoop becoming as militantly nationalist as the small parties of the extreme right. Anti-fascists and pro-fascists battled in the streets. The Communists convinced the Socialists to join with them again and once that happened, Communist discipline and propaganda so outshone the Socialists that they became the leaders of the French Left. The names of André Malraux and Pablo Picasso were widely publicized as Communist sympathizers. When the Soviet Union suddenly switched its line and signed a non-aggression treaty with Nazi Germany, the party in France lost thousands of members and sympathizers. After Germany occupied France, many Communists went underground to play important and heroic roles in the wartime Resistance. The Liberation found the Communists' reputation high among industrial workers, particularly in the reconstituted labor unions. Party cadres worked tirelessly to recruit members in factories and workshops. In 1946, more than one-fourth of the French electorate voted Communist. However, after 1948, as the Soviet Union's aggressive policies in Eastern Europe became apparent, its influence waned.

Shocked by the inroads Communism was making on French youth, the Church had decided to oppose the Left with a Christian democratic approach. The majority of Catholics were right wing, and their reactionary attitudes had turned off younger voters. Beginning in the early 30s, the Church established new organizations that supported social programs but also countered Communist propaganda in a drive to influence young French workers. Within ten years, the Young Christian Workers Party had succeeded in signing up 65,000 active members. Two additional organizations, the Young Christian Farmers and the Young Christian Independents (with a bourgeois base), were formed.

The Tango of the Archangel *reflects the gay romantic era known as* Les Années Folles *(The Crazy Years) before* World War II. *The artist Kees van Dongen loved the late night life and was a member of* Le Tout Paris *(high society).*

These organizations taught that Catholics owed a duty to the State as well as to God, and that going to Mass and contributing to the poor was not enough. If the Communists were not to take over all of the youth of France, Catholics had to take positive measures to prevent it. One's religious convictions were no longer enough; Catholics must have political convictions as well. During World War II, men and women in the Church and lay religious groups participated actively in the Resistance, and by their courage reinforced the impression among French workers of a militantly democratic Church.

A VISION OF THE FUTURE

France suffers through Nazi occupation until 1944 when it is liberated by Allied forces. De Gaulle returns in triumph. Fourth Republic is inaugurated. America's Marshall Plan speeds economic recovery. Nobel prizes for literature won by Camus (1957) and Sartre (1964). France joins the Common Market and gives independence to its colonies. De Gaulle is elected two-term president of the Fifth Republic. France enjoys a period of growth and prosperity. Student riots of May 1968 bring about social reforms.

HISTORICAL CHRONOLOGY		ART CHRONOLOGY	
1940—45	Germans occupy France. Liberation and victory.	1945	Picasso's The Charnel House reflects wartime brutalities. Jean Giraudoux writes the play "Madwoman of Chaillot."
1945—46	Women vote for the first time. Communists and Socialists win greatest electoral returns. Fourth Republic gets its constitution. De Gaulle resigns.	1946	Cocteau's Ballet "Death of Man" premieres in Paris.
1947—48	Communists dismissed from government. De Gaulle founds the Rally of the French People. United States Marshall Plan provides economic aid.	1947	Albert Camus's The Plague acclaimed. Christian Dior creates the "New Look" in fashion.
		1948	Le jazz hot becomes popular.
1949	France enters NATO and supports entry of West Germany.	1949	Women's changing role depicted in The Second Sex by Simone de Beauvoir.
1951	Suez Canal nationalized by Egypt. Industrial production regains pre-war peak.	1951	Paris celebrates its millennium, marking 2,000 years since Julius Caesar's conquest of Gaul.
1953	Reactionary party, the Poujadist League, appeals to small businessman and farmers.	1952	Playwright Samuel Beckett writes "Waiting for Godot."
1954—62	France quits Vietnam after defeat at Dien Bien Phu. Algerian War and struggle for independence. Saar is returned to German rule.	1953	Pierre Cardin opens his fashion establishment. Cocteau re-unites "The Six."
1957	Common Market formed.	1955	Concept of architecture as sculpture embodied in Le Corbusier's Notre Dame du Haut. Photographer Henri Cartier-Bresson honored by the Louvre.
1958	Fourth Republic ends with war in Algeria. Fifth Republic receives constitution from de Gaulle.	1956	Brigitte Bardot stars in And God Created Woman, directed by Roger Vadim.
1958—69	President Charles de Gaulle vows to re-establish French "grandeur."	1957	Nobel prize for literature awarded to Albert Camus.
1960	Atomic tests in Sahara.	1958	UNESCO building in Paris decorated by Picasso and others. Malraux appointed Minister of Culture.
1962	Algerian independence recognized. Presidency becomes a seven-year office.	1959	Hiroshima My Love by Alain Resnais and Four Hundred Blows by François Truffaut
1963	De Gaulle vetoes England's entry in Common Market.	1960	Career diplomat Saint-John Perse wins Nobel prize for literature.
1965	Elections return de Gaulle to the presidency.	1961	Edith Piaf sings at the Olympia Music Hall.
1966	French withdrawal from NATO. Technological cooperation with U.S.S.R. begins.	1964	Miniskirt introduced by designer Courrèges. Chagall paints ceiling of the Opera.
1967	De Gaulle encourages French-speaking dissidents in Quebec and vetoes second British application for entry into Common Market.	1967—68	Color television introduced in France. The American Challenge by Servan-Schreiber.
1968	May student riots explode into street fighting and general strike. De Gaulle calls for new elections and wins short-lived support.		

World War II

Even before he took power in Germany in 1933, Adolf Hitler had made it plain in his book, *Mein Kampf*, that he planned to rearm Germany, revoke the "injustices" of Versailles and change the map of Europe — even if it meant war. His threats were received in France, England and the United States with skepticism and timidity. In January 1935, the Saar voted for reunion with Germany, after a vociferous propaganda campaign by the Nazis. March 1936, saw the new German army march into the Rhineland, which had been demilitarized at Versailles. Hitler's next objective was Czechoslovakia, which had a German minority. His threats forced Daladier and Chamberlain to meet with him and Mussolini in Munich in 1938 where the French premier and British prime minister sacrificed Czechoslovakia. Returning to London, Chamberlain spoke of "peace in our time" while Daladier was received with cheers in Paris as the man who had saved France from another war. Three months later, German foreign minister Joachim von Ribbentrop was invited to Paris and signed a declaration of friendship. Many Frenchmen believed the Nazis were invincible, and that accommodation with them was inevitable. Some Frenchmen openly admired Hitler, who despised democracy for its weaknesses and promised to destroy Bolshevism.

In 1939, Nazi Germany and Communist Russia signed a non-aggression pact in a surprising and cynical turnabout. Now Hitler was free to move against Poland. In a *blitzkrieg* (lightning war) that stunned and horrified other countries, his opponents and neutrals alike, Hitler sent panzer divisions, motorized troop columns and Stuka dive bombers against the ill-equipped Poles, decimating them, to join up with his Soviet "allies" in eastern Poland. SS units rounded up Polish Jews, intellectuals and anti-Nazis for slave labor in Nazi war plants. Eventually, millions were murdered.

France and Britain declared war on Germany but neither was prepared to fight. For months, the French

In 1943, during the Occupation, Gilot painted a hawk as a symbol of the Nazis and, seen outside, Paris as a graveyard.

sat behind their Maginot Line and waited fearfully for the Germans to move. In this period of "the phony war," many Frenchmen and Britons hoped some kind of peace could be negotiated with Hitler. When the Germans finally moved, it was against Denmark and Norway on May 10, 1940 and into Belgium and France on May 14. By May 30, Belgium had surrendered, the Netherlands were occupied, the Maginot line had been

252

The grim aspects of the German occupation during World War II and the shortage of food are represented by leeks and a human *skull in a late Cubistic painting by Pablo Picasso in 1943. It now belongs to Paloma, his daughter by Françoise Gilot.*

turned and the fate of the French army sealed. The British expeditionary force was trapped on the Channel coast at Dunkerque, shielded by RAF fighters from Nazi raids. From England came boats of all kinds—naval vessels, yachts, fishing boats—to ferry the troops back to safety in England. On June 14, 1940, the French defenses collapsed and the Germans entered Paris and hoisted the swastika over its public buildings.

A few weeks later, the Nazis got their revenge for the ceremony at Compiègne twenty-two years earlier when they had surrendered to the French. In the same railroad car in which Marshal Foch had received the German delegation in 1918, General Wilhelm Keitel formally accepted the French surrender and granted an armistice. A jubilant Hitler visited the railroad car shortly afterward. The Reynaud government fled Paris, settling in Vichy, where Marshal Pétain, a hero of World War I, took over, promising to save as much of France's

dignity as he could. Eventually, he and Pierre Laval, the premier of the Vichy regime, obediently collaborated with the Germans—establishing a French version of a Nazi regime. The Third Republic was abolished, and secret police, torture chambers and roundups and deportations of its citizens replaced democratic traditions. Tens of thousands of Frenchmen were shipped to Germany as slave laborers.

The fight to liberate France was led outside the country by General Charles de Gaulle, who had flown to London and set up a government in exile. His Free French movement sent agents into occupied France to whip up resistance and recruited Free French military units for service in Africa. The resistance groups inside France were supplied by the Allies and led by French Communists, Catholic activists—Georges Bidault headed the Christian Democratic resistance—and Socialists. On the other side, collaborators like Charles

LIBERTÉ

By Paul Eluard

Sur la vitre des surprises	*On the window of surprises*
Sur les lèvres attentives	*On the lips that listen*
Bien au-dessus du silence	*Far above silence*
J'écris ton nom	*I write your name*
Sur mes refuges détruits	*On my refuges torn down*
Sur mes phares écroulés	*On my beacons all collapsed*
Sur les murs de mon ennui	*On the walls of my tedium*
J'écris ton nom	*I write your name*
Sur l'absence sans désir	*On the absence void of want*
Sur la solitude nue	*On the solitude stripped bare*
Sur les marches de la mort	*On the marches of death*
J'écris ton nom	*I write your name*
Sur la santé revenue	*On the health at last restored*
Sur le risque disparu	*On the danger gone away*
Sur l'espoir sans souvenir	*On hope that's gone for ever*
J'écris ton nom	*I write your name*
Et par le pouvoir d'un mot	*And by the power of a word*
Je recommence ma vie	*I start my life again*
Je suis né pour te connaître	*I am born here just to know you*
Pour te nommer	*To call you by your name*
Liberté.	*Liberty.*

Excerpted From "Liberté"
by Paul Eluard.
Translated by John Theobald.

These four huge panels by Fernand Léger illustrate the title of a poem by Paul Eluard: Liberty, Your Name I Write.

The lettering, color composition and semi-abstract face convey the idea of freedom—the theme of this long, mantra-like poem.

▲ *Sports, family outings and relaxation are the contemporary themes of this painting by Fernand Léger, a former Cubist.*

The reconstruction of France after the war was Léger's topical theme when his painted The Builders *in 1950.* ▶

Maurras, leader of the fascist Action Française, called the invasion "a divine surprise," while the followers of Jacques Doriot, a former Communist turned Nazi, wore SS uniforms. Many French industrialists and aristocrats consorted with the Nazi elite at parties, restaurants and in nightclubs. With food, clothing and gasoline scarce, black markets flourished. While its people grew hungry and sullen, the best of Paris was available to German officers and soldiers and the Germans took what they wanted. Nazi Field Marshal Goering came to Paris, visited its museums and then sent his art experts to the Louvre, other museums and to private collections to liberate priceless paintings and take them to Germany. Nazi doctrine branded the work of modern artists like Picasso and Matisse as "decadent" and "trash." Their

paintings were left alone. So were the artists themselves.

After the war, scores would be settled, and the hatreds and mistrust of the Occupation would divide people — and French politics — for years.

In the Allied invasion of France that began in Normandy on June 6, 1944, Free French troops participated, while resistance *maquisards* (guerrilla fighters) behind the German lines carried on acts of sabotage. A Free French armored division took on the job of leading the American advance to Paris and found the city already liberated by the resistance and the Paris police. Free French troops and resistance groups also played roles in the Allied invasion of southern France, redeeming the honor and glory of Frenchmen and women.

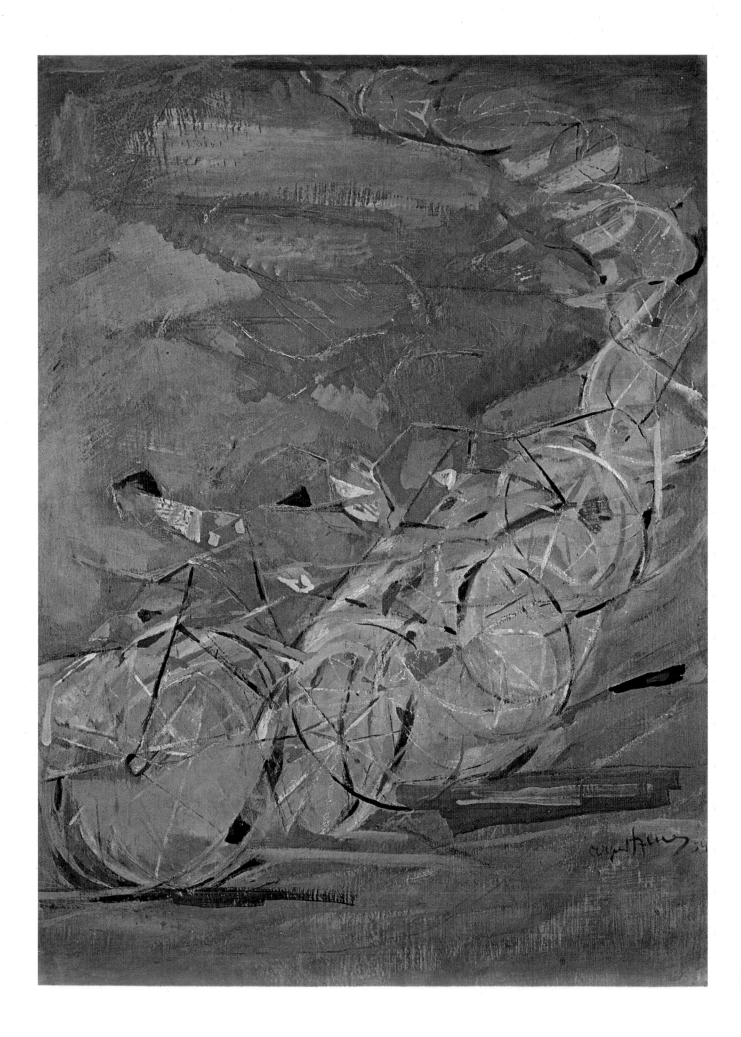

Entertainment In
Black And White

One evening in 1925, the *Théâtre des Champs Elysées* opened a new show: the *Revue Nègre*, the first troupe of black American entertainers to visit Paris. It featured Florence Mills, a New Orleans jazz band led by Sidney Bechet and a talented and beautiful eighteen-year-old singer and dancer named Joséphine Baker.

For her debut, a huge ball covered with flowers was lowered from the ceiling. As it reached the stage, it opened and there, nude except for a girdle of bananas, stood Joséphine Baker on an angled mirror. Her dancing brought the audience to its feet. Afterward, the sphere slowly closed, and she was raised up to the dome of the theater. Joséphine Baker went from the *Revue Nègre*

The incomparable Maurice Chevalier sang and danced his way
▼ *from the Folies Bergère to worldwide fame as a movie star.*

◄ *The high-speed motion of a long-distance bicycle race like the* Tour de France *is captured in this vivid painting.*

The American entertainer Joséphine Baker came to Paris in the 20s and stayed on to become one of its great monuments.

to the famed *Folies Bergère* and became a superstar in France. After thirty-one years of celebrity, Baker retired and adopted twelve underprivileged children. In 1959 needing money for their upkeep, she went back into show business to make her farewell appearance — which she continued to make for fourteen years.

Shortly after the singer Maurice Chevalier was hired by the *Folies Bergère*, he was paired with Mistinguett in a comedy-act which ended with the two of them rolled up in a rug. Very soon, they became lovers. When Chevalier was captured by the Germans in 1914, Mistinguett used her considerable charm to plead for his release. She succeeded when her friend, the King of Spain used his influence with the Kaiser. Chevalier was back at the Folies by 1916. He became world famous after his early film, *The Innocents of Paris*, but is best remembered for his singing of "Thank Heaven For Little Girls" in the film *Gigi*.

259

Colette who began as a dancer and actress, became one of France's most prolific and popular authors. From her *romantic yet realistic novels came plays and later, many motion pictures. Balzac and Proust were her literary idols.*

Colette

Probably because she married the wrong man, Sidonie-Gabrielle Colette became a writer. At the age of twenty, she married Henri Gauthier-Villars who, discovering that her writing talent was greater than his, published her first four "Claudine" novels under his pen name Willy. Colette divorced him after five years and became a performer at the *Folies Bergère*, where young Maurice Chevalier described her as "a superb example of the

1908 beauty." Between her scenes, Colette wrote in a corner of her dressing-room.

After remarrying, she made her living — a very good one — by writing a series of sensitive, passionate and popular novels. Among them were *Chéri, La Fin de Chéri, La Maison de Claudine, La Chatte, Duo* and *Gigi*.

She was the first woman writer to be made a member of the Belgian Royal Academy and the French Academy Goncourt, as well as grand officer of the Legion of Honor.

Edith Piaf, who had the look of a waif and the voice of an ▶ *angel, sang of love, broken hearts and the life in Paris.*

A Walk On
The Bright Side

In the Paris World's Fair of 1937, Raoul Dufy exhibited what may be the largest painting ever made. Its theme was Electricity. The painting covered two huge walls from floor to ceiling. After the fair, it went on display in its own great hall in the Paris Museum of Modern Art.

Born in 1887 in Le Havre, Raoul Dufy was one of eight children of an accountant who loved music, and was his church's organist and choirmaster. If Dufy had not become an artist, he would have been a musician like other members of his family. He studied at the *Ecole des Beaux Arts* and settled in Montmartre, spending his evenings at classical concerts and the Opera.

Dufy was greatly influenced by Matisse, moving from Impressionism to the Fauves, and then to a light, bright style that was completely his own.

When textile art interested him, he became a designer of fabrics for the couturier Poiret. There, he was in good company, for Picasso, Matisse and Léger at some time also designed fabrics. He illustrated a book of poetry by Mallarmé, painted murals for the *Jardin des Plantes* and designed ballet decors and costumes. But he became best known for his brilliantly lit paintings of race horses, landscapes and seascapes. In 1952, Dufy received the Grand Prize at the Venice Biennale. He said that his duty was "to make beauty accessible to everyone by putting things in order." One art critic wrote: "When he entered a room, it was like a flood of sunlight... there was an aura of majesty born of graciousness, simplicity and dedication."

◀ *Marcel Duchamp, portrayed here by his brother Jacques Villon, became world famous for his* Nude Descending a Staircase.

▲ *With splashes of color and figures outlined in black, Dufy gave a lyrical feeling to his painting,* Le Grand Concert.

Picasso

Pablo Picasso was a precocious genius who became a master of the Classic, neo-Classic, Impressionistic, Cubist and Surrealist schools. No matter what style he conceived or tried, his work was always distinctly Picasso. In his early works, he seemed instinctively to know more about painting than his teachers would ever learn. He understood how to select and absorb the appropriate elements of his environment to his vision. Picasso was able to translate his ideas into permanent images imbued with the spirit and temper of each passing decade.

Born in Malaga, Spain in 1881, he was christened Pablo Nepomuceno Crispiniano de la Santissima Trinidad Ruiz'y Picasso. At fourteen, he was admitted to the Barcelona School of Fine Arts where the time allowed for entrance examinations was a month. Pablo passed them in a day. At sixteen he won an award at the Fine Arts Exhibition in Madrid. At eighteen he had his own studio consisting of bed, chair, easel and paints. He shortened his impressive name and signed his early paintings P. Ruiz'Picasso, but in time dropped the P. Ruiz.'

In his late teens, he explored Barcelona's port and the brothels and cafés of its *Barrio Gótico* (Gothic quarter) with other young artists and writers looking for subjects to paint and write about. He began using large amounts of blue in his canvases and his "blue period" continued even after he moved to Paris at the age of twenty-three. In Paris, he rented a studio in Montmartre, and was fortunate in having as neighbors Max Jacob, an amusing and intelligent poet, and the Spanish artist Juan Gris. Even more fortunate was his proximity to the Circus Médrano, just a few minutes walk away. Three or four times a week, with sketch pad in hand, Picasso visited the circus with his friends. There he found subjects that interested him immensely. Picasso made many memorable paintings of the *Saltimbanques*, aerialists and acrobats who worked with the circus. About this time, he met a woman remembered only as Madeleine, and from the sensitive paintings Picasso made of her. She appears in several paintings he did in the Spring of 1904: with her dark hair piled on her head, at an ironing board and as the woman in the *Harlequin* family.

In those early days, Picasso met Matisse, Braque and *Douanier* Rousseau through the American collectors Gertrude Stein and her brother Leo. He was deeply influenced by the work of Toulouse-Lautrec who had died only three years before Picasso's arrival in Paris. He was also affected by the works of Rousseau, for whom — when he became a bit more prosperous — Picasso gave a banquet. At the banquet were his live-in companion Fernande Olivier, the critic Guillaume

In this painting of Picasso at seventy-five, Edouard Mac Avoy caught his remarkable energy and the intensity of his eyes.

Apollinaire, Gertrude Stein and his fellow-artists Marie Laurencin, Georges Braque, and Rousseau. After dinner, Rousseau said to Picasso: "You and I are the greatest painters of our time. You in the Egyptian style, I in the modern."

In Picasso's long life, he worked as hard as any manual laborer putting in long hours each day. He painted far into the night and in addition stretched his own canvases, made lithographs and worked on sculpture and ceramics. He was a lusty man continually on the prowl for women, but no matter how much he was taken with a woman, his ultimate love was for his painting, his studio, his brushes and the joy of working

In its subject matter and setting, this Paul Delvaux scene dates back to Ingres. But Delvaux's women are different: they *are free and uninhibited personalities who dominate the males around them. The Tumultuous Women is from 1968.*

with his hands. To Picasso, creation was both a physical and a mental process. He attacked each blank canvas as a matador attacks a bull. He brought out of himself and his brushes the raw vigor of sex, the gentleness of rapture, the horror of rape, the solace of peace and the beauty of motherhood.

Loyal to his friends, he went to visit Matisse on almost every Friday night for many years. Braque once said that he and Picasso worked together so closely, they were like "two roped mountaineers."

In 1936 when General Francisco Franco began his civil war against Spain's Republican government, the government welcomed Picasso's support and made him director of the Prado Museum. In that position, he was instrumental in saving the museum's treasures from destruction. At that time he wrote "Painting is not done to decorate apartments... It is an instrument of war against brutality and darkness." He was among the millions of persons horrified when on April 26, 1937, Nazi bombers aiding the Franco cause bombed the Basque town of Guernica, in a vicious demonstration of total war against civilians. Picasso struck back by painting a mammoth canvas, some 300 feet square, in which he protested against the cruelty and barbarism

of the war. Called *Guernica* after the destroyed town, it was displayed in the Spanish Pavillion at the 1937 Paris World's Fair. *Guernica* expressed Picasso's outrage at the violence of war and his compassion for suffering humanity. It will be remembered long after Franco and his fascism are forgotten.

Picasso chose beautiful and interesting women as his wives and lovers. Olga Koklova, a ballerina with the *Ballet Russe*, he married in 1918 and she bore him a son Paulo. By Marie Thérèse Walter, he had a daughter Maya. In 1946 Françoise Gilot, a gifted poet and painter, became his companion and bore him two children, Claude and Paloma. In March 1961, at the age of seventy-nine, he married Jacqueline Roque.

One of Picasso's very last paintings, done at the age of ninety, was of a mother and child. It was one of his favorite themes. Paintings titled *Mother and Child* had appeared as early as 1905 when he was only twenty-four. Its persistence provides a clue to one of Picasso's deepest feelings.

The Japanese artist, Foujita, who lived most of his life in ▶ *Paris recorded the various moods in* Le Bistro *in 1953.*

265

Aménagement du territoire (regional development) was a major priority in the economic and cultural growth of the

1960s that changed the face of France. Superhighways, faster trains and commuter airlines brought the cities and countryside closer together. Jacques Villon painted The Cranes of Rouen as a symbol of this era of expansion.

269

The Paris skyline changed in the 1960s with the appearance of new high-rise buildings, like these painted by Charbonnier.

These buildings were put up by the government as medium-cost housing at the Porte des Lillas on the periphery of Paris.

▲ *Spiky forms and somber colors are typical of Buffet who painted* The Artist and His Model *when he was twenty-years old.*

Like a cave painter transported into the twentieth century, ▶ *Jean Dubuffet uses graffiti style as a symbol of modern times.*

271

De Gaulle
Man Of France

On the morning of August 26, 1944, General Charles de Gaulle began his long walk of victory from the *Arc de Triomphe* to the *Place de La Concorde* celebrating the liberation of Paris. As the head of the Free French, he had fought the war from a distance, a new experience for a professional military officer who had seen combat in World War I and, before France fell, in World War II. For four years he had exhorted his countrymen from London to take heart, the war against Germany would be won.

Typical of de Gaulle, he had not bothered to inform the National Resistance Council, nor its leader Georges Bidault, of his intention to walk down the Champs Elysées that Saturday to the cheers of his countrymen. The Communists and other Resistance groups turned up anyway to participate in the victory march but, in tacit recognition of de Gaulle's supremacy, their leaders walked at a respectful distance behind the general. He later wrote, "I felt that I was fulfilling a function which far transcended my personality—for I was serving as an instrument of destiny."

Not a politician at heart, de Gaulle nevertheless had learned how to assume power. From the time of his adolescence and later in military school, he had pursued power, believing firmly in himself. He was inclined to disregard others' opinions, and developed a reputation for arrogance. For years he campaigned for a mobile armored force in the army, but not until France was collapsing in 1940 was his idea tried.

He served as premier of the provisional government of France after its liberation. However, in 1946, when the Communists won 26% of the votes and the Socialists 24%, de Gaulle felt he would be unable to govern and resigned. He formed the *Rassemblement du Peuple Français* (Gathering of the French People) and waited for a call to return. In 1958, in the first French election with universal suffrage, he was elected president by a great majority and then remodeled the constitution to suit France's need for stability and his own temperament. The new constitution specified that the government could not be overturned or dismissed for at least seven years. He devalued the franc so that French exports had a chance to compete in world markets. He presided over Algeria's last days as a French colony.

While president, de Gaulle helped to form the Common Market, unifying France, West Germany, Belgium, the Netherlands and Luxembourg in an economic union, but he opposed British entry. He insisted that France develop its *force de frappe* (nuclear striking force), even though it meant taking France out of NATO. On more than one occasion, his enemies plotted his assassination. He survived no less than thirty-one attempts on his life.

In his final days in office, de Gaulle came up against a new France, the postwar generation, with its own ideas of what the country should be like. In 1968, French university students were complaining about overcrowded classrooms and primitive laboratories (enrollments were up, but appropriations had lagged), the scarcity of jobs and the sorry state of the French economy. But de Gaulle's mind was on other things: a trip to Rumania and his plans for a national celebration of the tenth anniversary of his return to power.

At the University of Nanterre, a demonstration against United States intervention in Vietnam became violent. Windows were smashed and five students arrested. The students, led by red-headed Daniel Cohn-Bendit, demanded student representation in the government.

The government's response was to announce that future admissions to the university would be on the basis of an examination, instead of being automatic for anyone who had passed the *Baccalauréat*. The students protested again, the campus closed down and Cohn-Bendit was ordered to appear before a faculty council. He brought with him a number of supporters who were met by a right-wing group. A fight ensued and the administration called police to the campus—a violation of French university traditions. The entire Sorbonne shut down.

On May 7, the police were ordered by the government to enter the Sorbonne buildings and clear out the students occupying them. The students left quietly. Outside the gates the police were waiting. They rounded up over 500 students, put them into police vans and drove them away, whereupon watching students charged the police. In the fighting that followed, nearly 500 people were arrested. Between May 8 and 11, the students built barricades of paving blocks and repelled police charges. Persuaded by Georges Pompidou, de Gaulle accepted the students' demands to reopen the Sorbonne, withdraw the police from the Latin Quarter and release the arrested students. It was no longer enough. A twenty-four hour general strike was called in which nearly a million workers took part. De Gaulle gave in and promised a referendum, renovation of the educational system, increases in wages and a shorter work week.

It has long been said that generals die in bed—and de Gaulle came very close to it. He died in 1970 at the age of eighty sitting in an armchair at his home—watching television.

274

▲ *In this painting of de Gaulle (based on a photograph), the book represents the Constitution and the sword his military career.*

The artist Jean Hélion was an eyewitness to the Paris student riots of May 1968. A contemporary "Marianne" is in the center. ▶

Chagall was Russian by birth, French by choice. Characters in his dream paintings always looked toward a radiant future.

His fantasies often were set in the Russian villages of his youth. In 1964, he decorated the ceiling of the Paris Opera.

WORKS OF ART

279

25 (middle) Safety Pins; La Tène; 250-120 B.C.; bronze; Saint Germain-en-Laye, Musée des Antiquités Nationales.

(bottom) Belt; 1150-950 B.C.; bronze; found in Loir et Cher; Saint Germain-en-Laye, Musée des Antiquités Nationales.

26 Wild Boar; Gallo-Roman; bronze; found in Neuvy-en-Sullias; 35 x 46 cm; Orléans, Musée Historique et Archéologique.

27 Naked Man Running; Gallo-Roman; bronze; found in Neuvy-en-Sullias; 20 x 10 cm, Orléans, Musée Historique et Archéologique.

28 Coin With Head of Caesar as Pontifex Maximus; Gallo-Roman; silver; Paris, Bibliothèque Nationale, service photographique.

29 Coin With Head of Vercingétorix; Gallo-Roman; alloy of gold & silver; Paris, Bibliothèque Nationale, service photographique.

30 Roman Legionnaires; Gallo-Roman; bas-relief on stone; found in Saint Rémy de Provence; 59 x 83 cm; Lyon, Musée de la Civilisation Gallo-Romaine.

32/33 *Circus Games*; Gallo-Roman; mosaic; c. 175 A.D.; 129 x 316 cm; Lyon, Musée de la Civilisation Gallo-Romaine.

34/35 Nude Women and Juggler; Gallo-Roman; bronze; found in Neuvy-en-Sullias; 8.7 x 4.5 cm; Orléans, Musée Historique et Archéologique.

36 Jupiter Standing; Gallo-Roman; stone; found in Chécy-Loiret; 9.2 x 6 cm; Orléans, Musée Historique et Archéologique.

37 Bacchus; Gallo-Roman; bronze; found in Neuvy-en-Sullias; 23 x 13.5 cm; Orléans, Musée Historique et Archéologique.

38 *The Intoxication of Bacchus*; Gallo-Roman; mosaic; 125 x 125 cm; Lyon, Musée de la Civilisation Gallo-Romaine.

39 *Fight Between Eros And Pan*; c. 250 A.D.; mosaic; 110 x 110 cm; Lyon, Musée de la Civilisation Gallo-Romaine.

40 Bracelet; Gallo-Roman; gold; found in Isère; 7.5 x 5.5 cm; Lyon, Musée de la Civilisation Gallo-Romaine.

FIRST CHRISTIAN KINGS

41 Horsewoman Candleholder; brass; 12th c. Mosan art; Paris, Musée Cluny, on deposit from the Louvre.

42 *Baptism of Clovis*; illumination; 15th c.; 7.2 x 7.8 cm; From "The Great Chronicles of France;" Chantilly, Musée Condé.

43 *Scenes From The Life of Saint Rémi*; bas relief on ivory book cover; 9th/10th c.; Amiens, Musée de Picardie. Photo Gheerbrandt.

44 Charles The Great With His Son Pépin of Italy; 10th c. copy of Leges Salicae (...) Carolimagni; 24 x 14.5 cm; Modena, Biblioteca Capitolare. Photo Roncaglia.

45 Charlemagne; bronze; 9th/10th c.; 24 cm high; Paris, Musée du Louvre. Photo Documentation

photographique des Musées Nationaux.

47 Talisman of Charlemagne; gold, filigree, jewels, pearls; 9th c.; 7.3 x 6.5 cm; Reims, Palais du Tau. Photo Ann Munchow, Aachen.

48 Carolingian Soldiers; Codex 22, Psalterium Aureum; c. 875; 36.5 x 28 cm; Stiftsbibliothek, St. Gallen, photographic service.

49 Dagulf Psalter; ivory cover; end 8th c.; Rhine region; Paris, Musée du Louvre. Photo Documentation photographique des Musées Nationaux.

50 Saint Matthew; Ebo Gospels; c. 816-835; m 1, 178 fols, fol. 18 v 26 x 14.9 cm; Epernay, Bibliothèque Municipale. Photo Ann Munchow, Aachen.

51 Portrait of Louis the Pious; Reginense Latino fol.4v; c. 840; 36.5 x 29.5 cm; Rome, Biblioteca Apostolica Vaticana. Photo Biblioteca Vaticana.

52 Throne of Charles the Bald; Codex Aureus of St.Emmeram; Clm 14000 fol 5v; c. 870; 42 x 33 cm; Munich, Bayerische Staatsbibliothek, photographic service.

53 Frontispiece to Genesis; Grandval Bible; ms 10 546, 449 fols, fol 5v. c. 840.; London, 37.5 x 51 cm; The British Library, photographic service.

54 *Knight of the Crusades*; Codex Manesse, Cod. Pal. Germ. 848, fol 122 r; c. 1300; 18 x 24 cm; Universitats Bibliothek Heidelberg, photographic service.

THE CAROLINGIAN RENAISSANCE

55 Tannhauser; Codex Manesse, Cod. Pal. Germ. 848, fol 264 r; c.1300; 18 x 24 cm; Universitats Bibliothek Heidelberg, photographic service.

56/57 *Romanesque Normandy, Halley's Comet;* from the Bayeux tapestry; 1066; Bayeux, Musée de la Tapisserie de Bayeux. Photo, Musée de Bayeux.

58-59 *French Bishops at Cluny;* illumination; c. 1095; ms. Lat. 17716; Paris, Bibliothèque Nationale, service photographique.

60 Christ in the Midst of Exhultant Knights; illumination; ms .74 c. 13v; 20.5 x 17.5 cm; beg. 14th c.; Padova, Biblioteca del Seminario. Photo Alessandro Romanin.

61 Louis VII, the Young and Eleanor of Aquitaine; illumination; from the "Chronicles of St. Denis;" end of 14th c.; 8.5 x 7.7 cm; Chantilly, Musée Condé.

62 *The Laborer and His Plow;* illumination; from "The Miracles of our Lady;" beg. 13th c.; 34 x 24.2 cm; Nouv. Acq. Fr. 24541, fol. 172; Paris, Bibliothèque Nationale, service photographique.

63 *The Abduction of the Little Nun;* illumination; from "The Miracles of our Lady;" beg. 13th c.; 34 x 24.2 cm; Nouv. Acq. Fr. 24541, fol. 93; Paris, Bibliothèque Nationale, service photographique.

64-65 Carcassonne; walled city; built c. 1130

66 A Judicial Fight; enamel champlevé from Limoges; 14th c.; 11 x 14.5 cm; Orléans, Musée Historique et Archéologique.

THE POPE IN FRANCE — THE 100 YEAR WAR

67 *Froissart Offering His Book to the Duchess of Burgundy;* illumination; from "The Froissart Chronicles" Vol. 1; c. 1379; 17.7 x 19 cm; Chantilly, Musée Condé.

68 *The Charity of Saint Martin;* stained glass; Ile de France; c. 1230; Paris, Musée de Cluny.

69 Smiling Angels; sculpture; stone; Rheims cathedral; c. 1194.

70 *Court Scene — The Kiss;* fresco; 2nd half of 14th c.; school of Avignon; 147 x 182 cm; Avignon, Musée du Petit Palais, dépôt du Musée du Louvre.

71 *Charles V in Tournament;* illumination; end 14th c.; from "The Great Chronicles of France;" 8.5 x 6.2 cm; Chantilly, Musée Condé.

73 The Blessed Pierre of Luxembourg; oil; school of Avignon; c. 1470; 58 x 77 cm; Avignon, Musée du Petit Palais.

74 The Virgin of Mercy of the Cadard Family; school of Avignon; 15th c.; wood transposed on canvas; 66 x 187 cm; Chantilly, Musée Condé.

75 *The Circumcision;* Josse Lieferinxe a.k.a. the master of St. Sebastien; oil; school of Avignon; known since 1493; 78 x 59 cm; Avignon, Musée du Petit Palais, dépôt du Musée Calvet.

76 *Cathedral Building and Exorcism;* illumination; from "St.Vincent de Beauvais Chronicles;" beg. 15th c.; 9 x 10.5 cm; Chantilly, Musée Condé.

77 *The Devil and View of Hell;* illumination; from "St.Vincent de Beauvais Chronicles;" beg. 15th c.; 11 x 9.4 cm; Chantilly, Musée Condé.

78 *Witches on Their Brooms;* drawing in the margin of "Champion of the Ladies;" Martin le Franc; c. 1451; Paris, Bibliothèque Nationale, service photographique.

'79 Hommage to the Devil; Tractus Contra Sectam Valdensium; ms. fr. 961; Paris, Bibliothèque Nationale, service photographique.

80 *Pulse Checking;* illumination; from "Liber Notalilium Illustrissimi, Principus Philip VI Francorum Regis;" Guido de Vigerano de Papis; 1345; 24 x 11 cm; Chantilly, Musée Condé.

81 *Calendar Year;* detail; illumination; from "The Rustican;" Pierre de Crescens; c. 1456-60; whole 15.5 x 13.3 cm; Chantilly, Musée Condé.

82 *Defeat of the Duke of Lancaster;* illumination; from the "Froissart Chronicles;" 15th c.; Vol. 2; 18 x 8.3 cm; Chantilly, Musée Condé

83 Jean II the Good; oil; anon; mid. 14th c.; 57.5 x 35.5 cm; Paris, Musée du Louvre.

84/85 *The Arrival of Jeanne d'Arc in Chinon*; tapestry; 15th c.; 80 x 107 cm; Orléans, Musée Historique et Archéologique.

86 Charles VII; Jean Fouquet; oil on panel; c. 1444-1447; 86 x 71 cm; Paris, Musée du Louvre.

87 *The Duke of Berry With St. Andrew and John the Baptist Before the Virgin*; illumination; from the "Brussels Hours of Jean, Duke of Berry;" ms. 11060-61 p.14; c. 1402-09; 27.5 x 18.5 cm; Brussels, photo copyright Bibliothèque Royale Albert Ier.

89 *The Wedding of Philippe The Good of Burgundy and Isabelle of Portugal*; anon; oil; 15th c.; 161 x 177 cm; Château de Versailles.

90/91 *Assembly of the Burgundy Parliament Held By Charles the Daring*; anon; 1467-77; painting on copper; 21 x 66 cm; Château de Versailles.

92/93 *Last Communion and Martyrdom of St. Denis*; Henri Bellechose; c. 1398-1416; tempera on panel; 162 x 209 cm; Paris, Musée du Louvre.

94 Tombstone of John the Fearless, Duke of Burgundy and Marguerite of Bavaria; started in 1443 by Jean de la Huerta and finished by Antoine Le Moiturier in 1470; from the Chartreuse of Champmol; Dijon, Musée des Beaux Arts.

FRENCH RENAISSANCE

95 *Venus Presents Weapons To Enée*; Nicolas Poussin; 1639; oil; 107 x 146 cm; Rouen, Musée Des Beaux Arts.

96 Return From Hunting; tapestry; end 15th c.; 266 x 123 cm; Paris, Musée de Cluny.

97 *Arithmetic*; tapestry; 1520; 303 x 285 cm; Paris, Musée de Cluny.

98 *Concert*; tapestry; early 16th c.; 278 x 212 cm; Paris, Musée de Cluny.

99 *The Blacksmith*; tapestry; early 16th c.; 250 x 257 cm; Paris, Musée de Cluny.

100/1 *Grape Gathering*; tapestry; end 15th c.; 243 x 495 cm; Paris, Musée de Cluny.

102 François I; Jean Clouet; c. 1515; oil; Paris, Musée du Louvre.

103 Henri II as a Child; after Jean Clouet; c. 1523; oil on wood; 30 x 23 cm; Chantilly, Musée Condé.

104 *La Nature*; Le Tribolo; marble sculpture; 1528; Château de Fontainebleau.

105 Stairway Frieze; Francisco Primaticcio; Château de Fontainebleau.

106 *The Bath of Diana*; François Clouet; c. 1560; oil on wood; 133 x 192 cm; Rouen, Musée des Beaux Arts.

107 *The Seigneurial Bath*; tapestry; beg. 16th c.; 282 x 261 cm; Paris, Musée de Cluny.

108 *Gabrielle d'Estrées in Her Bath*; French school; beg. 17th c.; oil, 115 x 103 cm; Chantilly, Musée Condé.

109 *Diane de Poitiers as an Allegory of Peace*; Jean Capassin; Franco-Italian school of the Rhône Valley; c. 1568-70; oil; 75 x 100 cm; Aix-en-Provence, Musée Granet.

110 Equestrian Portrait of Henri II; French school of 16th c.; gouache on vellum glued on wood; 27 x 20.5 cm; Chantilly, Musée Condé.

111 Catherine de Medici; French school of 16th c.; oil on wood; 50 x 36 cm; Chantilly, Musée Condé.

112/13 *Ball Given at the Court of Henri II on the Occasion of the Wedding of Anne, Duke of Joyeuse, Admiral of France, With Marguerite of Spain on Sept. 24, 1581*; attributed to Herman Van der Mast; oil; detail; 122 x 185 cm; Château de Versailles.

114 Portrait of Michel Montaigne; French school of the 2nd half of the 16th c.; oil; 18.5 x 14.5 cm; Chantilly, Musée Condé.

115 *The Prodigal Son With the Courtesans*; Flemish School; mid-16th c.; oil; 128 x 78 cm; Paris, Musée Carnavalet.

211 *Café-Concert aux Ambassadeurs*;
Edgar Degas; c. 1876-8; pastel;
27 x 36 cm; Lyon, Musée des
Beaux Arts.

212 *Moulin de la Galette*; Pierre
Auguste Renoir; 1876; oil;
175 x 130 cm; Paris, Musée du
Jeu de Paume.

213 (left) *The Town Dance*; Pierre
Auguste Renoir; 1883; oil;
87 x 180 cm; Paris, Musée du Jeu
de Paume.

213 (right) *The Country Dance*; Pierre
Auguste Renoir; 1883; oil;
87 x 180 cm; Paris, Musée du Jeu
de Paume.

214 *The Bathers*; Paul Cézanne;
1890-92; oil; 80 x 59 cm; Paris,
Musée du Jeu de Paume.

215 *The Models*; Georges Seurat; oil;
48 x 39 cm; Paris, Musée du Jeu
de Paume.

216 (top) *Arearea*; Paul Gauguin; 1892;
oil; 93 x 75 cm; Paris, Musée du
Jeu de Paume.

216 (bottom) *The Church at Auvers*;
Vincent Van Gogh; 1890; oil;
94 x 74 cm; Paris, Musée du Jeu
de Paume.

217 *The Rouen Cathedral*; Claude
Monet; 1894; oil; 60 x 88 cm;
Paris, Musée du Jeu de Paume.

218/9 *The Wedding Party at the
Photographer's Studio*; A. Dagnan-
Bouvert; 1878-79; oil; Lyon,
Musée des Beaux Arts.

220 *Sarah Bernhardt*; Clairin; 1879;
oil; 51 x 31 cm; Paris, Comédie
Française.

221 *Between the Acts at the Comédie Française*;
Edouard Dantan; 1885, oil,
128 x 96 cm; Paris, Comédie
Française.

222 *The Bath*; Mary Cassatt; oil; Paris,
Musée du Petit Palais.

223 (top) *Annette's Soup*; Edouard
Vuillard; 1900; oil; 35.5 x 62 cm;
St. Tropez, Musée de
l'Annonciade.

223 (bottom) *The First Bath, or Birth of
Bernadette*; Maurice Denis; 1899;
oil; St. Tropez, Musée de
l'Annonciade.

224 *Liberty Inviting Artists to Participate in
the Exhibition*; Henri Rousseau;
1905-6; oil; 175 x 118 cm;
Tokyo, National Museum of
Modern Art.

SURVIVAL AND PROGRESS

225 *Two Laundresses*; Edgar Degas;
c. 1884; oil; 76 x 82 cm; Paris,
Musée du Jeu de Paume.

226 *The White Ball*; Marius Joseph
Avy; 1903; oil; Paris; Musée du
Petit Palais.

227 (top) *Les Champs Elysées*; Jean
François Raffaelli; c. 1900; oil;
Reims, Musée des Beaux Arts.

227 *Tabarin*; Georges Rouault; 1905;
oil; Paris, Musée d'Art Moderne
de la Ville de Paris.

228/9 *The Danse of La Goulue and Jacques
Renaudin Known as Valentin-le-
Désossé*; Henri de Toulouse-
Lautrec; 1895; 285 x 300 cm;
Paris, Musée du Jeu de Paume.

230/1 *Cinématographe Lumière*; poster;
153 x 117 cm; Paris, Musée du
Cinéma.

232 *Outside Shooting of a Movie*; H.
Ménessier; oil; 37 x 58cm; Paris,
Musée du Cinéma.

233 *The Accused*; Georges Rouault;
1907; oil; Paris, Musée d'Art
Moderne de la Ville de Paris.

234 *The Love Merchant*; Gustav Adolf
Mossa; 1904; watercolor;
50 x 26 cm; Nice, Musée des
Beaux Arts Jules Chéret.

235 *Self Portrait*; Pablo Picasso; 1906;
oil; Philadelphia Museum of Art,
A. E. Gallatin Collection. Photo
courtesy of the museum.

236 *The War*; Marcel Gromaire; 1925;
oil; Paris, Musée d'Art Moderne
de la Ville de Paris.

237 *Cathedral of Soissons in Ruins*;
François Flameng; May 18, 1915;
oil; 47 x 30 cm; Paris, Musée de
l'Armée.

238 *German Soldiers With Gas Masks*;
François Flameng; August 1917;
oil; 31 x 48.5 cm; Paris, Musée
de l'Armée.

239 *Verdun*; Félix Vallotton; 1917; oil;
115 x 146 cm; Paris, Musée de
l'Armée.

240 *The Group of Six*; Jacques Emile
Blanche; 1924; oil; 188 x 112 cm;
Rouen, Musée des Beaux Arts.

241 (top) Clémenceau; Auguste Rodin;
1911; sculpture; Paris, Musée
Rodin.

241 (bottom) *The Lovers*; Auguste Rodin; sculpture; Paris, Musée Rodin.

242 *A Storm in Nice*; Henri Matisse; 1919-20; oil; 72 x 59 cm; Nice, Musée Matisse.

243 *The Race Track*; Raoul Dufy; 1928; oil; 53 x 64 cm; St. Tropez, Musée de l'Annonciade.

245/6 *The Young People on the Beach*; Marcel Gromaire; 1927; oil; Paris, Musée d' Art Moderne de la Ville de Paris.

247 *Coco Chanel*; Marie Laurencin; 1923; oil; 92 x 73 cm; Paris, Musée de L'Orangerie; collection Walter Guillaume. Photo Documentation photographique des Musées Nationaux.

248 *The Church of Saint Peter of Montmartre*; Maurice Utrillo; 1931; oil; Paris, Musée d'Art Moderne de la Ville de Paris.

249 *The Sunday Stroll*; Jean Fautrier; Paris, Musée d'Art Moderne de la Ville de Paris.

250 *The Tango of the Archangel*; Kees van Dongen; c.1930; oil; 194 x 192 cm; Nice, Musée des Beaux Arts Jules Chéret.

A VISION OF THE FUTURE

251 *Builders*; Fernand Léger; stained-glass; Biot, Musée Fernand Léger.

252 *The Hawk*; Françoise Gilot; 1943; oil on canvas; 88 x 131 cm; New York, collection of the artist. Photo courtesy of the artist.

253 *Still Life With Skull, Leek and Pottery*; Pablo Picasso; 1942; oil on canvas; New York, collection of Paloma Picasso. Photo courtesy of Paloma Picasso.

255 *Liberty! Your Name I Write*; Fernand Léger; oil; Biot, Musée Fernand Léger.

256 *Leisure on Red Background*; Fernand Léger; 1949; oil; Biot, Musée Fernand Léger.

257 *The Builders*; Fernand Léger; 1950; oil; Biot, Musée Fernand Léger.

258 *The Bicycle Racers*; Arpad Szenes; 1954; oil; 71 x 99 cm; Dijon, Musée des Beaux Arts.

259 (top) Joséphine Baker; Paul Colin; 1925; poster. Photo © Jean-Loup Charmet and © Paul Colin.

259 (bottom) Maurice Chevalier; poster for the Folies Bergère 1963; Photo © EDIMEDIA, D.R.

260 Colette; Jean Texcier; 1912; drawing; Paris, Bibliothèque Nationale, cabinet des Estampes. Photo © EDIMEDIA, D.R.

261 Portrait of Edith Piaf; Claude Charpentier; 1970; oil; 40 x 53 cm; Paris, Musée Edith Piaf.

262 *Marcel Duchamp*; Jacques Villon; 1951; oil; 146 x 113 cm; Norway, Sonja Henie-Niels Onstad Foundations. Photo courtesy of the foundations.

263 *The Grand Concert*; Raoul Dufy; 1948; oil; 78 x 62cm; Nice, Musée des Beaux Arts Jules Chéret.

264 Portrait of Picasso; Edouard Mac Avoy; 1956; oil; Paris, Musée d'Art Moderne de la Ville de Paris.

265 *The Tumultuous Women*; Paul Delvaux; 1968; gouache; 72 x 106 cm; Paris, Galerie Isy Brachot.

266/7 *The Bistro*; Foujita; 1958; oil; Paris, Musée d'Art Moderne de la Ville de Paris

268/9 *The Cranes Near Rouen*; Jacques Villon; 1960; oil on canvas; 60 x 92 cm; Metz, Musée d'Art et d'Histoire. Photo Musée de Metz.

270 *The Lillas Porte*; Pierre Charbonnier; 1970; 72 x 99 cm; Lyon, Musée des Beaux Arts.

271 *The Artist and His Model*; Bernard Buffet; 1948; oil; Paris, Musée d'Art Moderne de la Ville de Paris.

272/3 *Opéra Batignol*; Jean Dubuffet; 1961; oil on canvas; 88 x 115 cm; New York, Barbara Mathes Gallery. Photo courtesy of the gallery.

275 De Gaulle; Roger Chapelain Midy; 1980; oil; 193 x 128 cm; Paris, Palais de l'Elysée. Photo Hubert Josse, © A.D.A.G.P. 1984

276/7   *Things Seen in May*; Jean Hélion;
        1968; acrylic on canvas; detail of
        triptych; 275 x 425 cm;
        Chateauneuf en Thymerais,
        collection of the artist.

278   *The Flight*; Marc Chagall; oil;
        125 x 90 cm; St. Paul de Vence,
        private collection, Maeght
        foundation.

279   *Court Scene — The Carole*; fresco;
        2nd half of 14th c.; school of
        Avignon; 166 x 188 cm;
        Avignon, Musée du Petit Palais,
        dépôt du Musée du Louvre.

288   *Resting Place of Artists From Lyon in the
        Isle of Barbe*; Antoine Duclaux; 1850;
        oil; Lyon, Musée des Beaux Arts.

Cover:
The Gallant Meal
16th-century School of Fontainebleau
Aix-en-Provence, Musée Granet

End pages:
(front) Paris, The Eiffel Tower seen from the Place de
la Concorde
(back) Paris, detail of fountain, Place de la Concorde
Photographs by Bradley Smith

Page 1:
Café-Concert aux Ambassadeurs
by Edgar Degas
Lyon, Musée des Beaux Arts

Title page:
View of the palace and gardens of Versailles
by Pierre Patel
Château de Versailles

SELECTED BIBLIOGRAPHY

Adam, George and Pearl, *A Book About Paris*. Jonathan Cape, London, 1927.

Allen, e.i., *From Plato to Nietzsche*. Fawcett World Library, New York, 1966.

Apel, Willi ed., *Harvard Dictionary of Music*. Harvard University Press, 1974 (2nd ed.).

Archambault, Paul, *Seven French Chroniclers "Witnesses to History."* Syracuse University Press, New York, 1974.

Archives Nationales, *La France du VIIe au XXe Siècle à Travers Soixante et onze Documents*. Archives Nationales, Paris, 1980.

Atkinson, R.J.C., *Stonehenge "Archeology and Interpretation."* Pelican Books Div., Penguin Books Ltd., Middlesex, England 1979.

Avril, François, *Manuscript Painting At the Court of France*. George Braziller, New York, 1978.

Barraclough, Geoffrey, *The Crucible of Europe "The 9th and 10th Centuries in European History."* University of California Press, Berkeley, 1976.

Bauer, Marion and Peyser, Ethel, *Music Through the Ages—An Introduction to Music History*. Elizabeth Rogers ed. G. P. Putnam's & Sons, New York, 1967 (third ed.).

Behrens, Catherine, *The Ancient Regime*. Harcourt Brace Jovanovich, London, 1968.

Bell, Susan Groag, ed., *Women From the Greeks to the French Revolution: An Historical Anthology*. Wadsworth Publishing Company, Belmont, 1973.

Beraud, Henri, *Twelve Portraits of the French Revolution*. Books for Libraries Press, Inc., Freeport, 1968.

Bitton, Davis, *The French Nobility in Crisis, 1560-1640*. Stanford University Press, Stanford, 1969.

Bloch, Marc, *French Rural History*, trans. J. Sondheimer. University of California, 1966.

Bowles, John, ed., *The Concise Encyclopaedia of World History*. Hawthorn Books, Inc., New York, 1958.

Boxer, Charles R., *The Dutch Seaborne Empire 1600-1800*. Alfred A. Knopf, New York, 1965.

Braudel, Fernand, *The Structures of Everyday Life: The Limits of the Possible*, trans. Sian Reynolds. Harper & Row Publishers, New York, 1981.

Brillat-Savarin, Jean Anthelme, *The Physiology of Taste*. Liveright Publishing Co., New York, 1948.

British Museum Publications, *The Gauls: Celtic Antiquities From France*. London, no date given.

Bronowski, J. and Mazlish, Bruce, *The Western Intellectual Tradition From Leonardo to Hegel*. Harper & Row, New York, 1960.

Caesar, Julius, *The Gallic War*, trans. Moses Hadas. Modern Library, New York, 1957.

Campbell, Joseph, *The Marks of the Gods: Primitive Mythology*. Viking Press, New York, 1959.

Carlyle, Thomas, *The French Revolution*. Random House, New York, 1857.

Castelot, André, *Queen of France "A Biography of Marie Antoinette."* Harper & Row, New York, 1957.

Castiglione, Count Baldassare, *The Book of the Courtier*, trans. Sir Thomas Hoby. E. P. Dutton & Co., New York, 1928.

Chambers, James, *The Devil's Horsemen: The Mongol Invasion of Europe*. Weidenfeld and Nicolson, London, 1979.

Chappell, George S., *Evil Through the Ages*. Frederick A. Stokes, Co., New York, 1932.

Chatzidakis, Manolis and Grabar, Andre, *Byzantine and Early Medieval Paintings*. Viking Press, New York, 1965.

Chronicles of the Crusades: Joinville and Villehardouin, trans. M. R. B. Shaw. Penguin Books, Baltimore, 1969.

Clark, Kenneth, *Looking At Pictures*. Holt, Rinehart and Winston, New York, 1960.

Clay, Jean and Contreras, Josette, *The Louvre*. Chartwell Books, Inc., Secaucus, 1970.

Cook, Don, *Charles de Gaulle*. G.·P. Putnam's Sons, New York, 1983.

Courthion, Pierre, *Impressionism*, trans. J. Shepley. Harry N. Abrams Inc., New York, 1977.

Davis, Nathalie Zemon, *Society and Culture in Early Modern France, eight essays*. Stanford University Press, Stanford, 1975.

Derval, Paul, *The Folies Bergère*. Methuen & Co., Ltd., London, 1955.

Dickens, Charles, *Child's History of England*. M. A. Donohue & Co., Chicago, no date given.

Dickens, A. G. ed., *The Courts of Europe. Politics, Patronage and Royalty 1400-1800*. McGraw-Hill, New York, 1977.

Dill, Samuel, *Roman Society in Gaul in the Merovingian Age*. Barnes & Noble, New York, 1966

Dimier, L., *French Painting in the Sixteenth Century*. Arno Press, New York, 1969.

Dimnet, Ernest, *The Art of Thinking*. Simon and Schuster, New York, 1932.

Douglas, David, *The Norman Fate 1100-1154*. University of California Press, Berkeley, 1976.

Douville, Raymond and Casanova, Jacques-Donat, *Daily Life in Early Canada*. Macmillan Co., New York, 1968.

Duby, Georges, *Foundations of a New Humanism 1280-1440*. Albert Skira, Geneva, 1966.

Duby, Georges, *The Making of the Christian West 980-1140*. Albert Skira, Geneva, 1967.

Duby, Georges, *The Age of the Cathedrals: Art and Society 980-1420*, trans. E. Levieux and B. Thompson. University of Chicago Press, 1981.

Duby, Georges, *The Early Growth of the European Economy. Warriors and Peasants in the Seventh to the Twelfth Century*, trans. H. Clarke. Weidenfeld & Nicolson, London, 1974.

Early Histories of Charlemagne: Einhard and the Monk of Saint Gall, trans. A. J. Grant. Cooper Square, New York, 1966.

Eccles, W. J., *The Canadian Frontier 1534-1760*. Holt Rhinehart and Winston, New York, 1969.

Edwards, Stewart, *The Paris Commune, 1871*. Eyre & Spottiswoode, London, 1971.

Einhard and Notker the Stammerer, trans. Lewis Thorpe. Penguin Books, Ltd., Middlesex, 1969.

Einstein, Alfred, *A Short History of Music*. Vintage Books, New York, 1954.

Evans, Joan, *Life in Medieval France*. Phaidon Press, London, 1969.

Fawtier, Robert, *The Capetian Kings of France*, trans. L. Bautier. Macmillan & Co., London, 1964.

Febvre, Lucien, *Life in Renaissance France*, trans. M. Rothstein. Harvard University Press, Cambridge, 1977.

Ferrante, Joan M., *Woman as Image in Medieval Literature From the 12th Century to Dante*. Columbia University Press, New York, 1975.

Fichtenau, Heinrich, *The Carolingian Empire*, trans. P. Munz. University of Toronto, 1978.

Flandrin, Jean-Louis, *Families in Former Times. Kinship, Household and Sexuality*, trans. R. Southern. Cambridge University Press, 1979.

Flanner (Genêt), Janet, *Paris Journal 1944-1965 and 1965-1971*. Atheneum Publishers, New York, 1965, 1971.

Ginzburg, Ralph, ed. Eros Magazine, Volumes 1 & 3. Eros Magazine Inc., New York, 1962.

Gordon, Benjamin Lee, *Medieval and Renaissance Medicine*. Philosophical Library, New York, 1959.

Gossman, Lional, (The John Hopkins Univ.) *French Society and Culture "Background For 18th Century Literature."* Prentice Hall, Inc., Englewood Cliffs, 1972.

Goubert, Pierre, *The Ancient Regime. French Society 1600-1750*, trans. S. Cox. Harper & Row, New York, 1973.

Goubert, Pierre, *Louis XIV and Twenty Million Frenchmen*, trans. A. Carter. Random House, New York, 1981.

Gramont, Sanche de, *The French: Portrait of a People*. G. P. Putnam's Sons, New York, 1969.

Gregory of Tours, *History of the French*, trans. E. Brehaut. Octagon Books, Inc., New York, 1965.

Gregory of Tours, *The History of the Franks*, trans. L. Thorpe. Penguin Books, New York, 1974.

Grun, Bernard, *The Timetables of History*. Simon & Schuster, New York, 1975.

Guedalla, Philip, introduction, *The Letters of Napoléon to Marie Louise*. Hutchinson & Co., Ltd., London, 1935.

Guerard, Albert, *France: A Modern History*. University of Michigan Press, Ann Arbor, 1969.

Harthan, John, *The Book of Hours*. Parklane, New York, 1977.

Hatt, Jean-Jacques, *Celts and Gallo-Romans*, trans. James Hogarth. Nagel Publishers, Paris, 1970.

Hay, Denis, *Europe in the Fourteenth and Fifteenth Centuries*. Holt, Reinhart & Winston, New York, 1966.

Hay, Denis, *Later Medieval Europe*. Longman, London, 1975.

Hayes, Carlton J. H. & Moon, Parker Thomas, *Ancient and Medieval History*. Macmillan & Co., New York, 1957.

Hays, H. R., *In the Beginnings "Early Man and His Gods."* G. P. Putnam's Sons, New York, 1963.

Heer, Friedrich, *Charlemagne and His World*. Macmillan & Co., New York, 1975.

Helias, Pierre-Jakez, *The Horse of Pride. Life in a Breton Village*, trans. J. Guichornaud. Yale University Press, New Haven, 1978.

Herm, Gerhard, *The Celts: The People Who Came Out of the Darkness*. Weidenfeld and Nicolson, London, 1975.

Hollander, Hans, *Early Medieval Art*. Universal Books, New York, 1974.

Hoyt, Robert S. and Chodorow, Stanley, *Europe in the Middle Ages*. Harcourt Brace Jovanovich, New York, 1976.

Hubbard, Elbert. *Elbert Hubbard's Scrap Book*. Wm. H. Wise & Co., New York, 1923.

Hughes, H. Stuart, *Contemporary European History*. Prentice-Hall, Englewood Cliffs, 1976.

Huizinga, Johan, *The Waning of the Middle Ages*. Doubleday & Co., New York, 1956.

Huyghe, René, ed., *Larousse Encyclopaedia of Byzantine & Medieval Art*. Prometheus Press, New York, 1963.

Ives, Colta Feller, *The Great Wave: The Influence of Japanese Woodcuts On French Prints*. The Metropolitan Museum of Art, New York, 1974.

Jung, Carl G., *Memories, Dreams, Reflections*. Random House, New York, 1963.

Kahler, Heinz, *The Art of Rome and Her Empire*. Crown Publishers, New York, 1963.

Kibler, William W., ed., *Eleanor of Aquitaine Patron and Politician*. University of Texas Press, Austin, 1976.

Kors, Alan C. and Peters, Edward, ed., *Witchcraft in Europe 1100-1700. A Documentary History*. University of Pennsylvania Press, Philadelphia, 1981.

Labarge, Margaret, *Saint Louis. Louis IX Most Christian King of France*. Little, Brown & Co., Boston, 1968.

Lacroix, Paul, *France in the Middle Ages. Customs, Classes and Conditions*. Frederick Ungar Publishing Co., New York, 1963.

Ladurie, Le Roy, *Montaillou. The Promised Land of Error*, trans. B. Bray. George Braziller, New York, 1978.

Lafayette, Madame de, *The Princess de Clèves*, trans. Nancy Mitford. Penguin Books, Middlesex, 1962.

Lasko, Peter, *Ars Sacra 800-1220*. Penguin Books, Ltd., Baltimore.

Latouche, Robert, *Caesar to Charlemagne. The Beginnings of France*, trans. J. Nicholson. Barnes & Noble, London, 1968.

Leeming, David Adam, *Mythology: The Voyage of the Hero*. J. B. Lippincott Co., Philadelphia, 1973.

Lefebvre, Georges, *The Coming of the French Revolution*, trans. R. R. Palmer. Vintage Books, New York, 1947.

Lenotre, G., *The Guillotine and Its Servants*, trans. R. Stawell. Hutchinson & Co., London.

Lewinsohn, Richard, M.D., *A History of Sexual Customs from Earliest Times to the Present*, trans. Alexander Mayce. Harper & Row, New York, 1958.

Lichine, Alexis, *Wines of France*. Alfred A. Knopf, New York, 1963.

Lough, John, *An Introduction to the Seventeenth Century France*. David McKay Company, Inc., New York, 1961.

Lucie-Smith, Edward, *Joan of Arc*. W.W. Norton, New York, 1977

Mair, Roslin, *Key Dates in Art History from 600 B.C. to the Present*. Phaidon, Oxford, 1979.

Malraux, André and André Parrot, ed., *The Arts of Mankind*. George Braziller, New York, 1970.

Marti-Ibanez, Félix, ed., *Tales of Philosophy*. Dell Publishing Co., New York, 1964.

Marty, Diana de, *The History of Haute Couture 1850-1950*. Holmes and Meier, New York, 1980.

Mc Laughlin, Terrence, *Dirt: A Social History As Seen Through the Uses and Abuses of Dirt*. Stein & Day, New York, 1971.

McNeill, W.H., *The Rise of the West*. University of Chicago Press, Chicago, 1963.

The Metropolitan Museum of Art, *The Vatican Collections: The Papacy and Art*. Harry N. Abrams, New York, 1982.

Mitchell, Sabrina, *Medieval Manuscript Painting*. The Viking Press, New York, 1965.

Mitford, Nancy, *The Sun King. Louis XIV at Versailles*. Harper & Row, New York, 1966.

Mollat, George, *The Popes at Avignon 1305-1378*, trans. Janet Love. Thomas Nelson & Sons, London, 1963.

Mongrédien, Georges, *Daily Life in the French Theater at the Time of Molière*, trans. C.E. Engel. Allen & Unwin, London, 1969.

Montagner, Hubert, *L'Enfant et la Communication*. Editions Stock, Paris, 1978.

Morrow and Cucuel, *Bohemian Paris of Today*. Chatto & Windus, London, 1899.

Muehsam, Gerd, compiler & ed., *French Painters and Paintings From the Fourteenth Century to Post-Impressionism*. Frederick Ungar Publishing Co., New York, 1970.

Mundy, John, *Europe in the High Middle Ages 1150-1309*. Basic Books, New York, 1973

Mütherich, Florentine and Gaehde, Joachim E., *Carolingian Paintings*. George Braziller, New York, 1976.

Napoléon Bonaparte: A Selection From His Written and Spoken Words, ed. and trans. J.C. Herald. Columbia University Press, New York, 1961.

Ogrizek, Doré, *The Paris We Love*. McGraw-Hill Book Co., New York, 1952.

Palmer, Palmer and Colton, J., *A History of the Modern World to 1815*. Alfred Knopf, New York, 1978.

Petit-Dutaillis, Charles, *The Feudal Monarchy in France and England. From the Tenth to the Thirteenth Century*, trans. E.D. Hunt. Routledge & Kegan Paul, London, 1949.

Pinkney, David H., *Napoléon III and the Rebuilding of Paris*. Princeton University Press, Princeton, 1972.

Previte-Orton, C.W., *The Shorter Cambridge Medieval History*. Cambridge University Press, 1979.

Quennell, Peter, ed., *Affairs of the Mind: The Salon in Europe and America From the 18th to the 20th Century*. New Republic Books, Washington, D. C., 1980.

Rank, Otto, *The Myth of the Birth of the Hero*. Alfred A. Knopf, New York, 1959.

Raphael, Frederic and McLeish, Kenneth, *The List of Books*. Mitchell Beazley Publishers, London, 1981.

Reff, Theodore, *Manet: Olympia*. Viking Press, Inc., New York, 1976.

Reynolds, Reginald, *Beards*. Harcourt Brace Jovanovich, New York, 1949.

Richardson, Joanna, *Colette*. Methuen, London, 1983.

Riche, Pierre, *Daily Life in the World of Charlemagne*. University of Pennsylvania Press, 1978.

Robertson, D.W. Jr., *Essays in Medieval Culture*. Princeton University Press, New Jersey, 1980.

Rosenberg, Pierre, *France in the Golden Age*. Metropolitan Museum of Art, New York, 1981.

Rude, George, *The Crowd in the French Revolution*. Clarendon Press, Oxford, 1959.

Rudorff, Raymond, *The Belle Epoque. Paris in the Nineties*. Saturday Review Press, New York, 1973.

Russell, Jeffrey Burton, *Witchcraft in the Middle Ages*. Cornell University Press, Ithaca, 1972.

Salmon, J.H.M., *Society in Crisis. France in the Sixteenth Century*. St. Martin's Press, New York, 1975.

Sawyer, P.H. and Wood, I.N., *Early Medieval Kingship*. University of Leeds, 1977.

Scutenaire, Louis, *La Chanson de Roland*. Editions l'Envers Sauvage du Réel, Paris, 1982.

Self and Society in Medieval France. *The Memoires of Abbot Guibert of Nogent*, trans. C.C.S. Bland. Harper & Row, New York, 1970.

Seward, Desmond, *The Hundred Years War: The English in France 1337-1453*. Constable and Co., Ltd., London, 1978.

Shaver-Crandell, Anne, *Cambridge Introduction to the History of Art: The Middle Ages*. Cambridge University Press, 1982.

Simone, Franco, *The French Renaissance. Medieval Tradition and Italian Influence in Shaping the Renaissance in France*, trans. H. Gaston Hall. Macmillan, London, 1969.

Soboul, Albert, *A Short History of the French Revolution 1789-1799*, trans. G. Symcox. University of California Press, Berkeley, 1977.

Soboul, Albert, *The Parisian Sans Culottes and the French Revolution 1793-94*, trans. G. Lewis. Clarendon Press, Oxford, 1964.

Stone, Donald, *France in the Sixteenth Century. A Medieval Society Transformed*. Prentice-Hall, Englewood Cliffs, 1969.

Strange, Mark, *Women of Power. The Life and Times of Catherine de Medici*. Harcourt Brace Jovanovich, New York, 1976.

Tapié, Victor-Lucien, *France in the Age of Louis XIII and Richelieu*, trans. D. Lockie. Praeger Publishing, New York, 1975.

Taylor, G. Rattray, *Sex in History. Society's Changing Attitudes to Sex Throughout the Ages*. Ballantine Books, Inc., New York, 1954.

Thomas, Marcel, *The Golden Age: Manuscript Painting at the Time of Jean, Duke of Berry*. George Braziller, New York, 1979.

The Brothers Duchamp, trans. from the French. New York Graphic Society, New York, 1975.

Tilly, Arthur, *Modern France. A Companion to French Studies*. Russell & Russell, New York, 1967

Tocqueville, Alexis de, *The Old Regime and the French Revolution*, trans. S. Gilbert. Doubleday, New York, 1955.

Treasure, G.R.R., *Seventeenth Century France*. Rivingtons, London, 1967.

Tyler, William R., *Dijon and the Valois Dukes of Burgundy*. University of Oklahoma Press, Norman, 1971.

Tuchman, Barbara, *The Proud Tower. A Portrait of the World Before the War 1890-1914*. Macmillan Co., New York, 1966.

Turner, E.S., *A History of Courting*. Michael Joseph, Ltd., London, 1954.

Vaughan, Redhard, *Philip the Bold*. Harvard University Press, Cambridge, 1962.

Wallace, David, et. al., *The Intimate Sex Lives of Famous People*. Dell Publishing Co., Inc., New York, 1981.

Wallechinsky, David and Wallace, Irving, *The Peoples Almanac*. Doubleday & Co., Inc., New York, 1975.

Weber, Eugene, *Peasants Into Frenchmen. The Modernization of Rural France, 1870-1914*. Stanford University Press, 1982.

Weiss, Millard, *The Limbourg Brothers and Their Contemporaries*. George Braziller, New York, the Pierpont Morgan Library, 1974.

Wilenski, R.H., *French Painting*. Dover Publications, Inc., New York, 1973.

Williams, Jay, et. al., *Knights of the Crusades*. American Heritage Publishing Co., New York, 1962.

Wright, Gordon, *France in Modern Times*. W.W. Norton, New York, 1981.

Wolf, John B., *Louis XIV*. W.W. Norton, New York, 1968.

Wood, Charles T., *Philip the Fair and Boniface VIII. State Versus Papacy*. R.E. Krieger Publishing Co., Huntington, 1976.

Wylie, Laurence, *Village in the Vaucluse*. Harvard University Press, 1974.

Zeuner, Frederick E., *A History of Domesticated Animals*. Harper & Row Publishers, New York, 1963.

INDEX

A Gemini Smith, Inc. Book

This book would not have been possible without the translations by Elisabeth Girard Smith who also accompanied me on my tour of research, painting selection and photography throughout France. I also owe a debt of gratitude to my editor Leonard Slater whose expertise and advice have been indispensable.

The text of *France: A History in Art* is set in Paladium.

Type set by Laura Lehman, Network Type, San Diego, California.